Media Amnesia

Media Amnesia

Rewriting the Economic Crisis

Laura Basu

PLUTO PRESS

First published 2018 by Pluto Press
345 Archway Road, London N6 5AA

www.plutobooks.com

Copyright © Laura Basu 2018

The right of Laura Basu to be identified as the author of this work has been
asserted by her in accordance with the Copyright, Designs and Patents Act 1988.

British Library Cataloguing in Publication Data
A catalogue record for this book is available from the British Library

ISBN   978 0 7453 3790 6   Hardback
ISBN   978 0 7453 3789 0   Paperback
ISBN   978 1 7868 0275 0   PDF eBook
ISBN   978 1 7868 0277 4   Kindle eBook
ISBN   978 1 7868 0276 7   EPUB eBook

Typeset by Stanford DTP Services, Northampton, England

Simultaneously printed in the United Kingdom and United States of America

Contents

Acknowledgements

This project was funded by a Marie Skłodowska-Curie research fellowship supported by Justin Lewis at Cardiff University. My thanks to Justin and to all my colleagues at Cardiff, especially my office mate Joe Cable. I'm also grateful for the institutional support I've received from the Institute for Cultural Inquiry, Utrecht University, the Department of Media and Communications, Goldsmiths, University of London and the Media, Economics, and Entrepreneurship program at the University of Southern California's Annenberg School for Communication and Journalism.

I want to thank all those who have contributed to this project, by reading chapters or proposals, giving important advice or helping me develop my ideas, especially: Ann Rigney, Astrid Erll, Nello Cristianini, Natalie Fenton, Des Freedman, James Curran, Danielle Rhodes, Fiona May, Christopher H. Smith, Chris Smith, Steve Schifferes, Christian Fuchs, Jonathan Hardy and Marko Ampuja.

A huge thank you to all the journalists who agreed to be interviewed and so generously gave of their time to share their insights and experiences. Likewise the economists, political scientists and activists who helped answer my difficult questions. And to my publisher, Pluto Press, especially my editor Anne Beech.

Thanks to my friends, either for letting me talk endlessly about my work or for providing much needed distraction – both types of support have been essential. As always, my wonderful family has been with me every step of the way – the LA crew: Jay, Tamara, Alita and Asha, and my unstoppable parents, Ann and Dipak Basu. Most of all, I want to thank the amazing giant, Erik Ros, who has been my partner on this adventure, and whose contribution to this book is incalculable.

Introduction

On 15 September 2007, the UK experienced its first run on a bank since 1866. Exactly a year later, Lehman Brothers filed the biggest bankruptcy in history. Over the course of 2008, global stock markets plunged nearly 50 per cent, wiping out $35 trillion in financial assets (McNally 2011: 13). Eight major US banks collapsed, as did more than twenty across Europe, many of which were taken over by governments. The entire edifice of the market system seemed to be crumbling before our eyes. Even the *Financial Times* ran a series on 'The Future of Capitalism', declaring that 'The world of the three past decades is gone' (quoted in McNally 2011: 14). A decade later, we are still feeling the effects of the banking meltdown, which has cost an estimated $13 trillion in bank bailouts (Blyth 2013: 5), and $50 trillion in asset values worldwide (Harvey 2011: 6). The economic crisis has now morphed into a political crisis, as authoritarian populist figures marshal people's anger and fear over their precarious finances into nationalist projects.

It is perhaps difficult to remember the sense of sheer panic and confusion in the initial stages of the crisis, swiftly followed by fury at a set of people who had styled themselves as 'masters of the universe' and reaped untold rewards creating what had turned out to be 'financial weapons of mass destruction' (in the words of master of the universe, Warren Buffett). We seem to have grown accustomed to a pervading sense of economic and now political turmoil. Not only that, we seem to have gotten used to the idea that it is we, the ordinary people, who will pay for it, via cuts to public services and lower incomes. Many now even believe that it was public spending that caused the crisis in the first place. It is widely thought that Labour lost the 2015 UK election partly because voters believed it had crashed the economy by spending too much public money, and was not committed enough to tackling the deficit through austerity. Some blame the poor or immigrants for the problems. We seem to have forgotten the origins of the banking meltdown, and its roots in the wider economic system. This is remarkable, not only because of the historical reality of the financial crisis, but because that crisis was *all over the news* at the time. How has history been so quickly rewritten, what role has the media played in rewriting it, and what effects might this have had for thinking about solutions to the economic problems?

These are the kinds of questions this book will address. It follows the UK news coverage of the crisis from the run on Northern Rock in 2007 until the present day, encompassing the global financial meltdown, the Great Recession, the UK deficit, the eurozone crisis, and falling living standards and rising inequality. It traces the twists and turns by which the media have taken us from a crisis produced by a form of capitalism that has created untold riches for those at the top to a situation in which the majority of people are struggling while those responsible have actually increased their share of global wealth.

In particular, it explores the phenomenon of *media amnesia*, which has been created purposely by politicians and sections of the press, and is often reproduced passively by the 'impartial' broadcasters and 'liberal' press. As the crisis has mutated over time, it has been continually reframed in the media. With each reframing, certain information is forgotten and other information is added, so that the crisis narrative is fluid, malleable and difficult to grasp in its entirety. It will be shown that this amnesia, which entails the media forgetting *its own very recent coverage,* has helped trap us in a neoliberal groundhog day. It has legitimised the implementation of the same kinds of policies that helped cause the crisis in the first place. These policies not only hit the poorest hardest but actually transfer resources upwards, from the 99 per cent to the 1 per cent. The 'strange non-death of neoliberalism' (Crouch 2011) since the 2008 crash has been widely observed (Mirowski 2013; Sum and Jessop 2013). This book explores the role of the media in this non-death.

There are three primary characteristics of the media coverage that contribute to media amnesia: a lack of historical explanation; an overly narrow range of perspectives privileging elite views; and a lack of global context. Each of these threads will be teased out through the following chapters. Media amnesia is not limited to the coverage of the economic crisis – it can be found in all kinds of reporting (the reporting of the Iraq War springs to mind), and is a defining condition of today's media. The economic crisis provides a rare opportunity to examine media amnesia over a time frame of several years continuously – it is one of the only phenomena that has stayed in the media eye constantly for that long a period. The workings of media amnesia in relation to a crisis that has become the backdrop of life for millions is thus the subject of this book.

MEDIA AMNESIA AND THE CRISIS

For some critical theorists, forgetting is a key feature of capitalism. Fredric Jameson, in his reading of Karl Marx, describes capital as a 'machine constantly breaking down, repairing itself not by solving its local problems, but by mutation onto larger and larger scales, its past always punctually forgotten...' (quoted in de Cock *et al.* 2012: 87). Prichard and Mir point out that this forgetfulness, a 'collective absent mindedness', lies at the heart of the economic regime that creates the conditions for ever more frequent and intensive crises. De Cock *et al.* argue that it is this forgetfulness that has allowed us to return to 'business as usual' after 2008 (de Cock *et al.* 2012: 87). Henry A. Giroux (2014) writes of 'the violence of organized forgetting', which has been perpetrated in the US by a range of institutions and sustains an increasingly destructive form of capitalism by short-circuiting critical thought.

Part of the reason capitalism creates amnesia is that the search for profit – capitalism's driving force – leads to the constant speeding up of our experience of time: what David Harvey (1989) has called 'time-space compression'. Companies are always searching for ways to produce more and faster. The current era has taken this acceleration to new levels, with finance capital's real-time transactions on the one hand and the just-in-time supply chains of transnational corporations on the other (Hope 2011). For social theorist Hartmut Rosa (2015), we are experiencing acceleration in multiple spheres of life, and this affects the ways we relate to each other and the world. For many, the speeding up of time under capitalism has wrought havoc on our ability to remember.

It is media, in the sense of information and communication technologies (ICTs), that have enabled the instantaneous transactions of finance and the transnational supply chains that are behind this acceleration (Hope 2011). In turn, media, including news media, have been profoundly affected by this phenomenon. In the age of 24/7 multi-platform news, journalists are having to operate at 'warp speed', constantly churning out stories while looking over their shoulders at what the competition are doing (Le Masurier 2015). This has led to problems with inaccuracy, cannibalisation of each others' stories and lack of contextualisation, as will be explored later on. The acceleration of news production has created a 'media torrent' and 'information overload' (Gitlin 2001).

Though there is now an abundance of information, that does not necessarily mean we can process and remember it – quite the reverse. In their book *No Time to Think*, journalists Howard Rosenberg and Charles S. Feldman (2008) argue that 'today's media blitz scrambles the public's perspective in ways that potentially shape how we think, act and react as a global society'. When it comes to news, acceleration has meant ultra fast-moving news agendas. As will be seen, new news doesn't only build on what came before it, but can actually serve to erase or write over past coverage. In the age of 'warp speed' this amounts to more than rewriting history: *history is being constantly rewritten as it is happening.* This book will show how, when it comes to the economic crisis, this media forgetting and rewriting has had ideological outcomes, coming to serve certain interests.

The acceleration of time within capitalism and information overload are not in themselves the focus of this book. Rather, they form the backdrop to the ongoing coverage of the crisis, with its amnesiac tendencies. The next part of this introduction gives an overview of the crisis itself. It is followed by an introduction to the key media issues that will be explored throughout. It ends with a description of the media study on which the book is based.

THE CRISIS

This section journeys into the economic processes resulting in the 2008 disaster. As mentioned above, the three major factors contributing to media amnesia are a lack of historical explanation, the dominance of elite perspectives and a lack of global context, so it is crucial that we avoid falling into the same trap by beginning with an understanding of the crisis that takes hold of its historical and global dimensions. Having said that, it is impossible to grasp fully in one introductory chapter the dynamics of global capitalism resulting in the crash, about which endless books have been written. In a sense, this section can be seen as a taster, and the issues raised here will be revisited in later chapters. We will start with a brief treatment of the immediate causes of the crash in the shape of toxic financial products, before moving to the deeper roots in the wider economy.

The 2007 run on Northern Rock was one consequence of a credit crunch which catastrophically went on to block the flow of money through the financial system. The problem was that banks relied not on deposits from their savers but short-term loans from each other to support their activities. When these money markets dried up, the banks did not have enough liquidity – cash and assets that can be quickly turned into cash – to continue functioning. Many also did not have enough capital – shareholders' equity and operating profits – to keep them going and so were actually insolvent. The big US banks had leverage ratios of around 30:1, meaning they borrowed $30 for every dollar they held in bank capital. The leverage of many European banks was even worse (McNally 2011: 106). Banking had become more indebted than any other sector of the economy (Harvey 2011: 30).

The banks stopped lending to each other because it had become clear that they had no way of valuing the more exotic assets on their books. These included types of mortgage-backed securities called collateralised debt obligations (CDOs). CDOs are a form of tradable debt made out of lots of other, particularly risky, bits of debt. Robert Peston (2012: 13) describes them as 'investments manufactured out of the offcuts and offal of other investments'. Banks had been creating and trading billions upon billions worth of these securities. They wreaked havoc in combination with a type of derivative called credit default swaps (CDSs). Derivatives are products that derive their value from the value of an underlying asset. The financial sector had been busy concocting more and more elaborate derivatives, eschewing what regulation existed by creating a shadow banking sector where much of this 'over the counter' trading took place. These markets were circulating up to $600 trillion by 2008 – compared with global output of $61 trillion (Harvey 2011: 21). If we think back to the questions of acceleration and time, it is the speed of financial transactions that means they are so voluminous, and therefore cumulatively so profitable – and so dangerous.

CDSs are a kind of insurance against debt default. If you make a loan and are worried that it might not be repaid, you can buy a CDS on the loan. The issuer of the CDS will, for a fee, refund you the amount of the loan in case of default. Only you don't have to be the holder of the debt to buy a CDS on that loan – anyone can buy the CDS, allowing them to be used for the purposes of pure speculation. Up to 80 per cent of the CDS market involved clients who were not themselves exposed to the relevant credit risks (Sayer 2015: 201). CDOs could be sold as very safe, AAA rated bonds by attaching CDSs to them. Together, CDOs and CDSs allowed risky loans to be repurposed into instruments billed as 'sound as a pound' (Peston 2012: 90). What is more, CDSs could also be used to bet against the risky loans contained in CDOs. The hedge fund Paulson & Co. made $15 billion from betting against the CDO market in 2007 (Peston .2012: 91). The speculators were right not to trust the CDOs' ratings. The credit rating agencies whose job it was to assess them – and who had given them AAA ratings – were paid by the same institutions they were supposed to rate.

Through CDOs and other securities – instruments supposedly designed to manage risk – the risk of loan default was diffused through the entire financial system. When people, particularly in the US, began defaulting on their mortgages, nobody knew where this bad debt was located, which is why the credit markets froze. But why was there so much bad debt in the first place? Banks had been conjuring enormous sums out of thin air to lend to businesses and households – at interest, of course. They then packaged up that debt into all kinds of different products and traded it back and forth to make vastly more profit out of it. The banks didn't care if those they were lending to could not afford to pay the money back, because the nifty securities spread (or at least hid) the risk. And in any case, it wasn't the loan issuer's problem as it had passed the debt on to who-knows-where. Predatory lending to those who couldn't afford it – in the form of subprime loans – was the order of the day.

As may have become apparent, for all this to happen, financial sector regulation had to have been somewhat lax. Regulation had been increasingly 'light touch' for the preceding thirty-odd years and especially from the 1990s. Many accounts of the crisis stop at around this point (as we'll see in chapter 1), with the recklessness of the financial sector, the building up of systemic problems in that sector and with the lack of adequate regulation of banks. However, to understand the crisis, we need to go deeper than that, and look at why finance had become so big and how it relates to movements in the wider economy. Marxian economic analysis helps grasp those deeper roots.

FINANCIALISATION

Finance had been actively deregulated ever since the breakdown of the Bretton Woods system of global financial governance from 1971. The Bretton Woods system had been set up after the Second World War to try to restabilise the world money system and prevent another

Great Depression. It had pegged the major currencies to the US dollar – confirming the US's place as the global economic hegemon – and the dollar to gold. This meant that the dollar was convertible to gold.

However, by the mid 1960s, new trends were shaping the global system. The Japanese and German economies, due in part to postwar support provided by the US, were developing at a much higher rate than the US. German and Japanese firms began seizing growing shares of the American market. In 1971, the US experienced its first postwar trade deficit with the rest of the world. The trade deficit overlapped with big deficits in the current account – the balance of inflows and outflows of money as well as goods – partly due to outward foreign direct investment and partly to massive military spending overseas on the Vietnam War (see glossary for definitions of trade and current account deficits). This meant more and more dollars leaving the US, many of them finding their way to central banks around the world. America's trading partners were now accumulating dollars they didn't need, and began cashing them in for gold. By 1971 foreign holdings of dollars were more than twenty times greater than all the gold the US government possessed (McNally 2011: 92). Once the reality of the trade deficit set in, the rush to convert dollars to gold intensified, and President Nixon had little choice but to break the link between the dollar and gold. Other currencies were in turn detached from the dollar.

The breakdown of the Bretton Woods arrangement led to enormous uncertainty for businesses operating multinationally and doing business in multiple currencies, as world money had begun to operate, in the words of the West German Chancellor, as a 'floating non-system' (McNally 2011: 93). The foreign exchange market duly exploded, becoming far and away the world's largest market. As monetary instability became the new normal, so did new forms of 'risk management', and with it, speculation. The extraordinary growth of foreign exchange trading thus drove the financialisation of contemporary capitalism – the growth of the financial sector relative to the rest of the economy.

Meanwhile, all the dollars washing around the world had led to the emergence of the eurodollar market, a unique space, unregulated by any state, in which dollars could be lent and borrowed. As this sector grew through the 1960s, states lost effective control of an increasingly large financial market, one which had grown to around $200 billion in deposits by 1984 (McNally 2011: 91). Governments followed suit with active deregulation. In 1986, the Big Bang interlinked London and New York and immediately thereafter all the world's major financial markets into one trading system. Banks could operate relatively freely across national borders. The Big Bang originated in the City, the UK's financial centre, sealing its place as one of the leading financial centres in the world. Then in 1999, the repeal in the US of the Glass-Steagall Act of 1933, which separated investment and commercial banking, further integrated the banking system into 'one giant network of financial power' (Harvey 2011: 20).

Since there were a lot of dollars sloshing around, the deregulated banks began conjuring up all kinds of exotic financial instruments for wealthy individuals and managers of pension and mutual funds to invest in – including securities like CDOs. The securitisation of mortgages really took off in the 1990s and went through the stratosphere from 2000. In 2005, the amount of debt Wall Street bought, packaged and sold equalled $2.7 trillion (McNally 2011: 102). It was the unquenchable thirst for mortgage-backed securities (such as CDOs) that drove the mania for subprime mortgages. By 2005 banks had made $625 billion in subprime loans, more than $500 billion of which was securitised. By 2006, 40 per cent of all US mortgages were 'non-traditional' i.e. pushed onto people who couldn't afford them and were likely to default.

Credit default swaps (CDSs) were being sold as insurance against these securities. Theoretically, there was no limit to the amount of CDSs that could be generated on a mortgage-backed security. By 2006, CDSs on mortgage bonds were eight times larger than the actual value of the bonds themselves (McNally 2011: 105). Astonishingly, the banks themselves believed in the products they were peddling, and kept billions worth of these junk bonds on their books. Some of them, including Lehman, kept buying mortgages and trying to securitise and sell them even as the market was clearly collapsing. Other financial institutions continued to sell CDSs on mortgage-backed CDOs even when the rise in mortgage default rates was common knowledge. The insurance company AIG sold $400 billion worth of CDSs on mortgage-backed CDOs, and was bailed out to the tune of $182 billion by US citizens. All the while, the 'Value at Risk' statistical models used to measure risk were signalling that everything was fine. All this shows that the bankers, in the words of one of the characters from Michael Lewis' *The Big Short*, were probably 'more morons than crooks' (quoted in McNally 2011: 107).

NEOLIBERALISM

The process of financialisation described above is one feature of the phase of capitalism that began at around the same time as the Bretton Woods monetary system collapsed, and with which we are still living to this day. It is known as neoliberalism – a term you may have come across and are possibly sick of by now. It is characterised by increasing marketisation of all aspects of life, i.e. turning what were previously considered public provisions into markets where goods and services are bought and sold for the profit of private individuals or companies. Liberalisation and deregulation, privatisation and reductions in social spending have all been central to this process. So have other so-called supply-side measures such as tax cuts for corporations and wealthy individuals, ostensibly to encourage them to invest in the economy, and other subsidies to the private sector. The Washington Consensus on economic policy was established by the late 1980s and supported by international bodies such as the IMF and World Bank. It was built around a set of principles emphasising regressive rather than progressive taxes; liberalisation of financial markets, trade and foreign direct investment; deregulation of markets and privatisation of state enterprises; strengthening of property rights; fiscal discipline (limitation of budget deficits) and the reduction of public spending (Screpanti 2014: 230).

These neoliberal policies have been accompanied by a potent ideology, promoting the private sector as more efficient than the public sector, individual responsibility and entrepreneurship, and competition. Central to the rise of this set of ideas have been certain strands of neoclassical economic theory (Weeks 2014). They espouse notions of 'public choice' and 'efficient markets' that must not be 'interfered with' by governments. The Chicago School of economic thought was an important site for the production of this economic theory (Quiggin 2010). It is important to note, though, that neoliberal ideology does not always correspond with neoliberalism in practice. It espouses a virulently anti-state ethos, for example, but relies heavily on the state to introduce and enforce the mechanisms by which it functions (Harvey 2011). These include the privatisation of public goods, particular tax and spend regimes, anti-union laws, (de)regulatory regimes, and a coercive apparatus to enforce the new status quo, including, in the US and increasingly in the UK, a prison system bursting at the seams. Thus, although neoliberalism is associated with 'free market' capitalism as opposed to state interventionism, markets in the neoliberal era are far from free. The key economists associated with neoliberalism are the Chicago School's Milton Friedman and his mentor Friedrich von Hayek. Its main political figureheads were Ronald Reagan in the US, Margaret Thatcher in the UK and Augusto Pinochet in Chile.

Many accounts of the 2008 financial crisis – those that go deeper than the greed and systemic problems within the banking sector – stop with neoliberalism. If it hadn't been for economic liberalisation and 'free-market fundamentalism' spawning a culture of greed, this disaster could never have happened. This may be true, but we need to ask why neoliberalism developed in the first place. It didn't happen by accident and it wasn't just down to the malevolence of Reagan, Thatcher and Pinochet. Neoliberalism developed because the previous form of capitalism, after two decades of buoyancy, was in crisis.

THE CRISIS OF SOCIAL DEMOCRACY

The Great Depression ended only with the massive stimulus to the economy that was the Second World War and its large-scale investment in 'mega-death' (Varoufakis 2015: 45). After the war, capitalist world leaders were worried about a possible return to depression, as well as the threat from communism, and they decided what was needed was a tightly controlled form of capitalism with strong public investment. The Bretton Woods system was part of this new compact. Some claim that the capitalist and communist regions of the cold war era were not that different in economic terms – both were in fact capitalist economies tightly managed by states and with state ownership of certain key resources (Kurz 2009). The combination of postwar rebuilding, state intervention, Fordist production techniques and mass consumption, decolonisation and leaps in world trade and investment led to high employment rates and spectacular economic growth in parts of the capitalist core. Worker productivity increased impressively, which meant that companies could pay their employees more whilst continuing to pocket higher profits. Living standards rose consistently. Under this social democratic form of capitalism, labour movements were strong and women and some other marginalised groups began making economic headway (Wolff 2012: 37–40).

However, from the mid-1960s the boom started to unwind (Streeck 2017: 25). The downturn conformed to a familiar pattern of declining profitability and over-accumulation identified by Karl Marx 100 years previously. In the drive for profit, accumulation of capital for production was ramped up to extraordinary levels in Japan, Western Europe and South Korea, where entire industries were built virtually overnight. This led to overcapacity, since there was not enough demand for the goods being produced. The hunt for profits paradoxically ended up hurting profits – unused buildings and equipment and stockpiled commodities cost money without making any. Businesses responded with a frenetic wave of downsizing as plants and equipment were written off and bankruptcies increased (McNally 2011: 30).

A US recession in 1971 was followed by a global slump in 1974. Over the course of the next two years, industrial output dropped by 10 per cent in the major capitalist countries and unemployment doubled to 15 million (McNally 2011: 31). Businesses were refusing to invest – they were on 'investment strike'. Recession meant that tax revenues were declining at the same time as social spending on unemployment was rising, which meant government deficits increased. New York City went bankrupt and in 1976 Britain received emergency loans from the IMF.

While economies were stagnating, inflation began to soar, creating the infamous 'stagflation' which until then was thought to have been impossible. Inflation was tied to the Keynesian policies governments pursued at the time, named after the economist John Maynard Keynes. He believed that recessions were caused by a lack of effective demand (especially consumer demand and business investment). This means that, at times when business investment is lacking, it makes sense for the government to step in to boost demand via both monetary policy (increasing the money supply) and fiscal policy (public spending). Under the Bretton Woods system, governments didn't have much leeway on these fronts, but after its collapse in 1971 they sharply increased their money supplies and spending. These expanded flows of money pushed up the prices of everything from food to housing, oil and gold.*

At the same time, unpegging the dollar from gold caused the dollar to lose value, leading oil and other commodity producers to raise their prices – which were denominated in dollars. Thus the notorious 'oil shocks' were unleashed, raising inflation further. As prices for everything increased, workers struck en masse in an attempt to keep wages in line

---

* McNally argues that expanding the money supply doesn't necessarily lead to inflation, but in this context it did. For a more detailed analysis of the dynamics of the period, see Mattick (1978) and Mandel (1978), cited in McNally (2011).

with the cost of living. Employers responded by raising prices to try to pass the costs onto consumers. A vicious inflationary spiral had set in. Governments continued trying to spend their way out of the crisis, creating a million public sector jobs a year in the core capitalist countries between 1971 and 1983 and running persistent deficits, fuelling inflation even further. By the late 1970s it was clear that Keynesian policies could not rescue capitalism from its present crisis.

CLASS WAR?

The inflationary spiral was finally broken in 1979 by the 'Volcker Shock' administered by Paul Volcker, the chairman of the US central bank, the Federal Reserve. According to political economist David McNally (2011: 35), the Volcker Shock marked the birth of the neoliberal era. The Fed pushed up interest rates from 10 to 20 per cent, knocking inflation down to 4 per cent. The price was a deep, deliberately induced recession. The prohibitively high borrowing costs led to sharp cutbacks in business investment and consumer demand, leading to mass unemployment and a full 17 months of economic contraction in the US.

What is crucial to understand is that all the policies and processes of neoliberalism described above were designed to restore profitability to capital, which, as discussed, had been falling. Restoring profitability meant taking away resources from labour and giving them to capital. Mass unemployment was deliberately induced to bring down wages – the greater supply of labour meant it became cheaper. If that weren't enough, a coordinated offensive between governments and employers around the world was launched to roll back union power, labour rights, wages, benefits and conditions of work. Workers resisted these attacks in huge numbers. But mass firings, jailings and large-scale policing were used to break the strikes. In 1985, Margaret Thatcher famously defeated Britain's National Union of Mineworkers. Union power was broken from Canada to Italy, Spain, Germany, France, Chile, Peru, Bolivia and Ecuador (McNally 2011: 43). The subsequent deregulation of labour markets meant 'flexible' employment arrangements, depriving workers of full-time wages and benefits. In the US, real wages were 15 per cent lower by 1993 than they had been in 1978 (44). In Chile, labour's share of national income plummeted from 47 per cent in 1970 to 19 per cent by 1989. At the same time, capital was receiving extra help in the form of tax cuts, privatisations and cuts to public spending – moving resources from the public to the private sector. All in all, this amounted to a large-scale shift in the allocation of wealth, from labour to capital. Inequality soared. Uber capitalist Warren Buffett recently commented, 'there's class warfare, all right, but it's my class, the rich class, that's making war, and we're winning' (Stein 2006).

As unions were busted, businesses were able to restructure their production processes in the quest for profits. This included downsizing, introducing new technologies to speed up production and relocation. Britain lost 25 per cent of its manufacturing industry between 1980 and 1984 (McNally 2011: 46). A core element in restructuring was a move to 'lean' production. The introduction of information technology was combined with flexible working arrangements, including contract-ing-out, casualisation, speed-up and longer working hours. In the US, productivity rose by 2 per cent a year between 1979 and 2007, while real wages increased by slightly more than 1 per cent. Thus, that period of thirty years saw an allocation to capital of much of the new wealth created by labour (48).

Profitability was restored in the 1980s, though never back to the glory days of the postwar period. However, the restructuring represented another problem for capital. If wages were stagnating or falling, how could people afford to buy the products capitalists were selling? Luckily, the answer presented itself in the form of unprecedented household debt. We have already discussed the rise in mortgages, but it wasn't just housing – consumer credit for everything from cars to university fees to shopping at Walmart soared. In the US in 1980, the average household owed around $40,000. By 2010 it was $130,000 (Harvey 2011: 18). At the same time, capitalists who had been reluctant to invest in productive industry due to declining rates of return had begun channelling more and more into the financial sector. Profits were much higher and there weren't the risks and waiting times involved in producing actual things. They invested in derivatives and securities – created out of household and corporate debt – as fast as the financial institutions could make them. We are back where we started, with debt, swollen, deregulated financial sectors and complex financial products.

GLOBALISATION

Capitalism is a world system, and some claim that different forms of imperialism have always been part of its development. The neoliberal phase of capitalism has been associated with what Marxist economist Ernesto Screpanti (2014) calls 'global imperialism', where multinational companies mainly headquartered in the advanced economies (and increasingly some of the emerging economies) extract wealth from around the world. One major way this is done is through ultra low wages, detailed below. Another way has been through debt. In the decade after 1973, Third World debt to global banks quintupled, rising by nearly half a trillion dollars. Then came the Volcker Shock. As interest rates soared, Mexico, Argentina, Poland, Chile, Peru and Venezuela defaulted. Throughout the 1980s and 1990s, more and more developing countries found themselves with unsustainable debts.

The IMF, the World Bank and Western governments stepped in with loans, on condition that the indebted nations carry out the now infamous 'structural adjustment programmes'. In line with the Washington Consensus, these included privatisation of basic resources, radical cuts to spending on public services and social security, removal of subsidies on prices for rice and other essential items, opening up the financial sector to foreign ownership, and labour market 'reforms' which disempowered unions and pushed down wages: in short, an ultra version of the neoliberal reforms carried out across the US and the global north. Whereas in the rich nations the reforms led to a transfer of wealth from the workers of those countries to their corporations, with structural adjustment in the global south, the wealth flowed from the workers and citizens of the south *also* to the corporations of the north. As inequality within countries grew, inequality between the richest and poorest people in the world likewise ballooned (McNally 2011: 127–9).

Another important part of the restructuring of capital has been the reorganisation of production geographically through foreign direct investment and outsourcing – which is at the heart of globalisation. Through what David Harvey (2011) calls 'accumulation through dispossession' and what Marx (1990) called 'primitive accumulation', hundreds of millions of people have been displaced in the global south – through enclosure and privatisation of land for commercial use. We are currently witnessing 'one of the great migrations in world history' (McNally 2011: 51), a demographic shift by which for the first time ever more humans live in cities than in the country. In East Asia, after 1990 the working class increased from about 100 million to 900 million workers. This gigantic pool of reserve labour is the key reason why wages in China's manufacturing industries are only around 5 per cent of the US level.

And cheap labour is key to the globalisation that is a primary feature of the neoliberal era. This great geographic reorganisation of global capitalism – with China at its heart – has seen industries such as textiles, electronics, furniture-making and steel becoming centred outside the old capitalist countries. The emerging economies are now the main drivers of global growth.

However, the investment boom in East Asia led in due course to another crisis of over-accumulation and profitability – the so-called Asian crisis of 1997. Excess capacity had been created in computer chips, autos, semiconductors, chemicals, steel, petrochemicals and fibre optics (McNally 2011: 59). What is more, by the early 1990s, this overheating economic expansion was fuelled by waves of speculative investment causing massive real estate and stock bubbles. Foreign investors had pumped $95 billion into the economies of Thailand, Malaysia, South Korea, the Philippines and Indonesia. The 1997 crash saw a *net outflow* of $20 billion from those countries. As foreign capital fled, currencies plummeted and trade crashed. At the worst point in the meltdown, 10,000 South Korean workers a day were losing their jobs.

The Asian crisis has been called the 'first great crisis of globalisation' (McNally 2011: 59). It sent out aftershocks – including crashes in Russia in 1998, Brazil in 1999, the US dotcom crisis in 2000 and in Argentina in 2000. These were offset by monetary stimulus by the world's central banks, and a frenetic shift in investment to China. The actions of the central banks succeeded in inflating asset bubbles across the globe. In addition, the global restructuring of capitalism led to some countries – most importantly the US – running huge trade and current account deficits with the new drivers of growth – especially China, causing 'global imbalances'. China recycled its surpluses back into the US via Wall Street, which contributed to the asset bubbles which ultimately burst in 2008 (Smith 2016: 287). If we take a global-historical view, then, we see that the 1929 crisis led to a new form of (social democratic) capitalism which found itself in crisis in the 1970s, which led to another new form of (neoliberal) capitalism which has led us to the mess we are in now. So what next?

THE AFTERMATH

We will be exploring what has happened since 2008 in this book – this section will provide a brief overview of some of the key trends. By the end of 2008 all sectors of the US economy were in deep trouble. The UK was just as badly affected, and Iceland went bankrupt. In 2009, Taiwan, China, South Korea and Japan saw their exports fall by 20 per cent or more in the course of two months (Harvey 2011: 6). World trade fell by a third. Oil-producing countries like Russia, Venezuela and the Gulf states found themselves in difficulty as commodity prices plummeted after riding high in the summer of 2008. The collapse of the oil revenue-driven building boom in the Gulf saw thousands of migrant workers from India, Palestine and south-east Asia sent home. Mexico, Ecuador, Haiti and Kerala in India, which depended heavily on remittances from those working abroad, found household incomes drying up as jobs overseas in construction and domestic work were lost (Harvey 2011: 38). Twenty million people found themselves unemployed in China.

Perhaps it was the sense of sheer panic that led to the banks being bailed out with very few strings attached (Varoufakis 2015: 165). In fact, the bailouts actually further empowered financial institutions, as states borrowed from those institutions – at interest – in order to bail them out. Private debt became public debt (discussed in Chapters 1, 2 and 4). Financial institutions then started speculating on the government debt they had created, especially on that of the weaker states of the eurozone (more on which in Chapter 4). Fiscal stimulus – government spending to try to stimulate the economy – which had been the consensus response in 2008 and 2009, swiftly turned to retrenchment and widespread attacks on public services. Austerity was imposed by governments and international bodies such as the European Union institutions and the IMF, which had once more stepped into the breach and 'bailed out' countries facing debt crises (Chapters 2 and 4). 'Structural reforms' including privatisations and deregulation of labour markets were imposed. At the same time, further tax cuts were awarded to the wealthiest, as in the preceding neoliberal decades, in the name of encouraging investment (Chapter 3). In short, in response to a crisis of neoliberalism we have seen not a reversal but an *escalation* of neoliberal measures. The role media amnesia has played in legitimising these measures is one of the main themes of this book.

Recall that these kinds of measures were originally brought in to transfer resources from labour to capital and restore profitability. Sure enough, inequality has intensified once more since 2008, with eight people now owning as much wealth as the poorest half of the world (Oxfam 2017a). In 2010, profits surged while an estimated 64 million people had been driven into poverty. As McNally (2011: 5) wrote, 'profits have improved... largely because working-class people have paid for them, through layoffs, wage cuts, reduced work hours, and the decimation of social services'.

Have these measures saved the economy? There has been a much-touted global 'recovery'. However, growth of the world economy remains below the pre-crisis period and that of past recoveries, and global debt has increased by $60 trillion since 2007 (Phillips 2016). Business investment is low. Growth in China, though three times the rate of that of the US, is slower than in the past. Cheap money washing around, partly due to central bank action designed to combat the recession, has led to a worrying increase in corporate debt in emerging markets. We have been repeatedly warned that the next crisis is just around the corner.

A deeper question might be, even if austerity, privatisation and more precarious working conditions had led to strong GDP growth, would the diminishing quality of life for the majority be worth it? What is the point of growth if most people don't benefit from it? There are strong international movements opposing austerity and the accompanying transfer of wealth upwards. Many of these movements take a Keynesian approach, advocating government investment to stimulate the economy, along with better regulation – in short, a return to the more social democratic form of capitalism of the postwar period. But here we should also ask, given what we know about the crises emanating from this form of capitalism, is a return to it a viable option? Especially if we consider that even during the postwar 'golden years' this economic approach was only able to benefit those in a small number of privileged countries? Is continued growth even feasible if the human species is to survive on this planet? Are there alternative options to both neoliberal and social democratic forms of capitalism? These are some of the most urgent social questions of the day, and we might wonder why the media are not asking them. To the contrary, as we will see, media amnesia effectively constrains us from asking the big questions. Part of countering amnesia means being prepared to put those questions back on the table.

THE MEDIA

This section will provide an introduction to some of the major trends within journalism today, some key concepts for analysing media, and the background to the rise of business and finance news, all needed to understand the workings of media amnesia in the coverage of the economic crisis. 'The media' is an elusive term, often bundling all communications technologies and formats into a singular noun. In this book, I will mainly be talking about the mainstream – by which I mean those with the most reach – news content providers.

Much has been made in recent years of the democratising threat posed by the internet to the dominant news outlets (Curran *et al.* 2016). Now anyone can start a news site or tweet the latest events. For many commentators, the 2017 UK general election results signalled the toppling of the press baron and media corporation. Left-wing Labour leader Jeremy Corbyn had done better than anyone expected (though Labour didn't win). While much of the press had branded him a terrorist sympathiser, he had managed to generate a lot of positive chatter on social media. The dark side of this media democratisation, 'fake news' spread on social media, has become a hot-button issue in relation to the rise of populism.

However, although the internet has led to a proliferation of voices online, the dominant media, for now, remain dominant. In fact, the top two sources of news in the UK are both TV channels: BBC One (with a reach of 48 per cent) and ITV (27 per cent). In the US, television is also the most popular way of consuming news, with 57 per cent often getting news this way, followed by 38 per cent getting news online, 25 per cent for radio and 20 per cent for print newspapers. For younger generations, though, the television figures are lower (Mitchell *et al.* 2016).

Perhaps more importantly, for those who get their news online, the mainstream brands still dominate. The biggest online source and third biggest source overall in the UK is the BBC website (with a reach of 23 per cent). The *Guardian*, *Daily Mail* and Sky News websites are all also in the top 20, as are newspapers like the *Sun*, the *Daily Mail* and the *Mirror*. In the US, 12 of the 15 most popular news websites are mainstream outlets, including CNN, the *New York Times*, Fox news, the Mail Online and BBC news.

Google, Yahoo, Facebook, YouTube and Twitter – which don't produce news but deliver it – were also in the UK top twenty (Ofcom 2015). These huge international distributors are no doubt changing the landscape of news, delivering more eyeballs to non-conventional outlets. However, they also often lead news consumers back to the mainstream brands (Freedman 2014: 99). Returning to the 2017 UK election, alternative news site the Canary achieved more Facebook shares than many mainstream brands. However, when it came to page views (i.e. articles actually read), 8 out of the top 10 websites were owned by traditional newspaper groups (Schlosberg 2017). The *Daily Mail* received 717 times as many page views as the Canary. BBC Online saw 1,053 times as many (Littunen 2017).

MEDIA CRISIS

Though still dominating the news landscape, the mainstream media are facing multiple crises, both financially and in terms of legitimacy. The latter crystallised in the UK in 2011–12 with the phone-hacking scandal, the subsequent closure of the *News of the World* newspaper and the Leveson Inquiry. Public trust in journalists has been low for several years, with a UK poll from 2015 placing trust in journalists to tell the truth at 22 per cent. This compares to doctors at 90 per cent, teachers at 86 per cent, the police at 66 per cent and even bankers at 31 per cent. Journalists tied with estate agents; the only profession with a lower rating was politicians at 16 per cent (Ipsos Mori 2015). In the US, only 18 per cent trust national news outlets and 22 per cent trust local news (Mitchell *et al.* 2016). There is a widely held belief that journalism is supposed to play a central role in democratic life, holding those in power to account and providing citizens with the information required to make informed decisions. The low trust scores indicate that, though people might think that journalism *should* fulfill such a function, it is often felt to fail in that capacity (Fenton 2010: 3).

The crisis of legitimacy is connected to trends in media markets. As we saw in the discussion about speed and acceleration, the media industries are not divorced from wider movements in the economy outlined above. Indeed, communications technologies have themselves been crucial in processes of financialisation, enabling real-time information and transactions which have been central to its development. Not only that, investment in communications has become among the main drivers of capitalism more broadly in the neoliberal period, as companies in all parts of the economy reorganised their businesses around digital networks (Chakravartty and Schiller 2010: 672), aiding the development of transnational business and globalisation.

And media – from telecoms systems to content provision – have undergone the same privatisation, deregulation and financialisation processes as the other sectors of the economy. Between 1984 and 1999, between $250 billion and $1 trillion of state-owned telecommunications networks were sold to investors worldwide (Chakravartty and Schiller 2010: 672). Meanwhile, public service media have been either part-privatised or made to operate in accordance with commercial market conditions (Hardy 2014: 83). It is the restructuring of media markets in the neoliberal era that forms the foundations for today's media amnesia.

This increasing marketisation is linked to growing media conglomeration. News media ownership is highly concentrated in countries as diverse as the US, Chile, South Africa, Malaysia, Argentina, Australia and Mexico (Freedman 2014: 52). News in the UK has long been oligopolistic, with three firms controlling 71 per cent of national newspaper circulation and five companies commanding 81 per cent of local newspaper titles (Media Reform Coalition 2015). Rupert Murdoch's News Corp and 21st Century Fox, which own the *Sun*, *The Times*, the *Wall Street Journal*, Fox News and are currently trying to take full control of Sky plc,* are perhaps the most notorious of these media conglomerates. There is deep concern that such concentration has resulted in a narrowing of perspectives offered to the public and a consolidation of the dominance of elite views (McChesney 1999; Hardy 2014: 105). The BBC and the *Guardian*, meanwhile, show that other kinds of media provision are possible and can prove successful. Neither the BBC nor the *Guardian* is immune from market pressures, however, and both have been undergoing changes in recent years, as will be explored later.

Neoliberal restructuring of the news industry has led to enormous pressures on journalists, as jobs have been cut while the 'news hole' they need to fill has grown ever bigger. In the UK, from the 1960s, a new generation of proprietors took over the newspaper industry, and promptly began indulging in 'corporate looting'. This really took off in the 1980s, when Rupert Murdoch, in one of the confrontations with workers characterising the shift to neoliberalism, defeated the print unions. With the defeat of the print unions, the journalists' union also lost much of its power. Free to impose their will, the new owners began cutting costs. Profits soared. Between 1985 and 1988, Murdoch's declared pre-tax profit on his UK titles rose from £35.6 million to £144.6 million. During the same period, staffing had been cut from 8,731 to 949 (Davies 2009: 63).

It wasn't just the commercial providers – the BBC was caught in the same logic. Between 1986 and 1994, 7,000 BBC jobs were cut. Then,

---

* Things though are in flux. At the time of writing, Disney is attempting to buy 21st Century Fox assets including the stakes in Sky. Trinity Mirror is also in talks to acquire 100 per cent of Express newspapers from owner Richard Desmond. These developments do not threaten to undermine the grip of press barons and corporations on media.

from the late 1990s and 2000s, more cuts were brought in just as news providers were moving into 24-hour broadcasting and online. According to one report, since 2001, between 27 per cent and 33 per cent of UK journalism jobs have gone (Slattery 2010). We therefore have increasing information overload on the one hand and not enough journalists on the other. Each of these situations individually contributes to media amnesia. The result of the combination of the two is exponential.

As in many other sectors, information technology has been used in the news industry to cut costs and increase revenue. However, the move online has ended up threatening the profitability of news outlets. Advertising revenues generated online are not enough to compensate for those lost in falling print newspaper sales. According to the *Financial Times*, in terms of subscription and advertising revenues, one print reader is worth ten online readers (Freedman 2010: 45). The main television channels are likewise losing viewers. Though the news industry is still profitable, its profitability is declining and there is a question mark over what a successful business model might look like in the medium term, with the link between news and advertising funding under threat. This has led to even more job cuts.

Things have worsened since the 2008 crash and the Great Recession (see Fuchs 2010). In the US, 300 newspapers went under in 2009 and 150 more in 2010. The *New York Times* cut 200 newsroom jobs in those same years (Williams 2013). In the UK, between 2007 and 2010 there were more than 9,500 reported job losses in journalism (Slattery 2010). The BBC announced 2,000 job cuts in 2011, many of them in news departments. The *Independent* closed its print titles in 2016. The same year, the Guardian Media Group announced 250 job cuts, 100 in editorial (Martinson 2016).

All of this has deeply affected the ability of journalists to provide quality news content. Journalists now work longer hours for less pay, with 20 per cent working at or below the living wage in the UK (Thurman *et al.* 2016). They are often working on casual contracts. They are now writing up to 13 stories per day (Phillips 2010: 100). Mark Deuze (2007) writes that journalists now work under conditions that are 'liquid', meaning that they are highly unstable. Perhaps this helps explain why the news narratives they produce are also 'liquid', shifting and sliding over time and liable to be hijacked to serve certain ends.

Nick Davies (2009: 60) describes the phenomenon of 'churnalism', whereby journalists are constantly churning out content as in a news factory, without conducting proper accuracy checks. Often content is fed to them by public relations sources. A study from 2008 (Lewis *et al.* 2008: 10–12) found that 41 per cent of broadsheet news items and 52 per cent of broadcast news items contained significant amounts of PR material, largely from politicians and the corporate world. It is thought that this figure is an underestimate since the full influence of PR is difficult to measure. Only 12 per cent of journalists' stories are their own work (Davies 2009: 69). News stories are thus less likely to be accurate, to provide historical or global context, to explore different viewpoints or challenge those in power. Elites are increasingly likely to be able to control the narrative. As will be seen, the lack of global and historical context and the dominance of elite views are the main contributing factors to media amnesia.

As well as cost-cutting, news firms have been busy revenue-raising. This has led to the rise of 'infotainment', some say at the expense of in-depth news (see McNair 1999: 44–50). Cost-cutting and revenue-raising are features of what McChesney (1999) calls the 'hyper-commercialisation' of media in the neoliberal era. In-depth, well-researched journalism still exists, and instances of good journalism will be highlighted throughout these pages. However, just as we have asked whether neoliberal or indeed any form of capitalism can serve the economic needs of people, we might ask whether today's media markets are capable of meeting our democratic needs (Curran 2002). We will explore the possibilities for changing or replacing these markets in Chapter 6.

ANALYSING MEDIA

Despite the problems with journalism outlined above, many journalists and some scholars subscribe to the 'liberal pluralist' model of journalism. They believe that a free press serves a vital democratic role, with markets catering to a plurality of views and helping citizens make informed decisions. Others, on the contrary, claim that the purpose of the media is not to enlighten but to 'inculcate and defend the economic, social, and political agenda of privileged groups that dominate the domestic society and the state' (Herman and Chomsky 1988: 33). Herman and Chomsky, in *Manufacturing Consent*, suggest applying a 'propaganda model' to analyse media. This has been criticised for giving an overly top-down view on the dynamics of media and power, though as will be seen the model is actually nuanced and helpful despite its controversial name.

Still others prefer to work with the term 'hegemony', developed by Antonio Gramsci in the 1930s while imprisoned under the Mussolini regime. Hegemony has to do with the processes by which consent is tacitly given by the majority of people to the existing social order (Gramsci 1971: 12). This consent is achieved through certain ideologies becoming dominant to the point where they are 'naturalised' and appear as 'common sense'. Ideologies are systems of beliefs and ideas, which filter our perception of reality (Jameson 1989, in de Cock 2018). Ideologies can serve the interests of particular social groups. There is constant struggle involved with an ideology becoming and remaining hegemonic – dominant ideas are always being negotiated and challenged and there is always the possibility that they might be uprooted and replaced by a new set of ideas. Gramsci thought that those critical of the status quo should strive to expose the power relations whereby ideas become 'common sense', and to construct a new, emancipatory, cultural mainstream – what he called 'good sense' (Freedman 2014: 27).

The media are primary sites where dominant ideas are continually being both reproduced and challenged. Thus, although journalism is associated with the idea of objectivity, the way stories are chosen and put together means that they are always ideologically encoded. Indeed, Stuart Hall and others have argued that the fact that news reporting is thought of as objective makes it all the more ideologically powerful (Hall *et al.* 1978). This idea of the construction in the news of 'common sense' will be central to the analysis in this book. The 'common sensification' of neoliberal ideas has been a key feature of media amnesia, and in turn, media amnesia has helped to 'commonsensify' neoliberal solutions to the crisis.

The media constructs or challenges common sense by 'framing' aspects of the world and thereby circumscribing our perceptions of reality. For a start, journalists and their editors decide what counts as a story and therefore what gets into the news. Media analysts have developed theories of *news values* – the values that influence what gets counted as news. News values that have been key to the coverage of the economic crisis include 'timeliness', favouring recent events; 'simplification' – the story should be easily simplified; 'cultural specificity', prioritising news about 'people like us'; and 'reference to elite nations', prioritising stories affecting rich countries (Stuart Allan 2004: 57–8). Although they are often taken for granted by journalists, news values are by no means objective (Cushion *et al.* 2016).

News values not only influence what gets counted as news, but also how news stories themselves are 'framed'. For example, journalists will often simplify stories, play up conflict and drama, focus on the very latest events, link stories to the lives of their readers and so on. Two other important news values are the privileging of event over process and effect over cause (McNair 1994: 60). Journalism tends to be much more focused on specific events than on ongoing processes (such as the dynamics of neoliberalism, for instance) and gives more attention to those events (especially spectacular ones) than their causes. These factors will be central in understanding media amnesia.

One way to analyse news coverage is through *framing analysis*. If framing theory suggests that news stories frame our perceptions of the world – in ways that may serve the interests of one group or another – framing analysis can help us discover how they do this, through looking at the way news items are constructed. Robert Entman, one of the media scholars most associated with framing analysis, writes that:

> To frame is to select some aspects of a perceived reality and make them more salient in communicating a text, in such a way as to promote a particular problem definition, causal interpretation, moral evaluation, and/or treatment recommendation for the item described. Typically frames diagnose, evaluate, and prescribe (Entman 1993: 52).

Thus, whenever we read, watch or listen to a news item, we can ask ourselves: what problem is being identified as important and how is it being defined? What explanations are provided for the problem and who is being held responsible? What possible responses or solutions are being offered? This way we can begin to understand what assumptions are contained within the item and consider whether they are valid.

As well as asking how media frames diagnose, evaluate and prescribe, two other questions are vital: who gets to speak? And what's left out? In respect to the first, the matter of news sources is paramount when analysing news. The sources journalists rely on for information operate as 'primary definers' (Hall *et al.* 1978: 57) – they give the initial definition of the problem and set the parameters of the debate. Primary definers are usually politicians and other official sources – their views will be given prominence overall, and structure the coverage.

In terms of the second question, just as particular sources with certain views play a key role in defining events, other views can be omitted altogether. Entman writes that 'most frames are defined by what they omit as well as include, and the omissions of potential problem definitions, explanations, evaluations, and recommendations may be as critical as the inclusions in guiding the audience' (54). We will see that the *narrowness* of the framing of the economic crisis – with so much information and so many perspectives excluded – not only contributes to media amnesia but constrains us from asking some of the most fundamental questions about how resources are allocated – questions that are arguably particularly urgent in this time of crisis. The approach to media in this book uses framing analysis to understand the workings of media amnesia and its ideological effects – how it comes to serve (not always intentionally) particular interests by making certain responses to the crisis appear as 'common sense' and excluding others from debate.

FINANCIAL JOURNALISM

The rise of multinational business and finance over the past decades has been accompanied by an 'extraordinary' rise in business and financial journalism, both within mainstream news and in the form of dedicated outlets. According to Chakravartty and Schiller (2010: 677), this has amounted to a structural reorientation of the news field towards finance and market developments, spanning the different segments of the news market. With this restructuring, news coverage overall began from the 1980s to prioritise sources from the financial sector and business community as well as 'pro-business' officials, to the detriment of voices from labour and other sections of society. This is a transnational phenomenon with its apex in the emerging economies of Asia (Chakravartty and Schiller 2010: 192). For critics, the growing dominance of financial and business news has played a strategic role in legitimising the unequal distribution of the benefits of globalisation. The celebration of Chinese and Indian millionaires and billionaires in the media of those countries is coupled with the message that the poor must pull themselves up by the bootstraps by tapping into their entrepreneurial potential.

Across the globe, wealthy business people, bankers and hedge-fund managers have been turned into 'experts' not only on the business matters that are their remit but on a whole range of social and economic questions. It is important to keep the fact of this repositioning of the news towards business and finance in mind when we come to the coverage of the different aspects of the crisis. It might seem inconceivable that those representing the sectors responsible for the crisis are the ones being called upon to make sense of it and to offer solutions. Bearing in mind the architecture that had been put in place during the decades preceding it will help to fathom the unfathomable.

We have seen that media have been intimately connected to the development of the latest phase of capitalism. Media, communications and information services have been some of the key areas of investment driving growth. They have played a major role in the processes of finan-cialisation and globalisation. They have also been subject to the same processes of deregulation, liberalisation and conglomeration as other sectors of the economy. In turn, the news has been a site through which neoliberal ideology – which in its early stages used to be marginal – has become 'common sense'. It is not surprising, then, that the media largely failed to foresee the 2008 crash.

JOURNALISM AND THE CRASH

News media have been roundly criticised for this failure, which led to some soul-searching by journalists during the early part of the crisis. Several explanations have been offered, many of which are linked to factors described throughout this section. Journalists were dependent on their financial sector sources for information and were thus reluctant to be too critical of what was happening within that sector (Davis 2011). Financial journalists were also often close to their sources in the financial sector, and unable to keep the critical distance needed to spot the risks building up in the system (Fay 2011: 52). Relatedly, finance journalists have been described as subject to 'ideological capture', uncritically taking on the views and values of their main sources (Schechter 2009; Starkman 2014). The growth of PR made it more difficult for journalists to scrutinise the sector properly. Damien Tambini (2010), meanwhile, claims that many finance journalists did not even see their role as that of 'watchdogs' serving the general public. Rather, they saw their job as providing market-relevant information to investors.

Apart from relationships with sources, another issue has been a lack of training, experience and basic understanding of how the financial sector operates which has made it difficult for journalists to explain increasingly complex financial products (Fraser 2009: 79). This lack of knowledge in turn resulted from the profit-maximising initiatives we have discussed, including the drive towards 'fast news', which have also had a negative impact on the kinds of investigative journalism that could have produced warnings (Schechter 2009: 25). The advertising revenues news businesses earned from both financial institutions and real estate were another important factor (Schechter 2009: 21). There have been claims of direct pressures from advertisers on journalists not to be critical of their activities, as well as softer forms of pressure leading to self-censorship (Mercille 2014; Starkman 2014). Knowles et al. (2017) claim that there has been a decline in financial journalism standards since the 1980s, as the media have faced increasing ideological, institutional and commercial pressures.

Finally, it must be remembered that journalists were far from alone in believing nothing was amiss in the world of finance. All those invested with authority on the subject – mainstream economists, central banks, treasury ministers, the IMF and the World Bank – also missed the signs, succumbing to a herd mentality which exacerbated both the inflating of bubbles and the scale of the resulting crash. Part of the process of neoliberal ideology becoming 'common sense' was the steady marginal-isation of sceptical voices – such as heterodox economists, for example – warning that the boom could not last forever. Journalism was thus just one element (though an important one) in a whole array of institutions communicating a blindly pro-business, pro-finance ideology. For this reason, it is necessary to consider journalism within the context of the neoliberal economy and culture more broadly. The issues outlined above affect not only specialist finance reporting but also journalism as a whole. We will return to each of them throughout the course of the book, as they are key to understanding the coverage of the crisis as it continues to unfold.

To sum up, the media industries have played a major role in the neoliberal phase of capitalism, and have in turn been characterised by increasing privatisation, deregulation and conglomeration. The quest for profit has led to ever more and faster news having to be produced by journalists. Concentration of ownership and depletion of resources mean that journalism is less likely to hold the powerful to account, investigate issues thoroughly or seek out a range of perspectives. Journalism is therefore perhaps more likely to fulfil a hegemonic role, legitimising existing social relations by presenting dominant ideas as 'common sense'. Journalists do not necessarily do this intentionally, but the choices they make about what counts as a story, what aspects of the story to emphasise or exclude, and who to turn to as a source, mean that the news frames the world in the interests of certain social groups. When it comes to reporting the economic crisis, the result of these dynamics is a powerful media amnesia that has tended to legitimate 'hyper-neoliberal' solutions to a neoliberal crisis – escalating the transfer of resources from the 99 per cent to the 1 per cent. I hope it has become clear that there is a close link between the kinds of economic movements causing the crisis and those impacting journalism. In fact, to some extent, *the same economic and political processes behind the crisis are also behind its hegemonic, amnesiac reporting.*

THE STUDY

At the heart of this book is a study systematically tracking the coverage of the crisis over time. Its sample comprises 1,133 news items from five UK outlets: the BBC TV *News at Ten*, and the *Guardian*, *Telegraph*, *Sun* and *Mirror* newspapers. These five cover the most popular news outlet in the UK (the BBC news) plus the broadsheet and tabloid newspapers leaning left and right with the highest circulations. It should be noted, though, that the kinds of conservative and 'free market' perspectives associated with the *Sun* and *Telegraph* are much more common in mainstream British journalism than the kinds of views associated with the socially 'liberal' *Guardian* and the *Mirror*, which styles itself as representing the labour movement.

The *Telegraph* is owned by the Telegraph Media Group, a corporation running a £51 million operating profit in 2015 (Greenslade 2016). It is known as a broadsheet appealing to the upper and middle classes, and has consistently supported the Conservative Party at general elections in modern times. The *Sun* is the newspaper with the highest circulation in Britain (Ponsford 2017). It is owned by Rupert Murdoch, whose companies News Corp (to which the *Sun* belongs) and 21st Century Fox are both listed among the top ten media companies worldwide in terms of market capitalisation (Seth 2015). The *Sun* is a right-wing tabloid usually supporting the Conservative Party at elections, though it switched over to New Labour for a period from 1997 after Tony Blair courted Murdoch and presented himself as suitably pro-business (Hesmondhalgh 2015: 374).

The BBC is a predominantly publicly-funded, non-profit organisation. It is mandated to be impartial and balanced. The *Mirror* is a tabloid owned by Trinity Mirror, the largest multimedia content publisher in the UK (Trinity Mirror website). The *Mirror* consistently supports the Labour Party during elections (*Guardian* 2010). The *Guardian* is owned by the Scott Trust, which became a limited company in 2008, and whose mandate is to keep the paper independent from political and commercial pressures. It tends to back the Labour Party at elections, though it supported the Liberal Democrats in 2010 (*Guardian* 2010). It is considered to represent the middle-class centre-left (Ashley 2008).

The research analyses coverage from the national edition of BBC news and the general news and comments sections of the newspapers, rather than specialist finance sections – the intention being to focus on the kinds of news that the average member of the public would be likely to access about these issues. Table 0.1 breaks down the sampled items by outlet and section.

Two one-week periods a year between 2007 and 2015 were selected for analysis. One was always the week of the budget in the UK – when the government announces its tax and spending plans for the year and reveals the state of the economy. In 2010 and 2015 there were two budgets because of the elections, and both were analysed. The other week is events-driven and covers the events of the crisis that received the most media attention. For 2008 two events-driven weeks were selected due to the sheer scale of the events and coverage.

The study was a framing analysis, of the kind described above. It analysed which economic problem or aspect of the crisis was the main focus of each news item, what explanations were offered for that problem and which possible solutions or responses were identified. The five aspects of the crisis receiving the most attention were the global financial meltdown, the UK deficit, the Great Recession and subsequent slump, the eurozone crisis and falling living standards and rising inequality and poverty. These form the basis of the following five chapters. As will be seen, they are entirely interconnected.

Table 0.1 News items by outlet and section

	Guardian	*Telegraph*	*Sun*	*Mirror*	*BBC*	*Total*
News	332	235	64	116		747
Comments	118	72	38	22		250
Total	450	307	102	138	136	**1,133**

Note was taken of whether each explanation and response was endorsed by the news item, rejected by it or mentioned more or less neutrally. For example, a response was considered as neutral if it was either mentioned simply as a measure that was being implemented or proposed without expressing any value judgement, or if evaluation of the measure by the news item was balanced, giving both positive and negative views equally. A response was considered as endorsed if the journalist explicitly supported a measure (more common in comments pieces) or if positive views on the measure were cited without being balanced by negative views. A response was also considered as endorsed if an opinion was expressed as a fact or taken as a given (e.g. 'austerity is necessary'). Responses were considered as rejected in the inverse way. When in doubt, the default category was 'neutral'.

As well as the framing analysis, semi-structured interviews were conducted with journalists from a range of news outlets. The journalists were at different levels of seniority, from current and former section editors from the *Daily Mail*, the *Guardian* and BBC news to young freelancers just starting out. They were asked about their experiences and views on the coverage, what factors they thought impacted their work, and their ideas for improving the quality of journalism.

The study makes no claim to be exhaustive or representative. The book's more modest aim is to provide an outline of the twists and turns of the coverage over the past decade, to illuminate the workings of media amnesia, and to explore what they mean for our media's role within contemporary society. While the focus of the investigation was on UK media, the book draws on studies from around the world, and explores trends that are transnational. That said, it is important to note that the kinds of critique found here pertain mainly to media systems found within liberal democracies. Asking questions about the extent to which media live up to democratic ideals may not be so relevant to regimes that do not even claim to be interested in such ideals. The rise in journalist casualties shows what can happen when journalists do attempt to pursue democratic goals such as holding power to account (Wahl-Jorgensen *et al.* 2016b: 801).

A last, brief point is that the book is about *both* the media and the economic crisis, which are intimately linked: the media frames the crisis and the crisis impacts the media. It weaves together discussions of the news content, why the coverage is how it is – including the political and economic conditions of journalism and professional routines and values – and the economic crisis itself. It also explores alternative explanations and possible solutions to the problems that have not made it into the news coverage but are offered by heterodox scholars and activists. Hopefully this kind of narrative will prove of interest to those interested in both media and the crisis economy, and in politics or current events more broadly. Although I have tried to minimise and explain economic jargon, it seems impossible to talk about the economy without it making an appearance – so a glossary of terms is included.

Chapters 1 to 5 deal with the coverage of the major flashpoints of the crisis mentioned above. Chapter 6 is dedicated to potential cures for media amnesia. It explores a range of solutions to the problems of journalism, focusing on three areas in particular. First, it explores the 'new news ecosystem' brought to life by the internet. Secondly, it engages with debates around social media. Thirdly, it considers a range of possible media reform options, from mild behavioural remedies to ideas for restructuring news provision to serve the public interest. Ultimately, the book shows that the control of media is part of the wider social struggle over the control of resources that is at the heart of the economic crisis, necessitating joined-up action on multiple fronts to achieve change. One thing's for sure: we will need real change in both the media and the wider society if we are to avoid further economic crisis and deteriorating quality of life for the global 99 per cent.

1

Crash

A tone of escalating panic marks the coverage of the financial crisis. After Lehman Brothers collapsed in September 2008, headlines like 'Nightmare on Wall Street', 'Titanic has hit iceberg' and 'The only thing we have to fear is not feeling fearful enough' were common. Phrases like 'financial apocalypse', 'economic armageddon', 'financial tsunami' and 'naked terror' litter reports. Little wonder. The financial system was in fully-fledged meltdown. Worldwide credit had seized up as financial institutions refused to lend to each other for fear of the toxic assets they had on their books. By the end of 2008, global stock markets had plunged nearly 50 per cent, wiping out around $35 trillion in financial assets. All five of Wall Street's investment banks – and many more around the world – had vanished (McNally 2011: 13). For the first time in 70 years, the world was witnessing a fully-blown crisis of capitalism. Governments came to the rescue with hundreds of billions of dollars in bailouts, while central banks pumped in liquidity and cut interest rates to near zero.

Given the sheer scale of the meltdown, journalists and their editors must have been flabbergasted. Probably for that reason, this first phase of the crisis saw the most open media framing. Rage against the 'masters of the universe' appeared alongside attempts to explain the systemic problems with finance. Some coverage even grasped the roots of the crisis in the neoliberal or 'free market' capitalism of the previous three decades. Demands for bankers to be held to account joined widespread calls for financial reform. Full public ownership of the banks was even approved of in some quarters of the press. The global nature of the crisis and its effects was conveyed.

Unfortunately, these explanations and demands were quickly forgotten. Even at this early stage, several of the problems with the coverage that later become all-too-apparent were identifiable. Explanations were too often shallow, confusing or absent altogether. Measures taken by the establishment were too often accepted without proper scrutiny. And the range of debate, though broader than in later stages of the crisis, nevertheless excluded discussion of some of the most fundamental questions about our global economy – questions that a crisis should arguably bring out into the open. In some ways, then, the coverage of this first phase of the crisis is the starting point from which media amnesia is explored in the remainder of the book – it was the coverage from this period that was later forgotten and rewritten in subsequent months and years. However, as will be seen, the elements of media amnesia were already discernible in 2008.

GREEDY BANKERS

The most common explanation for the crash was the bad behaviour of those working in the financial sector, or the 'greedy bankers' frame (Thompson 2009; Schifferes and Knowles 2015). In coverage focusing on the financial crisis, this accounted for 29.3 per cent of explanations given. Headlines blazed, 'Arrogance and greed of bankers lie at the heart of financial meltdown' and 'so many suffer for the grimy greed of a few'. The *Mirror* referred to 'greedy, immoral bankers' and 'grasping bankers' who had 'infected the system with financial foot-and-mouth' to fund their 'obscene lifestyles' (Maguire 2008b).

The sense of outrage expressed here is perfectly understandable, and there is a good argument that journalists should give voice to public anger directed towards those implicated in causing hardship to millions. In 2007, Goldman Sachs paid its leading employees $20–$25 million each in bonuses, with some traders getting as much as $50 million. Real-life pantomime villains like RBS's Fred 'the Shred' Goodwin made for good headlines. We might wonder where this anger has gone, after years of austerity. Those claiming that there is no 'magic money tree' to fund public services might do well to remember the bankers and their bonuses.

The problem with this approach, though, is that the tales of greed, arrogance and stupidity tend to distract from the more systemic problems with the financial sector. As Steve Schifferes and Sophie Knowles (2015: 48) write: 'the moralizing of the crisis in the press allowed popular anger to focus on individuals, rather than on the financial system as a whole, or on the politicians and regulators who had created the structures that had permitted abuse of the financial system'. While there is certainly a place for anger, then, a more systemic understanding of the crisis is necessary.

SUBPRIME AND SECURITIES

The majority of media items failed to provide these systemic explanations. Nevertheless, they were the second most frequent category of explanation for the crash, representing 24.4 per cent of the causes mentioned. Some journalists made a valiant effort to explain to their audiences in plain English what was going on, no easy task in the small space available in the conventional news format. In the *Telegraph*, Edmund Conway explained the issue in some detail during the Bear Stearns collapse in March 2008. It is worth quoting at length:

> Quite simply, we have borrowed too much over the past decade or so. Individuals and businesses alike are guilty. When banks ran out of money to lend to their customers, rather than closing the floodgates they came up with an ingenious solution. They found they could continue to lend mortgages and loans if they sliced up the debt and sold it on to other canny investors. They did so, and it was this 'securitisation' that helped drive house prices ever higher both here and in America ...
>
> The only problem was that those investors weren't as canny as they thought. They paid massive prices for these bundles of debt, despite the high probability that a certain proportion of the debtors would default. When house prices in America started to fall, inevitably, after so many years of break-neck inflation, all too many investors found themselves landed with these toxic packages, no longer worth much more than the paper they were written on ...
>
> Unsurprisingly, as a result of all this chaos, banks have pretty much given up on securitisation and this is where our rather vulnerable economy comes in ... until recently mortgage companies were relying on this funny money for almost a third of their lending ...
>
> The fact that none of the banks has any idea how badly their competitors have fared has only served to intensify the crisis. The interbank lending markets – the oil that lubricates the financial system – have been all but frozen for months (Conway 2008).

This article lays out concisely the problems with banks overborrowing and overlending, securitisation and the subsequent collapse of confidence and liquidity. Other journalists also detailed the failures of the regulators – the Financial Services Authority (FSA) in the UK –

to spot the problems. Regulatory failure was the fifth most frequently mentioned cause of the crash.

Unfortunately, Conway begins his article by blaming ordinary consumers for borrowing too much. In one respect, blaming consumers makes sense. After all, this debt would not have existed had consumers not borrowed the money. However, this ignores the fact that real wages had been falling or stagnating. Both in the US and in the UK, individuals were regularly borrowing not for luxury goods but to spend on services like education or healthcare, or just to makes ends meet (BBC Radio 4 2011).

Nevertheless, the rest of Conway's account is reasonably comprehensive, accurate and clear. Elsewhere, the coverage made no attempt to explain the systemic problems in finance. When explanations were offered, they were often given in a fleeting and off-hand way, which would not have shed much light on the situation for the average reader or viewer. With others, the most striking thing about them is how incomprehensible they are:

> It is not just that Lehman had $110bn of senior bonds that are now virtually valueless; it had written an estimated additional $440bn credit default swaps on top, which it cannot honour ... Nobody knows where these losses will end up. It has suddenly become obvious that the Paulson plan cannot simultaneously handle this together with the fallout of the sub-prime crisis. And in addition there is the impossible challenge of financing trillions of dollars of asset-backed securities which are maturing when the world's interbank markets are shut (Hutton 2008).

Bear in mind that these items are not from the specialist finance sections but the main news and comments pages. Moreover, this article was published during the height of the collapse in October 2008, so terminology to which we may now have become more accustomed would have still been relatively new. The jargon of 'credit markets', 'liquidity', 'subprime', 'asset-backed securities' and 'credit default swaps' would probably not have enlightened the average reader as to what was going on. Only those already familiar with the system would understand the language, and it is likely that these people already knew what was happening – in fact only the kinds of people *giving* the journalists the information would understand these explanations.

Why was it so difficult for journalists to explain the systemic problems with finance in a way that made sense? One reason is that most of them didn't understand what was going on, and so were reliant on sources within the finance sector. Much of the generalist coverage was not produced by financial journalists but by those working in politics sections or the news desk, who would have had even less knowledge of the subject. One former BBC correspondent stressed to me that the compartmentalisation of news production into different sections, operating in silos, and the prioritising of some sections over others (i.e. politics over economics), led to a lack of clear and thorough explanation.

But there may be another reason: the system does not make sense. Henry Ford once remarked about the US that 'it is well enough that people of the nation do not understand our banking and monetary system, for if they did, I believe there would be a revolution before tomorrow morning' (in Byttebier 2017: 14).

Over the decades, those working in the financial sector had erected a scaffolding of incomprehensible jargon with which, in the words of journalist Max Hastings, they told people that 'only they knew how to manage capitalism'. Behind that scaffolding, they were engaging in some truly nonsensical behaviour. Heterodox Cambridge University economist Ha-Joon Chang explains just how surreal 'financial innovation' had become. Mortgage-backed securities (MBSs) were created by bundling together up to several thousand mortgages. Then, some of these MBSs, up to 150 of them, were bundled into collateralised debt obligations (CDOs). Then, CDOs squared were created by using other CDOs as collateral. Then, CDOs cubed were created by combining CDOs with CDOs squared. Ever higher-powered CDOs were created (Chang 2011: 238). Credit default swaps (CDSs) were created to protect against default on CDOs. Only you didn't have to be exposed to the risk in order to buy one.

These antics were carrying on within institutions that were 'too big to fail' and threatened to bring down the entire system if they collapsed – something they knew very well. The regulations governing financial institutions were designed according to their wishes. Many of the transactions were taking place in the shadow banking sector, which evades even this regulatory regime. According to journalist Joris Luyendijk (2016), who interviewed 200 people working in finance, the system was riddled with 'conflicts of interest' and 'perverse incentives'. In particular, the shareholder-value model of banking prioritises return on equity over all else. It encourages excessive leverage and risk-taking. While the rewards have been harvested by shareholders and managers, the risks have been borne by society (Haldane 2011: 2).

Economist and former Greek Finance Minister Yanis Varoufakis (2015: 132) argues that complex financial instruments came to function as a kind of 'private money', which flooded the world economy. In 2007, for every $1 of world income, $12 worth of derivatives circulated. In the words of Varoufakis: 'the world of finance had evidently grown too large to be contained on planet earth!' (130). Finance had seemingly lost any connection to reality. However, as Tony Norfield (2016: 84) explains, that connection hadn't been broken, it had just been 'stretched'. All the private money that the banks had created was based on debt. The ability of the debtors to repay the debt with interest was dependent on the creation of value in the 'real' economy – their wages. When they started defaulting on their loans, the system came tumbling down.

FINANCIALISATION

To understand the crisis, journalists did not just have to get to grips with the impenetrable financial system but with how that system had become so dominant, and its relationship to the wider economy. Curiously, in the 412 media items with a primary focus on the global financial crisis, the size and dominance of the financial sector was only given as an explanation for the problems three times – all in the *Guardian*. For the entire sample of 1,133 items focusing on all the different aspects of the crisis, this explanation was only given 18 times – 1.8 per cent of the explanations mentioned. Eleven of these mentions were in the context of the eurozone crisis, especially when it came to Cyprus, whose financial sector was 7.5 times the size of its economy (Strupczewski 2013).

However, the UK also had, and still has, a very large banking sector. The City is one of the world's leading financial centres and is the most international in its reach (Norfield 2016: 4). This has implications for other sectors of the economy, and for the stability of the economy as a whole. As Ashley Seager (2008a) wrote in the *Guardian*:

The sector has grown 57 per cent since 1997, in sharp contrast to manufacturing, which has spent most of the past 10 years in or close to recession as a result of the strong pound limiting its ability to sell products abroad.

As well as its magnitude, contemporary finance is extraordinary in terms of its penetration into all areas of the economy and everyday life, and its influence over policy. In other words, contemporary capitalism has become financialised. Economist and former Syriza MP Costas Lapavitsas, who has written one of the best-known books on financialisation (2013), explains that financialisation is the sum of three fundamental tendencies that are widespread in mature capitalist countries. First, financial institutions have come to focus more on trading in financial assets than lending to companies for production. Second, non-financial corporations have financialised themselves, using their profits to engage in financial transactions. And third, households and individuals have increasingly been drawn into the financial system through debt. Financialisation has been accompanied by increased inequality, as financiers have managed to stake more and more claims on the profits of non-financial businesses and people's incomes, in the form of fees, commission and interest. Financialisation was not in itself a subject for media discussion at this time. However, one set of reforms that had enabled the sector to grow so excessively was: deregulation.

'CASINO CAPITALISM'

The deepest media explanations for the crisis frame the problems with the banking sector in the context of the policies and processes characterising neoliberalism, like deregulation, liberalisation and globalisation. These 'neoliberal' explanations were the third most frequent type of explanation given for the financial crisis, though only accounting for 10.7 per cent of causes mentioned.

Most of these explanations focus on financial deregulation. The *Guardian's* Polly Toynbee (2008) fumed: 'It began with Margaret Thatcher's Big Bang deregulation and now it has nearly brought the world's economy crashing to destruction.' It wasn't only the left-leaning *Guardian* that contained this kind of explanation, however. While this category of explanation represents 15.4 per cent of causes mentioned for the financial crisis in the *Guardian*, for the *Telegraph* the figure is 7.7 per cent, 6.1 per cent for the *Sun*, 9.7 per cent for the *Mirror* and 4.3 per cent for the BBC news.

A piece from the free-market bastion the *Telegraph* quotes a 'surprisingly candid' hedge-fund manager asking why better regulations weren't in place (Raynor 2008a). The tabloids had their own version too.

One piece from the *Mirror* makes a common juxtaposition between good old-fashioned manufacturing-based capitalism and bad new-fangled finance capitalism:

> This was once a country where people built things, and made things ... Then Thatcher arrived and proclaimed that the jobs where people got their hands dirty were old-fashioned and that the financial sector would generate the money we needed to pay our way. New Labour went along with it. It has not worked. That kind of casino capitalism, a culture of unfettered and unapologetic greed, has brought us to this wretched point (Parsons 2008).

Even the *Sun* blamed deregulation, pointing the finger at

> a Prime Minister who spent a decade as Chancellor letting the credit industry run riot ... It hasn't happened in Canada, Australia or Sweden because THEIR banks were properly regulated ... That is Gordon's fault. He failed to lock the stable door. Now the horses are trampling all over the economy (Kavanagh 2008b).

The political affiliations of the newspapers are evident here. The *Sun* and the *Telegraph* blame Gordon Brown and New Labour, while the *Guardian* and the *Mirror* point the finger at Thatcher. The fact that such flexibility for allocating blame is even possible suggests that both parties not only acquiesced in financial deregulation but actively promoted it. While Thatcher had been responsible for the 1986 Big Bang deregulation of the sector, New Labour further deregulated in 1997 and established the Financial Services Authority (FSA), which was tasked with 'light-touch' regulation.

DIGGING DEEPER

Regardless of the political partisanship, the attention to the role of financial deregulation in the crisis is welcome. As we saw in the introduction, however, the crisis can't be understood in relation to financial policy alone. Financial deregulation and financialisation happened alongside other processes defining the neoliberal era beginning in the 1970s: corporations relocating overseas and the attendant liberalisation of trade and investment across national borders (i.e. globalisation); and the deregulation of labour markets, privatisation of public resources, reductions in social spending, and tax cuts for corporations and the rich to boost the profitability of capital.

A minority of the coverage, especially in the *Guardian* and *Mirror*, did nod towards these wider transformations. The *Guardian*'s Seumas Milne, for example, was one of the handful of journalists to use the term 'neoliberal' at this time. He criticised the political establishment for not grasping the full extent of the crisis and the need for reform:

> Britain's political class appears to be wedded to the politics of the 1990s and the glory days of neoliberalism, clinging to the economic legacy of Thatcherism and unable to make the shift from deregulation to intervention that the times demand (Milne 2008).

In the same piece, Milne also uses other language commonly deployed to describe the neoliberal model of capitalism, like 'laissez-faire capitalism', 'the free market model', 'market fundamentalism' and 'economic liberalism'. Other journalists also complained about 'Thatcherism', 'casino capitalism', 'free market capitalism', and cultures of greed, individualism or consumerism. These implicitly take their criticism beyond financial deregulation to the deeper form of capitalism. Nevertheless, this kind of framing was rare.

HISTORY WILL TEACH US SOMETHING

This relative lack of explanatory depth is related to what we will discover to be one of the major elements of media amnesia: a lack of historical context. Most of the coverage blaming deregulation situates the crisis in the context of the past decade or so, when 'light-touch' regulation of finance entered its heyday (though the coverage isn't usually specific about time-spans). Those articles pointing the finger at Thatcherism implicitly stretch back to the late 1970s. Certainly none of the coverage goes further back than that. This is noteworthy, especially given that there was a great deal of historical *analogy*. Media scholar John Tulloch noted that 'the press and the blogosphere is full of articles recalling everything from Tulipmania, the crash of Overend and Gurney in 1866 to 1929' (Tulloch 2009: 100). From the time of the Lehman collapse, it became common for journalists and commentators to compare events with the 1929 Wall Street Crash and the Great Depression: 'This is without doubt the most serious financial shock since 1929' (Elliott 2008b); 'a financial crisis comparable to the Wall Street Crash of 1929' (Winnett 2008); 'This is now clearly the most serious crisis of the capitalist system since 1929–33' (Hobsbawm 2008).

Historical *analogies* with 1929 were abundant, but historical *context* certainly didn't go that far back. Analogy and context are very different things. The first is used in this case as a kind of benchmark or point of comparison – to indicate the seriousness of events, make predictions and offer lessons from history. The latter helps explain how we got to where we are.

Some economists and other academics do trace the origins of the 2008 crash to the crash of 1929. Varoufakis (2015) shows that the postwar, Keynesian, more tightly-controlled economic system was established in response to the 'laissez-faire' form of capitalism that caused the 1929 crash. The breakdown of the postwar settlement in turn led to the neoliberal transformation of capitalism, which created the instability that culminated in the 2008 meltdown. Marxian scholars might go back even further, and trace the origins of the crisis back to the establishment of capitalism itself. They maintain that capitalism is an inherently unstable system that never resolves its crises but only moves them around. In many cases, the causes of each crisis can be found in responses to the previous crisis (Harvey 2011). In subsequent chapters we will see how responses to the crisis in 2008 and 2009 sowed the seeds for future crises.

Thus, only a minority of coverage gave in-depth explanations that situated the problems of finance within the broader transformations taking place over the preceding decades, and certainly not further back than that. Most of the explanations offered were more superficial, focusing either on the systemic problems within the financial sector or, most frequently, the greed and recklessness of individual bankers.

In fact, a large portion of the sample didn't give any explanations whatsoever. Of the media items focusing primarily on the financial crisis, 42.6 per cent of them offered no explanations at all. This figure increases over time. In September 2007, during the run on Northern Rock, some kind of explanation was given in 81.1 per cent of the items. By October 2008, the figure was only 44.8 per cent. In later periods, the percentage is even lower. When all the coverage dealing with all the economic problems for the entire period is taken together, no explanation at all is given in 48.9 per cent of the items – almost half. In the *Guardian* 45.8 per cent of items give no explanation, for the *Telegraph* 51.5 per cent, the *Sun* 58.1 per cent, the *Mirror* 43.1 per cent and the BBC news 52.6 per cent. The reasons behind the chronic lack of historical context in journalism are explored in Chapter 2.

'TECTONIC CHANGE'

The coverage of the crisis at this time was contradictory. On the one hand, it conveyed the enormity of the situation, and frequently claimed that things would never be the same again. On the other, through the framing of possible responses to the crisis, it tended to contain the debate and thereby possibly enable the restoration of the status quo. Later on we will look more closely at which specific responses to the crisis attracted attention – punishing the bankers, the bank bailouts, banking reform and the part-nationalisations of the banks. This section considers the tone and parameters of the debate as a whole.

The entire economic system was under threat. Under these circumstances, politics had been turned upside down. In the US, the citadel of 'free market' capitalism, George W. Bush was partially nationalising the financial system. In the UK, the Labour government, after having spent more than a decade carefully building up a 'market-friendly' image, had already begun that process. The Conservatives, the party of Margaret Thatcher, were pushing the government to take more control over bonuses. One *Guardian* correspondent quoted MP George Galloway: 'The Liberals sound like Labour and the Conservatives like communists – the kaleidoscope has definitely been shaken' (Watt 2008). This sense of upheaval was reflected in the media.

When the UK government bailed out its banks, a BBC headline announced: 'It's the day the system changed forever' (BBC 2008c). The *Telegraph* solemnly declared: 'OCTOBER 13, 2008 will go down in history as the day the capitalist system in Britain admitted defeat' (Raynor 2008b), adding that things had 'changed irreversibly'. In the *Mirror*, Kevin Maguire wrote, 'in a hundred years from now students will be studying this cataclysmic upheaval in the same way our kids learn about the Jarrow March, the General Strike and the Industrial Revolution' (Maguire 2008a). A *Guardian* piece quoted Labour's Tony Lloyd: 'The tectonic plates have shifted and we will never again be in the position of the Thatcher and Reagan years. That has been swept away by the excesses of the private sector.' It proclaimed:

An unfinished and not necessarily propitious tectonic change is still in train ... these are clearly now new times. Under pressure of events the limits of the possible have been redefined – or at least reopened (Watt and Treanor 2008).

The extent of the shock felt was reflected in the fact that, for perhaps the first time in years, the word 'capitalism' started to appear frequently in the media. Journalists and pundits wrote of 'a major failure of market capitalism' (Hastings 2008), 'capitalism gone wrong' (Leeson 2008) and a 'full-throttle crisis of capitalism' (Hunt 2008).

Journalist Nick Davies explains that, before the 1980s and 1990s, the structure of society – capitalism – had generated 'the most powerful global debate of the twentieth century' (Davies 2009: 128). Since the ascent of neoliberalism, however, that social structure had become invisible. It had simply become taken for granted or 'naturalised'. In 2006, the word 'crap' made it into the news more frequently than the word 'capitalism' (Davies 2009: 128). The 2008 crash jolted commentators into remembering that our economy and society are arranged in a certain way, and that the arrangement had a name. In the media coverage focusing primarily on the global financial crisis, the word 'capitalism' featured 25 times in the *Guardian*, 15 in the *Telegraph*, 5 in the *Mirror* and 3 in the *Sun*. The c-word even slipped into the BBC news on 3 occasions, with Robert Peston telling viewers that 'the wheels of capitalism are seizing up' (BBC 2008a).

The memory did not last long, however. In October 2008, 12.7 per cent of the items analysed in this study mentioned the word 'capitalism'. In January 2009, it was 7.8 per cent. By April 2009, when the debate shifted to the deficit and austerity, it was zero.

There was also an extraordinary amount of talk about socialism. The *Guardian*'s economics editor pointed out that 'Ben Bernanke, chairman of the Federal Reserve, and Hank Paulson, the Goldman Sachs tycoon who became US treasury secretary, have done more for socialism in the past seven days than anybody since Marx and Engels' (Elliott 2008a). Another *Guardian* piece claimed that the US bailout had provided a 'socialist solution to capitalistic problems' (Sorrell and Butselaar 2008). Jonathan Freedland (2008) described the US rescue package as 'red-blooded Bolshevism'.

The *Telegraph*'s copy expressed a similar idea only with more hostility. After the UK bank bailout was announced, Andrew Gimson (2008) asked, 'what kind of a place London will become with Brown and Darling's reinvention of socialism. The Leningrad of the West?' A report on the bailout claimed that we were now 'living in a country which is part capitalist, part socialist' (Raynor 2008b). The *Sun*'s Trevor Kavanagh (2008b) wrote that 'Old Socialists and Labour MPs will have danced a jig at the death of capitalism – until they realised that, like John Prescott, we are all middle class now.' It was left to the *Telegraph*'s Charles Moore (2008) to point out that:

> To me, it does not look like socialism that the Government is ready to take shares in banks. They are non-voting shares, and the idea is to sell them later. The plan does not attempt to direct the banks' decisions. This looks like a huge effort to shore up capitalism, not to replace it. It is the Left that should be annoyed: some of them are.

Indeed, as journalists were waxing lyrical about 'tectonic change', the authorities were doing everything in their power to shore up capitalism and return to business as usual. Many of the policies they have implemented since have been desperate measures to keep the system afloat, often to the disadvantage of the 99 per cent. The lightning-speed media forgetting of capitalism, making the system once again invisible and therefore off the table for discussion, may have helped to enable this situation.

Even at the time, despite all the talk of socialism and 'irreversible change', some commentators expressly set out to contain the debate within the parameters of capitalism. John Tulloch analysed the historical amnesia and the complex rhetorical manoeuvring taking place within the right-wing broadsheets at this time to rescue capitalism's reputation – by positing a 'good capitalism/bad capitalism' split and blaming the bad capitalists, and by refocusing blame onto the Labour Party (in Hoskins and Tulloch 2016: 73–83). This recuperation also took place in the *Guardian*. Max Hastings (2008) wrote that 'Market capitalism has delivered amazing prosperity to the west', and endorsed Margaret Thatcher's slogan that 'There Is No Alternative'. Another piece warned against 'fundamentalisms of right and left' and sought to remind *Guardian* readers that 'as Churchill said of democracy, the capitalist market economy is the worst economic system ever invented, apart from all the others' (Marquand 2008).

As we will see below, the idea that capitalism should be reformed to curb its 'excesses' was mooted, especially in the *Guardian* and the *Mirror*.

But despite the talk of capitalism and socialism, the idea of moving beyond capitalism was off limits. The only item that got anywhere close to such an idea was a piece from October 2008 by George Monbiot in the *Guardian*. In it, he warns that the infinite economic growth demanded by capitalism is incompatible with the planet's capacity to sustain human life. The question of economic growth, and its ecological implications, will return in Chapter 3.

Thus, the coverage conveyed the extremity of the crisis, and predicted momentous change. But at the same time, despite the recognition that capitalism had failed, there was no discussion of changes that might go beyond capitalism. While there was talk of reopening the 'limits of the possible', the media were simultaneously helping to close those limits down.

BANKER-BASHING

Corresponding to the 'greedy bankers' explanation, there were calls for those responsible to be punished. However, this was only the seventh most frequently mentioned possible response, making up 3.6 per cent of the possible responses to the crash mentioned. It was seen not so much as a solution to the problems but as a means of putting right an injustice and giving the taxpayer some form of catharsis. It found most support in the *Guardian*, and also found endorsement in the *Telegraph* and the *Mirror*. Interestingly, although the *Sun*'s copy quite frequently blamed greedy bankers, it did not endorse punishment – at least not in the sample analysed here. Recommended punishments ranged from run-of-the-mill sackings and imprisonments to the more creative:

I estimate that there is about £1bn worth of coppers in circulation that no one's using. I think we should give all these coppers to the masters of the universe to help them out of their troubles, on the understanding that they count it. By hand. I am confident that by the time they've finished, if not before, they will have rediscovered the forgotten art of adding up (Browning 2008).

To the more morbid:

Let them relive the Dark Ages they're dragging the world economy back to. Put them in stocks (to remind them what got them into this mess) and invite everyone whose home has been repossessed to pelt them with bricks (Reade 2008).

In Iceland, where the banking sector had grown to 10 times the size of the economy before collapsing, several senior bankers were sent to prison (Simanowitz). In the UK, Andrew Sayer (2015: 272) notes that Fred Goodwin of RBS cost society £45 billion and 9,000 jobs. He had his pension cut to £342,500 per year and lost his knighthood (given to him by New Labour for services to banking!). Meanwhile, Nicholas Robinson was jailed for six months for stealing bottles of water worth £3.50 during the 2011 London riots.

In June 2017, four former executives from Barclays Bank, and the bank itself, were charged with fraud over the bank's actions during the bailouts. It is the first time criminal charges related to the financial crisis have been brought against a bank in the UK. This is despite scandal after scandal, from Libor-rigging to insurance mis-selling, hitting the headlines.

BANK BAILING

Table 1.1 Mentions of bank bailouts as possible response to the global financial crisis. Sample size: 412. Percentages show proportion endorsed, rejected or reported neutrally by outlet.

Solution				Outlet			Total
		Guardian	Telegraph	Sun	Mirror	BBC	
Bank bailouts	Endorsed	31	27	4	8	27	97
		19.9%	24.8%	12.1%	16%	67.5%	
	Rejected	0	2	1	0	0	3
		0%	1.8%	3%	0%	0%	
	Neutral	125	80	28	42	13	288
		80.1%	73.4%	84.8%*	84%	32.5%	
	Total	156	109	33	50	40	388

*Note: Percentages might not always add up to exactly 100, due to rounding.

By far the most frequently cited response to the crash referred to the bank bailouts. They accounted for 39.5 per cent of possible responses mentioned. In September 2008, US Treasury Secretary Henry Paulson proposed a bank rescue plan costing $700 billion, the bulk of which entailed buying up toxic mortgage-backed securities. In October, the

UK Chancellor Alistair Darling announced a £500 billion bailout. This included £50 billion in direct state investment, £200 billion in short-term loans and £250 billion in guarantees. Several other governments followed suit. This was only after a series of banks had already collapsed or been taken over, and central banks had pumped in tens of billions of liquidity into their financial systems.

The UK bailouts were the focus of attention in the UK coverage. Table 1.1 shows that the bailouts were overwhelmingly reported neutrally or endorsed. As explored below, the accompanying idea of nationalisation was often framed negatively, but there was virtually no opposition voiced to the bank rescues themselves – i.e. handing over the money. Governments justified them on the basis that they had no choice – the bailouts were necessary to prevent unimaginable catastrophe. That argument was accepted and reproduced in the coverage. When there was criticism, it was not around the idea of giving the banks money but about whether it was sufficient and whether it had arrived too late. In the days building up to the UK bailout announcement, the government came under repeated attack for dithering – not only in the right-wing press but also the *Guardian*. One report stated that:

> Instead of exuding authority, as he did last week with the appointment of the national economic council, the government has been playing catch-up ... Instead of being on top of events and acting decisively, the chancellor has been criticised for dithering (Wintour 2008a).

That criticism had come from within the financial sector itself! Then-Bank of England chief Mervyn King had also been criticised for dithering the previous year when Northern Rock was in meltdown. Events were moving so fast and their possible effects were so massive that action had to be taken at a speed the authorities found difficult to handle.

Once the rescue plan was announced, it was generally agreed to be 'bold' and 'comprehensive'. As can be seen in Table 1.1, the BBC was particularly supportive of the bailouts. The political editor commented that, 'after a year of ad hoc solutions, this plan's designed to be comprehensive and long-term', adding, 'there was barely a murmur of opposition in Westminster today, for a simple reason. Most politicians know that if the City fails, so too does the entire economy.' The business editor expressed his relief: 'I think we have narrowly avoided disaster' (BBC 2008b).

The chancellor and prime minister came in for praise. Gordon Brown entered perhaps his sunniest period as prime minister, hearing his handling of the situation heralded as 'world leading'. His political fortunes would not last long.

The endorsement of the bailouts across the media was to some extent understandable. The scale of what was happening caused panic in elite circles, including journalists. It must have been a relief to think that governments were getting the situation under control. Were they right to believe that any amount of public money was worth spending to avoid a complete meltdown of the system? Today, the consensus seems to remain that the bailouts were necessary to prevent disaster. What would have happened in cities, for example, if money had stopped circulating through the economy, preventing supermarkets stocking their shelves with food? On the other hand, political scientist Mark Blyth (2013: 234) believes that in hindsight, given the economic and social devastation that has occurred as a result, and the fact that the banks are still on shaky ground, the bailouts were a mistake: 'we may have impoverished a few million people to save an industry of dubious social utility that is now on its last legs.'

Whether or not bailouts were preferable to letting the banks fail, what is certain is that the form the packages took and their possible implications should have come under much more scrutiny. At the time, there were repeated assurances that public services would not suffer as a result of the huge injection of public money into the banks. Authorities made it clear that the banks would 'pay the money back'. As will be seen in the next chapter, some pundits did anticipate that the bailouts would mean tax rises and spending cuts. But this was not followed by any discussion of how to prevent such unacceptable consequences.

There was even talk of the taxpayer making a profit from the bailout. In a *Guardian* report, the UK Shareholders Association was quoted describing the bailout as 'a socialist leftwing agenda to get hold of the banks without paying anything like a realistic price for them' (Treanor *et al.* 2008). On the BBC news, the association also expressed its disgust at the victimisation of shareholders.

This 'profit' presumably referred to the possibility that the government would see a good rate of return on its direct investment in shares and loans, now estimated at £123.93 billion. In 2017 the government sold the last of its shares in Lloyds for a total return of £21.2 billion – roughly breaking even. In 2011 Northern Rock had been sold to Virgin Money, owned by tax exile Richard Branson, at a loss. In 2015, £2 billion of the state's £45 billion of RBS shareholdings were sold at a loss.

However, these kinds of returns pale into insignificance compared with the full cost of the bailout, which includes an estimated £332.4 billion in guarantees and liabilities and £5 billion a year just to service the loan for the bailout (Curtis 2011). By the end of 2009, the total value of the bailouts in the US, UK and eurozone equalled an estimated $14 trillion – almost a quarter of the world's GDP (Sayer 2015: 229). Keep these sums in mind when we come to Chapter 2 and austerity. The impact of the crash on the wider economy has been even more serious. In 2010, the Bank of England's Andy Haldane estimated the present value of expected future losses to the world economy at between $60 trillion and $200 trillion (Sayer 2015: 229). Some people may have made a profit from the crisis, but it was not the average citizen.

According to Varoufakis (2015), the rescue money came with few strings attached. This is unlike after the 1929 crash, when far-reaching international measures were adopted to control the banking sector. In the postwar period, when these measures were in place, there were far fewer financial crises. This time round, finance was able to make a 'mighty comeback'.

Meanwhile, in bailing out the banks, states were indebting themselves. To whom? 'Investors' often within the same financial institutions they were bailing out (Sayer 2015). Moreover, the crisis caused economies to shrink and tax receipts to fall, meaning governments borrowed even more from these financial markets – at interest. There was no discussion in the mainstream media at the time as to whether the public should be expected to pay interest to those they were rescuing. These 'markets' were now in a position to pressure the governments who had saved them to make cuts to public spending programmes and privatise public resources. As attention shifted to the deficit, the fact that it was the banks that had caused the damage to public finances was promptly forgotten and the blame placed on profligate states. The role of media amnesia in this extraordinary revisioning is the subject of the next chapter.

There was some irritation aired in the media at this situation of 'socialism for the rich'. Both the BBC news and the *Guardian* reported Labour MP Colin Burgon's comment that 'What I see is the invisible hand of the market putting its hand into the pocket of the taxpayer and taking £50bn away, and maybe putting two fingers up as well' (Watt 2008). Despite this, as seen above, there was near consensus in support of the rescue packages at the time, both politically and in the media. Not everyone failed to appreciate the implications. In a short piece on the US bailouts, Naomi Klein wrote in the *Guardian*:

> Nobody should believe the overblown claims that 'free market' ideology is now dead. During boom times it is profitable to preach laissez-faire, because an absentee government allows speculative bubbles to inflate. When those bubbles burst, the ideology becomes a hindrance, and it goes dormant while government rides to the rescue. But rest assured: the ideology will come roaring back when the bailouts are done. The massive debt the public is accumulating to bail out the speculators will then become part of a global budget crisis that will be the rationalisation for deep cuts to social programmes, and for a renewed push to privatise what is left of the public sector (Klein and Butselaar 2008).

LOOSE MONEY

The fourth most talked about possible response to the crash concerned the interest-rate reductions made by central banks across the globe. These accounted for 7.8 per cent of possible responses mentioned. The idea behind cutting interest rates is to make borrowing cheaper and thereby to get money flowing through banks and the economy in an attempt to fight off recession. On 8 October 2008, the central banks of the US, UK, the eurozone, Canada, Sweden and Switzerland cut their rates by 0.5 per cent at the same time. By early 2009, rates in many places were close to zero, approaching what economists call the 'zero lower bound'. Although the US has been raising rates since 2015, in many places, including the UK, rates remain at or near rock bottom.

It might strike the reader as odd that the response to a crisis caused in large measure by private sector debt was to make borrowing easier. This question will be explored further in Chapter 3. Researchers from the Centre for Research on Socio-Cultural Change (CRESC) claim that ultra loose monetary policy – low interest rates and quantitative easing – combined with tight fiscal policy (austerity) is 'almost certainly technically wrong' for dealing with this sort of recession. However, it is 'politically right for the financial markets because it provides them with cheap feedstock for trading' (Froud *et al.* 2011: 10). Like the bailouts, interest-rate cuts were deemed necessary in an emergency, and there was no opposition at all to this measure in the sampled media items at the time.

REGULATION, REGULATION, REGULATION

Table 1.2 Mentions of bank reform as possible response to the global financial crisis. Sample size: 412. Percentages show proportion endorsed, rejected or mentioned neutrally by outlet.

Solution				Outlet			Total
		Guardian	Telegraph	Sun	Mirror	BBC	
Bank reform	Endorsed	33	7	2	8	3	53
		35.5%	16.3%	25%	53.3%	33.3%	
	Rejected	1	3	0	0	0	4
		1.1%	7%	0%	0%	0%	
	Neutral	59	33	6	7	6	111
		63.4%	76.7%	75%	46.7%	66.7%	
	Total	93	43	8	15	9	168

The second most discussed solution to the banking crisis after the bailouts was banking reform, which accounted for 17.1 per cent of possible responses mentioned. This was widely endorsed or reported neutrally across the media spectrum, as seen in Table 1.2. Calls for reform were often lacking in detail. Yet they were in many cases strongly worded, declaring that irresponsible behaviour must be prevented, and often centring on curbs on bonuses. On other occasions, detailed proposals were outlined, especially in the *Guardian*. There was talk, for example, of a new Glass-Steagall law, to separate retail banking from investment banking. Larry Elliott, the *Guardian*'s economics editor, was an advocate of this option.

However, as the crisis evolved from a banking meltdown to recession and public debt crises, banking reform dropped off the media agenda. If we take the entire sample covering all aspects of the crisis, in September 2008, banking reform comprised 19.5 per cent of the possible solutions mentioned. By January 2009, it had fallen to 10.7 per cent. In the week of the budget of April 2009 – when media hysteria about the deficit really got into gear and austerity became the dominant narrative – the figure was 1.3 per cent. In March 2011, it was zero. Banking reform had been relegated to jargon-filled discussions in the specialist finance pages.

This was convenient for the financial sector and the politicians it was busy lobbying. It is not that there has been no regulation since the crash. In fact there has been a profusion of new regulation on both national and international levels. In the UK, the Independent Commission on Banking was established under the newly-formed coalition government in 2010. It recommended that banks be made to 'ring fence' their high street businesses from their 'casino' investment banking arms, increase capital ratios and submit to a competition investigation, as well as recommending the creation of a 'bail-in' option.

In the US, the Dodd-Frank Act was enacted in 2010 by the Obama administration. A key component, the Volcker Rule, aimed to separate the investment and commercial functions of a bank, in a push-back in the direction of Glass-Steagall. The legislation also subjected institutions deemed 'systemically important' to extra oversight and regulation, set up a Consumer Financial Protection Bureau, contained a provision for regulating derivatives, and established an office tasked with monitoring credit ratings agencies.

Basel III is an international, voluntary accord agreed in 2010–11. It strengthens capital requirements including 'bail-in capital', and introduces leverage and liquidity requirements, and counter-cyclical measures – banks are required to set aside more capital during credit expansion, while during credit contraction capital requirements can be loosened. Some countries, such as France, also introduced a financial transaction tax after the crash: a small tax of around 0.2 per cent on certain financial transactions, designed to slow down financial speculation while raising revenue. Ten EU countries are exploring the possibility of an EU financial transaction tax.

However, much of this new legislation has been repeatedly delayed or watered down. Some claim that it was not adequate in the first place. Bank of England maverick technocrat Andy Haldane has criticised Basel III for embracing the complexity of the financial system, arguing instead for simplicity in regulation. The CRESC authors claim that the UK is trapped in a 'groundhog day' when it comes to finance. For them, the Independent Commission on Banking was limited by its remit to investigate how to meet the objectives of increased 'stability' and 'competition' in the banking sector. It did not ask deeper questions about what the role of finance should be. The report fell short of recommending full separation between banks' investment and retail arms, which would have broken up financial conglomerates that are 'too big to fail', or any large-scale branch divestment by the big four retail banking chains.

For the CRESC researchers, despite the slew of new regulations, nothing major has changed. Conflicts of interest and perverse incentives remain. They argue that the crash has led not to the diminution but to the *consolidation* of the power of the elites responsible for causing it. First, the core executive became stronger after the crash, especially the Treasury and the Bank of England – a 'highly traditional nexus of power in the Westminster governing system'. Secondly, because of the lack of strings attached to the bailouts, the metropolitan financial elite became more powerful (Froud *et al.* 2011: 12). The domestic banking system became concentrated in the hands of a small number of London-based institutions. In 2008, the four biggest institutions had a 64 per cent share of the retail market, and that share had been falling. By 2010, it was 77 per cent (12). The financial elite had entered the crisis with a professional and well-resourced lobbying network, facilitated by the Corporation of the City of London. The concentration of market share made lobbying even easier.

At the same time, the political parties had become increasingly reliant on rich donors, often from within finance. In 2005, when David Cameron became leader of the Conservative Party, the financial services industries were the source of just under a quarter of total cash donations to the party. By 2010 the figure had risen to just over 50 per cent (Froud *et al.* 2011: 16). Following the 2010 UK election, 134 Conservative MPs and Lords were employed in the financial sector (Davis 2013: 180). An estimated £92.8 million was spent by the sector lobbying the British government in 2011 alone. Given the alliance of political and financial elites, and the increased strength of both after the crash, it is no wonder that financial reforms have made little impact.

The situation is similar in the US. When Obama came to power he summoned the very people who had been responsible for the deregulation of Wall Street under Bill Clinton – Larry Summers and Tim Geithner – to devise a plan to rescue the banks. According to Varoufakis (2015: 173), this plan was based on the creation of new derivatives – 'new forms of private money underwritten by taxpayers' public money'. As will be explored in Chapter 4, the eurozone created its own version of the Geithner-Summers plan. Again, rather than diminishing the power of the financial institutions, it allowed them to make a 'mighty comeback' (Varoufakis 2015: 174). Wall Street promptly used its new strength to lobby against strong reform and back Obama's political opponents. Consequently, the Volcker Rule component of the Dodd-Frank legislation was passed only in a watered-down form.

In a mind-bending case of media amnesia, Dodd-Frank has since come to be framed not as the consequence but as the *cause* of ongoing economic problems in the US. At the time of writing, President Donald Trump is trying to do away with the legislation, seven years after it was passed. Journalist and media scholar Adam Cox (2018) has analysed US news coverage of the Dodd-Frank reforms between 2009 and 2012. He found that, during the early part of the period, 'market-interventionist' frames endorsing bank reform were much more common than 'market-fundamentalist', neoliberal frames. However, in the early months of the 2012 election campaign, market-fundamentalist frames began to overtake interventionist frames, tending to ignore the reason for the reforms and concentrating instead on possible negative consequences. They suggested that the regulation would stifle the economy by preventing banks from lending to businesses and consumers. During and after his election campaign, Trump – channelling Reagan's characterisation of government as the problem – reframed the issue again. He presented the job-choking effects of Dodd-Frank as actually happening rather than as a possibility. Absent from his framing were the reasons why Dodd-Frank existed in the first place.

Despite the enormity of the meltdown, therefore, banking reform, though prolific, has been modest. In the CRESC researchers' formulation: 'big crisis/small reform'. Though the idea of reform was prominent and consistently endorsed in the media at the time of the crash, even then it tended to be incommensurate to the scale of the crisis. Since then, media amnesia – whether in the form of forgetting to pay attention to the issue or actually misremembering the circumstances of reform – has no doubt helped those wanting to resist more robust regulation.

Other options have certainly been proposed in the years following 2008. Yet these rarely make it into the non-specialist news, certainly not in a sustained way. These include breaking up banks that are 'too big to fail', much higher capital and especially equity requirements, stronger leverage ratios, changing control rights in banks and changing the basis of performance targets and remuneration to reduce 'perverse incentives' (Haldane 2011: 17), banning complex financial products that cannot be proven safe and beneficial to society (Sayer 2015: 354), regulating the shadow banking sector, appointing regulators who are truly independent and not 'captured', and tackling tax havens where much of the riskiest trading takes place (Shaxson 2011). In addition, financial transaction taxes – resisted by both UK and US politicians – have been called for by a wide range of constituencies.

TURNING THE CLOCKS BACK

Others claim that even these proposals are too timid. They argue that it is financialisation that is the problem. Therefore, the solution is to try to reverse financialisation, to reduce the size of the financial sector and the involvement of finance in the rest of the economy and everyday life. Lapavitsas (2014) explains that in the postwar, pre-neoliberal era, far tighter controls were placed on finance, under the auspices of the Bretton Woods agreement. First, there were controls on interest rates paid to financial institutions, and on the amount of credit generated by financial institutions. Second, there were controls on the range of functions that financial institutions were allowed to undertake. And third, there were controls on international capital flows. Lapavitsas proposes that these kinds of controls be reinstated.

The idea of bringing back credit controls, and especially capital controls, is unthinkable for most mainstream economists. It might not sit well with members of the public either, since it would mean having limits placed on money that could be spent overseas. De-financialising everyday life might also mean not being able to pay for everything by card. However, Lapavitsas and others argue that, difficult as it might be to achieve, it could help recreate a more equal and less unstable form of capitalism. In an interview with journalist Paul Mason, he claimed: 'The benefits of the dynamic globalised financial economy are very hard to pin down. It is very difficult to see what free movement of capital has contributed to the growth of the global economy' (BBC Radio 4 2011).

This interview was broadcast on BBC Radio 4. However, these kinds of ideas almost never make it into the news. A former head of BBC news told me that the news bulletins should be thought of like the front page of a newspaper. Other current affairs programming is like the inside pages, giving more in-depth insight. The problem is, however, that a programme like *Newsnight* or a Radio 4 segment reaches a far smaller audience than the *Ten O'Clock News*. Moreover, as the journalist pointed out, current affairs programming is in decline.

THE RETURN OF THE PUBLIC?

Table 1.3 Mentions of public ownership as possible response to the global financial crisis. Sample size: 412. Percentages show proportion endorsed, rejected or mentioned neutrally by outlet.

Solution			Outlet				Total
		Guardian	Telegraph	Sun	Mirror	BBC	
Public ownership	Endorsed	13	4	0	8	0	25
		27.1%	10.5%	0%	50%	0%	
	Rejected	1	5	2	0	0	8
		2.1%	13.2%	28.6%	0%	0%	
	Neutral	34	29	5	8	6	82
		70.8%	76.3%	71.4%	50%	100%	
	Total	48	38	7	16	6	115

As part of the bank bailout, the British government bought shares in RBS, HBOS and Lloyds TSB, thus part-nationalising them. Northern Rock had been nationalised the previous February, and Bradford & Bingley in September. Other governments, including the US, Iceland, Ireland, France, Germany, the Netherlands, Belgium and Luxembourg, also nationalised banks. Nationalisation was the third most frequently covered possible response to the crash, accounting for 11.7 per cent of possible responses mentioned.

During the bailout negotiations in October 2008 there was widespread discussion about how much control the government would and should take in return for its investment. The Labour government was in a pickle because on the one hand it wanted to be seen as being tough on the banks but on the other it was loath to lose the free-market-friendly image it had been so desperate to cultivate. Prime Minister Gordon Brown claimed that there would be 'strings attached' in the form of curbs on executive pay and obligatory lending to small businesses and households (Roberts and Manning 2008). At the same time, ministers stated that the government would take an 'arms-length' approach and was 'not in the business of running banks' (Treanor *et al.* 2008).

Table 1.3 shows that the *Guardian* and the *Mirror* endorsed the nationalisations more frequently than they rejected them, while it was the other way round for the *Telegraph* and the *Sun*. The BBC reported the moves neutrally – in contrast to its coverage of the bailouts. In the *Guardian*, some opinion pieces pressed the government to go further.

John McDonnell, now Shadow Chancellor, complained that 'this is handing over taxpayers' money to the very people who led banks to the brink of collapse', and asserted, 'We should have nationalised to stabilise, with control for the taxpayer' (2008). Another interesting piece suggested turning the Post Office – at that time in line for privatisation – into a publicly-run 'people's bank' instead (Cruddas 2008). Copy in the *Mirror* also supported public ownership and control. In September 2008 – before the bailout – Paul Routledge (2008) wrote about the bankers, 'put them on trial and take over their banks, in the public interest'.

The *Sun* and the *Telegraph* displayed the most opposition to the idea of bank nationalisation. One *Telegraph* columnist was disgusted at the idea that the government might take a controlling stake:

> The Left is on a roll. Just when you thought it was safe to go back into the political debate – free forever from time-wasting ideological arguments about why the state rather than the individual was the source of moral good – back it all comes. And this time it is rampant with sanctimonious self-satisfaction (Leonard 2008).

Most of the coverage was not so overtly hostile. But most of it did accept without question the government's stance that it should have as little direct involvement as possible, and that the nationalisations should be temporary (see also Berry 2012). And this is precisely what transpired. According to the CRESC authors (Froud *et al.* 2011: 7), the management of the public holdings acquired in the crisis has since been governed by entirely traditional shareholder-value assumptions of the sort that guided the markets before the crash. And the British government is reprivatising the banks as quickly as possible.

There are those who believe that the public ownership of the banking sector should go much further. For them, even the stronger proposals for regulation discussed above are insufficient to transform finance so that it serves a socially useful purpose. For Lapavitsas (2014), public ownership of banks would be an important step in reversing financialisation. He argues not only for nationalising failed private banks but for establishing new institutions based on public-service principles. Public banks would provide credit as a public utility. Public credit would be allocated to enterprises engaged in production and to households for housing, education and health, as well as to smooth general consumption. Interest rates would be determined democratically and could vary among borrowers according to social policy objectives. Public banks could also provide the usual range of monetary services to businesses and households. In addition, they could engage in longer-term lending for large-scale investment, thereby helping to build sustainable infrastructure. The Labour Party under Jeremy Corbyn has pledged a national investment bank that would aim to fulfil some part of this vision for investment in infrastructure (though falling far short of Lapavitsas' larger vision).

Others have suggested that the money supply itself be taken into public hands. Currently, 97 per cent of new money in the UK is created not by the state but by banks. In the US, around 95 per cent of new money is created by banks. Each time a bank makes a loan, it creates money. This means that the vast majority of money *is debt*, created by private banks for the sole purpose of accruing interest. Peter Stalker (2015: 129) makes the point that the UK money supply is effectively controlled by 56 unelected individuals – the directors of HSBC, Barclays, RBS, Lloyds and Standard Chartered banks. A poll by research and campaign organisation Positive Money found that 9 out of 10 MPs did not have an accurate idea of where money comes from. Positive Money argues that the money supply should be entirely in the hands of the democratically elected government, and the amount of money produced decided by an independent body (Stalker 2015: 132–3).

Lapavitsas goes even further. He argues that not only should there be public provisioning of credit and banking services, but that other areas of the economy should also be taken into public ownership. As we have seen, non-financial corporations are highly financialised. This means that privatisation and financialisation are closely connected. Reversing financialisation means reversing privatisation. Lapavitsas proposes the restoration and broadening of public provision of housing, health, education and pensions. This would also mean services would become more affordable, thus helping to de-financialise households. Thus, for these academics and activists, not just banking but the economy as a whole needs to be changed. And public ownership is at the heart of that change.

Of course, these ideas might not be to everybody's taste, and they may sound extreme. However, we shouldn't let media amnesia make us forget that this was an extreme crisis, and the conditions causing it have not yet significantly changed. Indeed, as we will see in future chapters, in many ways they have intensified. Lapavitsas' proposals sound a lot like 'going back to the 1970s'. We must ask if this is either possible or desirable. Some may think this sounds like state socialism run by authoritarian, centralised bureaucracies. However, he emphasises the need to avoid centralisation and instead 'instigate new public mechanisms of provision that could also have communal and associational aspects' (Lapavitsas 2014: 16). Perhaps especially at times of intense economic crisis, the media should provide a forum for debating precisely these kinds of questions.

The *Guardian* did and still does feature pieces advocating public ownership. And in 2008 it published articles calling not just for banking reform but reform of capitalism on a deeper level. John Tulloch perceived a dialogue taking place among *Guardian* journalists at that time about 'free-market' capitalism and what might replace it (Hoskins and Tulloch 2016). The late Marxist Eric Hobsbawm, for example, penned a piece with the headline 'Ditch the free market model' (2008). In the *Mirror*, Kevin Maguire (2008a) urged Labour to abandon privatisation and 'remould Britain'. However, these voices were relatively peripheral even at the time. They did not manage to open the door to sustained, widespread discussions of ambitious and long-term solutions. And as seen above, even these voices stopped short of raising possibilities beyond capitalism, despite understanding how far capitalism had failed.

SAFE IDEAS

It seems odd that an open acknowledgement of a crisis of capitalism and predictions of momentous change could coexist with a refusal to give sustained attention to serious solutions. If the purpose of the media is to facilitate the formation of public opinion through an 'open market of ideas' (McNair 1994: 30), surely this would be precisely the time to give free range to as many ideas as possible? Instead, establishment responses were accepted without proper scrutiny.

This has to do with one of the central problems with the mainstream media: its lack of *pluralism*. We will see that this is one of the major elements of the media amnesia plaguing later coverage of the crisis. In the UK, we have newspapers that represent the 'left' and the 'right'. The public service broadcasters are mandated to represent the full spectrum of society's views in an impartial and balanced way. Despite this, only a relatively narrow range of views was represented in any sustained way in the mainstream media. And these views tended to be ones held by elites.

Why is this? The interests of the press barons who own much of the UK media are a major factor – they will be considered further in Chapter 2. We can begin with the beliefs and values of news-makers themselves. Journalists tend to come from privileged backgrounds. A report from the Sutton Trust (cited in Robertson 2011) revealed that 54 per cent of the top 100 UK journalists was educated in independent schools while only 7 per cent of the general population was educated in such schools. Of those journalists who attended university, 56 per cent attended either Oxford or Cambridge and 72 per cent attended one of the 13 top-ranked UK universities. Often journalists go to university with the people who become politicians, civil servants or bankers. Owen Jones (2015: 111) points to a dangerous revolving door between media and politics. In short, journalists tend to be part of the elite.

One freelance journalist I spoke to, who wrote regularly for the *Guardian* and had written for *The Times* and the *Independent,* said that journalists with an elite education were more likely to get a staff job with benefits and sick pay. She said she used to call it Gosford Park, referencing a film about a wealthy family and their servants, because: 'the Oxbridge privately educated journalists were the ones who get the salaried jobs, with the holiday pay, sick pay and pensions, and disability. And if you aren't part of that world, then you're scraping by on commissions you get.' The values and priorities of this elite class could not help but filter into coverage. In the words of *Guardian* columnist George Monbiot (2017), 'whatever their professed beliefs, [journalists] tend to be drawn towards their class interests.'

We saw that the BBC news was particularly supportive of the bank bailouts, at least implicitly. This sits with critiques of the BBC that, although it is supposed to be impartial, in times of crisis those running it feel that its role is to support the 'national interest' – meaning the interests of the state. The common historical example given to illustrate this is the 1926 General Strike – the UK's only such strike. The BBC suspended impartiality and sided with the state. The BBC's founding father, John Reith, famously remarked that the government 'know that they can trust us not to be really impartial' (Mills 2016). Tom Mills' (2016) *The BBC: Myth of a Public Service* argues that the BBC is not and never has been fully independent, and traces its complex and intimate relations with the state.

Even when journalists do not automatically share establishment values, according to Nick Davies, they tend to 'play it safe'. They do this in several ways. They rely on official sources. They avoid annoying any organisation or individual with the power to hurt news organisations. They also 'select safe ideas'. This happens in two ways: 'first, moral and political ideas generally are not expressed overtly in the story but are the undeclared assumptions on which it is built and, being undeclared, are safe from scrutiny. Second, they reflect the surrounding consensus' (Davies 2009: 125).

The issue of sources is crucial. Herman and Chomsky argued in *Manufacturing Consent* (1988) that the media function to legitimise the views of the establishment. This is not necessarily done consciously. Rather, it is a process that occurs by way of five 'filters'. The third filter is sourcing practices. The others are ownership and profit orientation, advertising, flak and anti-communist ideology. All of these are relevant to the patterns of media coverage described in this book (yes, even anti-communist ideology), and will crop up in different chapters.

When it comes to sourcing, studies have consistently found that journalists rely heavily on official sources (Hall *et al.* 1978; Philo 1995; Wahl-Jorgensen *et al.* 2016a). The research for this book found the same. Politicians and other official sources made up by far the biggest category of sources cited in the coverage. For the sample as a whole, they made up 50.9 per cent of sources cited. Trade unions, by contrast, accounted for only 2.3 per cent. Activists and protesters accounted for 0.6 per cent.

For those news items focusing primarily on the financial crisis, the figure for politicians and other official sources was 48 per cent. The other major category of sources for those items was financial sector representatives, making up 28 per cent. Just those two categories account for 76 per cent of all the sources cited in the news items focusing on the crash. Each of the other categories of sources – members of the public, activists, charities or campaign groups, think tanks, economists or other academics – accounted for less than 5 per cent. Similar numbers were found across the outlets.

This means that official sources and representatives of the financial services had enormous power to set the terms of the debate. They were, in Stuart Hall *et al.*'s terminology, the 'primary definers' of the events. Hall and his colleagues argued that there was a 'systematically structured *over-accessing* to the media of those in powerful and privileged institutional positions' (Hall *et al.* 1978: 58). With reporting, which is supposed to be objective, two opposing views on an issue are often sought, to provide balance. However, both views will usually come from within the elite – usually the government and the opposition party. The views of those in powerful positions will organise the coverage and determine the parameters for debate.

The issue of sourcing is related to the issue of public relations (PR). Aeron Davis (2002) claims that, during the neoliberal period, a 'public relations democracy' has emerged. Angela Phillips (2010: 95) writes that 'in the day-to-day world of journalism, every single major public announcement can be classified as "PR" and every organization wishing to address journalists will use public relations techniques.' Journalists are continually being sent information by sources who are trying to promote stories. When a new story breaks, organisations concerned will send out packaged responses to an entire press list in an attempt to control the narrative. Phillips writes that this isn't necessarily evidence of a democratic deficit. It depends on where the PR comes from. However, most PR comes from officials and corporations (Lewis *et al.* 2008).

On one level it makes sense that these sources get to be the primary definers. Officials are in charge of running things, so they know what is going on and should be responsible for explaining things. Politicians are democratically elected so they represent the rest of us. This was certainly the view expressed by some of the journalists I spoke to. Those working in the financial sector were uniquely placed to shed light on the financial crisis. However, each of these groups has its own agenda, which is not always declared. In his research on the BBC coverage of the bank bailout, Mike Berry (2012) found that financial services figures were treated as objective experts rather than as representing an interest group. Since we were in the middle of a meltdown emanating from this sector, the idea that they could be considered 'experts' on anything is perplexing.

Allowing politicians to set the agenda is particularly problematic if the main parties have little to distinguish them from one another. This means that they all represent the interests of the same social groups, while the rest of society is unrepresented. In many parts of the world, this has been the case during the neoliberal era. For sociologist Colin Crouch (2000), the political correlative of neoliberalism is 'postdemocracy'. This is where democratic processes such as elections continue to exist but cease to be truly representative, as states orient themselves increasingly to the interests of corporations instead of citizens. Rather than truly serving their constituencies, politicians employ marketing techniques and 'spin' to win votes. Publics feel disenfranchised and so become detached from mainstream politics.

Politics in postdemocracy is geared less towards those harmed by the crash and more towards the interests of those who caused it – and who comprised the second largest chunk of sources used to report it. Of sources cited in the coverage, therefore, 76 per cent represented an alliance of elites whose interests do not necessarily align with those of the majority of people. At the time of writing it appears that political parties are diverging from each other, and are once again starting to represent different sections of society. Time will tell how far any of the parties will be willing or able to serve interests that are not aligned with those of corporations, financial or otherwise.

Journalists also selected safe ideas and reflected the surrounding consensus. Several of the journalists I spoke to from different news outlets acknowledged the problem of 'pack mentality' – they don't want to stray too far from the crowd in their reporting or even opinion pieces. One former senior editor at the *Guardian*, the paper perhaps most likely to give voice to alternative economic ideas, talked to me about the importance placed on credibility by journalists there. In particular she spoke of the need for journalists to be seen to have 'grown-up politics'. This was another way of saying 'politics that aren't too left wing'. Certain ideas – for example Keynesian economics – are accepted and seen as 'grown up'. But often, more creative ideas are not. Journalists were engaged in a constant, unspoken struggle over what was 'grown up' and what was not. This struggle is similar to the struggle over 'common sense', discussed in the Introduction.

Credibility is another reason that official and other elite sources are so dominant (Allan 2004). A former BBC journalist, for example, spoke about the need for credible sources and the inappropriateness of giving prominence to a 'wacky view'. The more powerful a source, the more 'credible' it is perceived as being, and the more influence it has over the public discourse.

According to Davies, 'playing it safe' has intensified in the age of 'churnalism'. This brings us to one aspect of Herman and Chomsky's first filter: the profit orientation of most news providers. Market pressures mean journalists are having to produce news at 'warp speed'. This means that they will use established networks of sources they can rely upon to give a quote quickly and in a convenient format. These tend to be officials and other powerful groups that have well-resourced communications departments. And journalists and editors are more likely to want to avoid lawsuits or flak, and will adjust their content accordingly.

The *Guardian* and BBC are examples of news providers with different business models, and in some ways this does allow them to escape some of these pressures. *Guardian* journalists I spoke to, especially senior ones, felt that they had a lot of autonomy relative to other organisations. However, they are by no means immune from market pressures, as explored in the case of the BBC in Chapter 3.

'EVERYTHING IS SO INTRINSICALLY LINKED'

During this period of intense crisis, the economy came into focus as thoroughly global. News items were littered with references to the 'global financial crisis', the 'global economy', the 'global turmoil' and 'international markets'. BBC news correspondents explained that we live in a 'globalised, interconnected' system, and that 'everything is so intrinsically linked' (BBC 2009). It was important to explain to the public how problems seemingly originating in the US housing market were having such a huge impact on the UK and the rest of the world. 70.6 per cent of the media items focusing primarily on the financial crisis made at least some attempt to convey the global nature of the economy.

As well as these attempts to express the global interconnectedness of the economy, there was also an unusual amount of attention paid to countries other than the UK. Of course, the US was a primary focus. Iceland's collapsing financial system also made headlines, especially as money belonging to UK citizens and local councils was at stake. The eurozone was likewise very much in the media's sights. This is crucial to remember when we get to the coverage of the eurozone crisis in Chapter 4. The actions of the European Central Bank in cutting interest rates and injecting liquidity were high profile, as were huge bailout pledges by several eurozone countries in the middle of October 2008. For example, a €500 billion rescue package by the German government was widely reported, and Chancellor Angela Merkel was quoted as saying 'drastic action' was needed to shore up the financial system (Levitin and Samuel 2008).

The pending problems within the eurozone, including the question of the sovereign debt of Greece and other southern states, were even foreshadowed at this time:

> The credit crunch should test conclusively whether it is sustainable for countries to share a single currency outside a political union. The

financial markets seem to be sceptical. The difference (or 'spread') between the yields on German government bonds and those of many of the other member states have widened steadily over the course of 2008. In Greece's case, the spread over German bunds is now almost a full percentage point, while in Italy it is 0.9 and Spain 0.6. A year ago, the differences were negligible. What these spreads tell us is that investors have more confidence in the ability of the German government to service its debts than the Italian, Spanish or Greek governments. And since they share the same currency, this means investors believe there is a growing risk that the euro area will unravel (Whyte and Tilford 2008).

As the eurozone went into recession in November 2008, before the UK, that also made it into the main news pages. The effects the crunch was having all over Europe were in full view. As will be seen, by the time the European 'debt crisis' hit in 2010, its starting-point in the financial crisis had been forgotten.

Western countries – especially the UK, US and eurozone members – were by far the main focus of attention. However, the situation in non-Western countries was also occasionally reported. Unsurprisingly, given its importance for the global economy, Asia got most attention outside the West. Reports of Singapore falling into recession, Asian stock markets falling and central banks slashing borrowing costs in China, Taiwan, Hong Kong and South Korea (as well as Australia) made it into the main news pages in October 2008 (Moore 2008).

Regions of the world that usually receive very little media attention were also covered. A piece in the *Telegraph*, also from October 2008, hinted at possible geopolitical implications as it reported on the depletion of Pakistan's foreign reserves, Ukraine's shaky banking system and steel mill closures, tumbling stocks in the BRICS (Brazil, Russia, India, China, South Africa), and the Hungarian government intervention after a run on one of its banks and the plummeting of its stock exchange (Evans-Pritchard 2008). An exemplary piece in the *Guardian* dealt with the economic situation in Europe, Russia, India, Japan, Brazil, Venezuela, Cuba, Zimbabwe, Iraq, the Middle East and south-east Asia (*Guardian* 2008).

Meanwhile, the president of the World Bank issued a warning, which was widely reported, that the banking meltdown had created a 'human crisis' in many of the poorest countries, requiring a coordinated response.

The number of malnourished people was predicted to increase by 44 million in 2008, to 967 million, as a result of high food prices (Elliott and Stewart 2008b). What was not mentioned was the role of financialisation in those high food prices, specifically speculation over the future price of wheat, rice and soya beans (Varoufakis 2015: 163).

Global solutions were also very much the order of the day. The fifth most frequently mentioned possible response was 'multilateral action', meaning that the importance of governments acting multilaterally was emphasised over the form that action might take. This accounted for 7.2 per cent of possible responses to the crash mentioned. Internationally coordinated interest-rate cuts were welcomed, as were calls for synchronised bailouts. The need for multilateral action was seen to be a lesson learned from the failures of the Great Depression, during which protectionism was thought to have worsened the crisis. This question of protectionism versus 'open markets' has come back in more recent years, and is explored further in Chapter 3. Gordon Brown, meanwhile, used his moment in the sun to call for a new international governance system (Wintour 2008b).

The attention to the global picture at this time corresponds with media scholar Peter Berglez's (2009) concept of 'global journalism'. For Berglez, global journalism is a rare phenomenon within media systems, which remain stubbornly nationally oriented. Global journalism not only covers events outside the news organisation's national remit, it situates and explains events in terms of their global interconnections. It is the journalistic representation of 'complex relations', and sees the world as a 'single place'. This approach is essential when it comes to understanding the economy, which is inescapably global. Journalists during the height of the crisis tried to illuminate this global dimension. Unfortunately, this attention to global interconnectivity evaporated as time wore on and the crisis became normalised. Only 57.5 per cent of the sample as a whole made any attempt to provide even the shallowest global context. We will see that the lack of global context in reporting as the crisis wore on is one of the main contributing factors to media amnesia.

GOING GLOBAL

Journalists' attempts to shed light on the global nature of the crisis during its initial stages were admirable. However, these attempts themselves had limitations that meant they failed properly to explain the crisis to the public. The *Financial Times*' Martin Wolf (2014) has been among those highlighting the role of 'global imbalances' in producing the financial crisis. Some countries – China and emerging Asian countries, Germany and Japan, and the oil-exporting countries – had accumulated large current account surpluses. Others – most notably the US but also the UK – had run up corresponding trade and current account deficits. The trade imbalances created financial imbalances. Surpluses were recycled back into the US, via Wall Street, as surplus countries built up dollar reserves. Before the crash the US trade deficit was by itself absorbing 60 per cent of the surpluses of the rest of the world. This was a contributing factor to financialisation and the ensuing financial crash. The 'global imbalances' explanation for the crisis – which both grasps the global nature of the crisis and the interconnectedness of finance with the rest of the economy – rarely found its way out of specialist publications like the *Financial Times* at this time.

However, in his *Imperialism in the Twenty-first Century*, John Smith (2016) accuses even this explanation of being superficial. Smith points out that the prime contributor to 'global imbalances' was the shift of production to low-wage economies like China by transnational corporations (TNCs). The globalisation of production was rarely presented as a factor in the crash.

TNCs relocated production during the neoliberal era to profit from squeezing wages. TNCs, though transnational, are still linked to specific countries. According to *Fortune*, in 2011, of the 500 biggest multinationals, 164 were based in Europe, 133 in the US, 68 in Japan and 61 in China (Screpanti 2014: 100). They manufacture goods in low-wage countries and sell them in high-wage countries, profiting from the difference. The states where the products are sold also benefit, through value added tax. These corporations and the states in which they are based are thus engaged in a contemporary form of *imperialism*. For some Marxian scholars, to understand the crisis fully it is necessary to understand capitalism not just as a global but as an imperialist system.

Tony Norfield, former banker and author of *The City*, writes that:

A country does not have to rule politically over another for it to be imperialist, and imperialism did not die out with the end (almost) of colonialism. Today, imperialism is characterised by economic privileges in the world economy, reinforced by monopolistic control over industry, commerce and finance, and backed up by powerful states, directly or indirectly (Norfield 2016: 117).

Norfield explains that finance plays a key role in contemporary imperialism. This is especially the case for the UK, where the international role played by the country's financial sector helps fund its chronic current account deficit. This is the reason why UK governments, regardless of the party in power, continue to back the City, block international regulation and refuse to tackle tax havens. Understanding the crisis in this way raises questions about the options for reform discussed above. Financialisation at least partly arose out of the globalisation of production. Thus, can it be tackled without tackling the global conditions under which goods are produced and services supplied? Moreover, if states are protecting their imperialistic interests by defending both their finance sectors and their non-financial corporations, can the problems be tackled through the framework of nation-states? These are very complex issues that require a great deal of research and deliberation. They would later play a role in the Brexit debates. Though the mainstream media made a valiant attempt to convey the global dimensions of the crash, it got nowhere near to even asking these fundamental questions.

CONCLUSION

Relative to what came after, the reporting of the financial crash displayed rigorous analysis, awareness of structural, global problems and openness to creative solutions. As well as expressing justifiable anger, there was an attempt to explain the systemic problems with finance, and these problems were sometimes placed in the context of neoliberalism. The kinds of state control that might accompany the bank bailouts were sometimes debated, as were proposals for banking reform, and there were public demands for bankers to be held to account.

However, the limitations of the coverage were already serious. Explanations were often historically and geographically shallow, riddled with jargon or absent. Emergency responses taken by the authorities, namely the bank bailouts and the interest-rate cuts, were endorsed without proper scrutiny or consideration of the consequences. Long-term, far-reaching ideas for social change were given virtually no airtime or column inches, despite the fact that capitalism was clearly malfunctioning. Thus, the three major elements of the media amnesia characterising the later coverage of the crisis were already present at the beginning of this story: the lack of historical context, the narrow range of elite perspectives and the lack of global context.

In January 2009 the UK officially entered recession. UK unemployment reached 1.9 million. Despite this, a piece in the *Telegraph* told readers to buck up: 'there are no soup kitchens or children without shoes; people are not going hungry' (*Telegraph* 2009). This echoed a sentiment expressed by Tory politician Boris Johnson the previous October. He had mocked predictions that it would be 'back to the 1930s, with barrels for trousers, soup kitchens and buddy can you spare a dime'. The UK government offered £20 billion to small firms to stimulate the economy. Germany provided a €50 billion stimulus package. The Bank of England cut interest rates to 1.5 per cent, the lowest level in its history. There were mass protests all over Europe at austerity measures being brought in. There was outrage at the nationalised Northern Rock paying out £8.8 million in bonuses. Deflation looked likely to set in. The Irish government nationalised the Anglo Irish Bank, guaranteeing all loans and deposits and thereby saddling Irish citizens with their bankers' almost infinite losses (Varoufakis 2015: 158). And that's just January.

In February, President Obama signed his $787 billion Geithner-Summers plan. Insurance giant AIG declared a $61.7 billion loss during the previous quarter, and was promised another $30 billion from the US Treasury. In March the Federal Reserve announced it would purchase another $2 trillion of banks' bad debts. In April, amid mass protests, the G20 met in London. Prime Minister Gordon Brown looked like he'd saved his skin (and, in his words, 'the world') as world leaders announced a $1.1 trillion global rescue plan. However, as it became clear that the package was having a limited impact on the global recession, Brown's reputation lost its sheen, and a new economic monster arrived: the deficit.

2
Deficit

The financial crisis led to a deep global recession. The damage done by the recession to public finances was even worse than the billions directly spent on bailing out the banks. Tax revenues were falling as spending on unemployment benefit rose. The consensus response of governments at first was Keynesian fiscal stimulus on top of monetary easing, meaning that as well as lowering interest rates, governments supported their economies with public spending to boost demand. China committed 13 per cent of GDP, Spain 7 per cent, the United States around 5.5 per cent and Germany almost 3 per cent (Blyth 2013: 55). The UK under New Labour was one of the major economies leading calls for fiscal action at the time.

However, Mark Blyth (2013: 54) describes the major capitalist countries as 'twelve-month Keynesians'. In 2010, with the European Central Bank, the German government, Canada and Britain's newly elected coalition leading the charge, the balance of international opinion shifted to austerity, with the emphasis on spending cuts over tax rises. By the end of 2008, Spain, Portugal and Greece had already had their debt downgraded, and several countries – including Latvia, Lithuania and Bulgaria – had begun making cuts to public spending. Some countries were forced to implement austerity measures by the international institutions bailing them out. Other countries, such as the UK, imposed austerity on their own citizens.

Austerity has meant that ordinary people are paying the price of the financial crisis, raising stark questions about fairness and democratic process. On top of this, it is important to remember that cutting spending while the economy is weak contradicts much established macroeconomic theory (Wren-Lewis 2015). Those economists supporting austerity used the argument that public spending 'crowds out' private sector investment, so cutting public spending can lead to increased private sector investment and thereby to economic growth. However, Mark Blyth points out that this theory is unconventional and is not supported by much historical evidence. On the contrary, according to established Keynesian theory, reducing public spending during recessions takes demand out of the economy. This leads to further economic contraction, which leads to tax receipts falling further, which means further damage to public finances. Thus, *pursuing austerity while the economy is weak increases rather than decreases public debts* (Blyth 2013). This is precisely what has happened since 2008.

As the debts were transferred from the private to the public sector, media attention shifted from the banking crisis and resulting recession to public deficits and debts. In the UK, in April 2009, the chancellor revealed borrowing figures of £175 billion, up from a projected £43 billion in March 2008. This generated a media hysteria around the deficit, which was framed as requiring urgent action (Berry 2016a and b). For reasons both of fairness and economic prudence, it has always been difficult to justify austerity. Because of this, those pursuing austerity had to manufacture an extraordinary bout of media amnesia, involving a smörgåsbord of soundbites and linguistic fudges, vagaries and slippages. Most often, no explanation for the deficit was given at all. At the same time, the idea that the deficit was caused by too much public spending began to creep in, and became the most common explanation for the deficit. This rewriting of history happened with breathtaking speed.

Austerity became by far the dominant solution to the deficit discussed in the media. Other possible options were sidelined. Not only that, other options were framed not as alternatives but as *supplements* to austerity. Even though austerity has been controversial, some level of austerity was presented as necessary and inevitable, even in the 'left-wing' press and certainly the BBC. The economic argument in favour of cutting public spending – that it can boost growth by allowing more room for the private sector – was not the main one heard in the mainstream media, though it was expressed in specialist publications. Mainly, the government was presented as having no choice but to impose austerity to cut the deficit. It was not always clear why it was so essential to tackle the deficit immediately, but the argument was often given that those countries with high levels of borrowing might be punished by 'the markets'. The debt interest the governments had to pay to these 'markets' might rise, and in any case it was wrong for governments to saddle future generations with big debts.

One of the other options for tackling the deficit – taxing the rich – was dismissed as 'class war'. The debate around taxing the wealthy was moreover highly contained. While Labour's policy of raising the top rate of income tax received substantial coverage, other possibilities for taxing the 1 per cent were rarely expressed. Meanwhile, a deeper, historically-informed analysis of the functioning of debt in the global economy was entirely absent.

REWRITING THE CRISIS

'They didn't fix the roof'

In the UK, the media hysteria about public finances really began in April 2009. However, the 'fiscal irresponsibility' frame had been present long before then. This is the idea that the problems originated not in a financial crisis caused by greedy bankers, structural problems within the banking sector and decades of economic liberalisation, but in overspending by the Labour government. It was evident, though in a minor way, right from the start of the financial crisis. This revisionist history of the crisis was thus being written even while the crisis was still in its infancy. It would become a key means of justifying austerity.

This narrative was strongest in the right-wing press. During the run on Northern Rock in September 2007, the *Telegraph* featured a piece by 'free market' economist Ruth Lea, identifying potential weaknesses in the economy and blaming Gordon Brown's 'public-spending spree'. In March 2008, when the fledgling banking crisis was already having an impact on the economy, Trevor Kavanagh wrote in the *Sun*: 'it is Gordon Brown who has spent all our lolly. It is the ex-Chancellor who hurled our money down the drain in misbegotten social experiments on the NHS, schools and welfare' (Kavanagh 2008a).

While the financial crisis was in full throttle in late 2008, it was uncommon to blame it on public spending since this would have been absurd. However, the fiscal irresponsibility frame reappeared with a vengeance as soon as the financial panic started to die down and the debts were transferred from the private to the public sector. This was in part thanks to the slipperiness of political language. For example, it is fascinating to chart the evolution of the Conservative soundbite 'Labour's decade of debt'. The phrase does not in itself make clear which kind of debt is referred to – public or private. It started life during the run on Northern Rock in 2007 and at that time was actually associated with both public and personal debt. The role played by reckless bank lending and high household debt in the financial crisis was at that time beginning to be exposed. The following item in the *Telegraph* with the headline 'Politics as Tories blame Labour's "decade of debt"' explicitly associates the soundbite with personal debt:

> George Osborne, the Shadow Chancellor, also suggested soaring personal debt under a decade of Labour could be a key factor in the crisis. Vince Cable, the Liberal Democrat Treasury spokesman and a former chief economist at Shell, joined the attacks by warning that Gordon Brown as Chancellor had presided over mounting personal debt in Britain, which now stood at £1.3 trillion (Carlin *et al.* 2007).

This interpretation could still be found at the end of 2008 (Reece 2008). The following *Telegraph* piece from January 2009 mysteriously conflates personal, corporate and public debt:

> On the issue of his backing Labour's spending plans until very recently, despite warnings that they were unsustainable, Mr Cameron admitted he should have distanced himself from them 'a bit faster'...
>
> He added: 'In terms of personal and corporate debt Britain is, I think it is true to say, the most indebted nation on earth, in fact not just now but for all time. That is truly frightening stuff and we need to address that.'
>
> George Osborne, the Shadow Chancellor, yesterday used a speech at the Institute of Chartered Accountants to announce Tory plans to curb 'wasteful' government spending by using finance directors to rein in Whitehall departments' budgets (Porter 2009).

Other news items simply reproduced the 'decade of debt' phrase as-is, without interpreting what kind of debt is meant (e.g. Brignall 2007). Over time, the personal debt component was dropped and attention focused solely on public debt. At the time of the April 2009 budget, 'Labour's decade of debt' was reconfigured to mean public debt and used to impressive effect in Cameron's savage response to Chancellor Alistair Darling's budget statement:

> This Prime Minister has certainly got himself in the history books – he's written a whole chapter in red ink: Labour's decade of debt ... The fundamental truth is that all Labour governments run out of money.

> The last Labour government gave us the Winter of Discontent, this Labour government has given us the Decade of Debt (Prince 2009).

The speech was repeated in all major media outlets, with no interrogation of the meaning of 'Labour's decade of debt'. As personal debt was forgotten, public debt was brought to the fore, and Labour's irresponsible borrowing fingered as the culprit.

Another well-known Conservative soundbite was 'they didn't fix the roof while the sun was shining'. This is even vaguer than 'Labour's decade of debt' and was used to insinuate government profligacy without actually saying so. On top of that, a third displacement can be identified. The Conservatives and the right-wing press began to frame the *bank bailouts* as fiscal irresponsibility, even though just a few months previously they had been in support:

> David Cameron warned that Britain could go bankrupt and would have to be rescued by the IMF because of the Government's handling of the economic crisis ... the Tory leader said that 'the money will run out' soon if Gordon Brown was allowed to continue with his expensive bank bail-outs' (Winnett 2009).

This bailout irresponsibility was then conflated with general profligacy to create a generalised image of Labour as fiscally incompetent. These displacements and conflations were for the most part repeated uncritically by the media, which allowed and in some cases helped the Conservative Party to control the narrative.

Soon after, these fudges were no longer necessary, and it became more common directly to blame the state of the public finances on Labour overspending. As we have seen, the *Sun* had never had much of a problem doing this, here blaming welfare instead of the 'misguided' health and education projects referred to above: 'We are trillions in debt and still borrowing as much as we raise in tax to pay for a bloated welfare state and a ballooning army of unemployed ... Huge sums of precious cash have been squandered' (Kavanagh 2009).

John Tulloch identifies a 'two nations' theme in the *Daily Mail* at the time of the G20 summit in late March/early April 2009, in which the comfortable public sector continues its 'ever more insane spending of your money' while the rest of the country is 'in the worst Recession since the Thirties' (Hoskins and Tulloch 2016: 179–80). Even pieces in the *Guardian* referred to 'Labour's misguidedly optimistic spending plans in 2005' and its habit of 'excessive borrowing' (White 2010). This shows how important the initial framing of a problem is. Once the initial definition was established, Labour was unable to change it.

This kind of framing evidently had an effect. Mike Berry (2018) conducted focus groups with members of the general public. He found that nearly 70 per cent of respondents thought that increased public spending had caused the deficit. In fact, as noted, it was the reduction in the tax base due to the recession that was the main immediate cause.

Blaming Labour overspending was reinforced with countless off-hand allusions to 'the economic mess left by Labour' (Laws 2011), 'Labour's disgraceful stewardship' or its 'mismanaged economy' (Kynaston 2010). These cases do not blame overspending specifically but evoke an image of Labour as economically incompetent in general. The party had gained this reputation after a Labour government had to take a loan from the IMF in 1976 and subsequently presided over the 'Winter of Discontent' in 1978–9. New Labour under Tony Blair and Gordon Brown had fought hard to shake off the reputation by being 'pro-business', but now sections of the media were frequently invoking the 'bad old days' of the 1970s to discredit Labour economically (Biressi and Nunn 2013). Never mind that in the 1970s inequality was lower and real wages were growing (Sayer 2015: 190–1).

In fact, before the financial crisis, government debt was actually *not that high* in historic terms. According to the Institute of Fiscal Studies, the fiscal record of the 1997–2010 Labour administration had followed a similar pattern to that of the 1979–97 Conservative administration. Both entered office facing sizeable structural deficits (deficits that persist even after an economy recovers from recession) and both went on to achieve sizeable surpluses before slipping back into structural deficits. In 2007, Britain had the second largest structural deficit in the G7, but the second lowest debt-to-GDP ratio (debt in relation to economic output), at 30.4 per cent in 2007 versus 40.4 per cent in 1996 under John Major. Labour increased spending from 39.9 per cent of national income in 1996–7 to 41.1 per cent in 2007–8. The majority of this spending went on the NHS and education. Social security spending actually fell, from 13.1 per cent of national income in 1997 to 11.1 per cent in 2007–8 (Pirie 2012: 348). It is true, then, that Labour had allowed the public finances to slip into deficit in the years before the crisis, during a period of economic expansion. However, Labour's pre-crisis record hardly revealed an orgy of spending and was similar to those of former Conservative prime ministers Margaret Thatcher and John Major. Misremembering the crisis thus required some impressive semantic gymnastics.

Forgetting the banks

The crisis could not have been rewritten, however, without a considerable amount of full-blown amnesia. Overall, fiscal irresponsibility has been the dominant explanation for the UK deficit. In coverage focusing on the deficit, this explanation accounted for 33.3 per cent of explanations mentioned, whereas the second most common explanation, the financial crisis, accounted for 20.2 per cent of the explanations mentioned. Non-specific blaming of the Labour Party made up a further 11.6 per cent, and was the third most common explanation for the deficit. As shown in Table 2.1, the fiscal irresponsibility explanation was strongly endorsed in the *Telegraph*, the *Sun* and even in the *Guardian*. *Mirror* journalists mainly chose to ignore this position, while the BBC mostly reported it neutrally – simply reporting Tory claims without endorsing or rejecting them.

However, it should be noted that, though fiscal irresponsibility was the main reason given for the deficit, direct blaming of this kind was not actually that frequent. In 52.4 per cent of the sampled news items with a primary focus on the deficit, no explanation was given.

Table 2.1 Mentions of fiscal irresponsibility as cause of the UK deficit. Sample size: 191. Percentages show proportion endorsed, rejected or mentioned neutrally by outlet.

Cause		*Guardian*	*Telegraph*	Outlet *Sun*	*Mirror*	*BBC*	*Total*
Fiscal irresponsibility	Endorsed	5	15	7	0	1	28
		45.5%	75%	100%	0%	20%	
	Rejected	1	0	0	0	0	1
		9.1%	0%	0%	0%	0%	
	Neutral	5	5	0	0	4	14
		45.5%	25%	0%	0%	80%	
	Total	11	20	7	0	5	43

The downturn accounted for 10.9 per cent of the explanations for the deficit – the fact that the recession had led to falling tax revenues. As mentioned, the financial crisis was the second most cited cause of the deficit. But the structural causes of the financial crisis in turn – those explored in the previous chapter – are hardly mentioned. The misconduct of the financial sector made up 10.9 per cent of the explanations for the deficit. The systemic problems within the sector lying behind that misconduct accounted for only 0.8 per cent. The longer-term context of 'free market' capitalism since the 1980s only comprised 3.1 per cent of the explanations given for the deficit. As the crisis evolved and attention shifted from the banking meltdown to the deficit, the timeline of the crisis was being erased and rewritten.

This was happening at incredible speed. By the end of the budget week of April 2009 – six months after the announcement of a £500 billion bank bailout in Britain – 'fiscal irresponsibility' had become the dominant explanation for the deficit, comprising 32.6 per cent of explanations. The financial crisis was at 28.3 per cent and financial sector misconduct 8.7 per cent. Systemic problems in finance weren't offered as an explanation at all, and economic liberalisation accounted for only 6.5 per cent of explanations – given three times.

In the vacuum created by the lack of any other explanations, the Labour overspending framing dominated, even though it was only repeated in a (sizeable) minority of news items. Thus it was a potent mix of media amnesia and active misremembering that allowed the history of the crisis to be rewritten while that history was still unfolding. Here we see two of the main elements of media amnesia at work: a lack of historical context and a lack of pluralism – a narrow range of elite-dominated views. These two elements intersect. Because Conservative politicians wanted to impose austerity, they purposely left out or misremembered even the most recent past of the crisis in their public statements. Because the views of political elites structure media coverage, this forgetting and misremembering was reproduced on a large scale. And the chronic inability of the media to provide historical context meant that they did not correct the narratives of the politicians. How do we explain the persistent lack of historical context in journalism?

To begin with, we can go back to the news values outlined in the introduction. For journalists, getting the very latest news tends to be the priority. When the crisis mutated from a financial to a public debt crisis, journalists were more preoccupied with the headline borrowing figures than with the processes that had caused the problems. This helps to explain why they failed to identify not only the deep, long-term causes of the financial crisis but later on frequently even the financial crisis itself as the cause of the mounting deficit.

Another important news value is simplicity. Several journalists told me that the narrative of Labour overspending and austerity, with its household finance analogies ('living within our means'), was attractive because it was simpler than the actual roots of the crisis in the inscrutable world of finance and the movements of global capitalism. They also privileged event over cause, creating a spectacle out of events without examining how those events happened.

These news values are in turn connected to the market orientation of news providers. Their cost-cutting practices mean journalists are not necessarily knowledgeable about their subject, and don't have time to acquire knowledge. Revenue-raising leads, many claim, to extreme simplification and 'dumbing down' (Franklin 1997).

AUSTERITY BRITAIN

Table 2.2 Mentions of top 5 possible responses to UK deficit. Sample size: 191. Percentages show proportion endorsed, rejected or mentioned neutrally by outlet.

Solution		Outlet				Total
	Guardian	Telegraph	Sun	Mirror	BBC	
Austerity						
Endorsed	26	31	18	2	9	86
	18.6%	39.7%	48.6%	6.3%	20%	
Rejected	35	7	3	26	1	72
	25%	9%	8.1%	81.3%	2.2%	
Neutral	79	40	16	4	35	174
	56.4%	51.3%	43.2%	12.5%	77.5%	
Total	140	78	37	32	45	332
Tax rises and spending cuts on the wealthy						
Endorsed	11	3	1	8	0	23
	18%	11.1%	6.7%	53.3%	0%	
Rejected	6	18	7	1	1	33
	9.8%	66.7%	46.7%	6.7%	6.3%	
Neutral	44	6	7	6	15	78
	72.1%	22.2%	46.7%	40%	93.8%	
Total	61	27	15	15	16	134
'Business-friendly' measures						
Endorsed	7	7	6	1	4	25
	29.2%	77.8%	66.7%	25%	44.4%	
Rejected	4	0	0	0	0	4
	16.7%	0%	0%	0%	0%	

Neutral	13	2	3	3	5	26
	54.2%	22.2%	33.3%	75%	55.6%	
Total	24	9	9	4	9	55

Government investment in economy

Endorsed	8	1	0	2	1	12
	29.6%	14.3%	0%	100%	10%	
Rejected	0	1	0	0	0	1
	0%	14.3%	0%	0%	0%	
Neutral	19	5	4	0	9	37
	70.4%	71.4%	100%	0%	90%	
Total	27	7	4	2	10	50

Tackle tax evasion/avoidance

Endorsed	1	0	0	0	0	1
	10%	0%	0%	0%	0%	
Rejected	0	0	0	0	0	0
	0%	0%	0%	0%	0%	
Neutral	9	4	0	1	3	17
	90%	100%	0%	100%	100%	
Total	10	4	0	1	3	18

Table 2.3 Mentions of top 6 possible responses to all problems combined. Sample size: 1,133. Percentages show proportion endorsed, rejected or mentioned neutrally by outlet.

Solution			Outlet			Total
	Guardian	Telegraph	Sun	Mirror	BBC	
Austerity						
Endorsed	40	59	26	3	19	147
	12.4%	38.3%	45.6%	3.8%	19.4%	
Rejected	90	8	5	56	2	161
	28%	5.2%	8.8%	71.8%	2%	
Neutral	192	87	26	19	77	401
	59.6%	56.5%	45.6%	24.4%	78.6%	
Total	322	154	57	78	98	709
Bank bailouts						
Endorsed	36	33	6	10	36	121
	20.5%	26.8%	15.4%	18.2%	64.3%	
Rejected	1	2	2	0	0	5
	0.6%	1.6%	5.1%	0%	0%	
Neutral	139	88	31	45	20	323
	79%	71.5%	79.5%	81.8%	35.7%	
Total	176	123	39	55	56	449
'Business-friendly' measures						
Endorsed	30	64	27	14	12	147
	22.6%	78%	79.4%	46.7%	31.6%	

Solution			Outlet			Total
	Guardian	Telegraph	Sun	Mirror	BBC	
Rejected	37	0	0	8	0	45
	27.8%	0%	0%	26.7%	0%	
Neutral	66	18	7	8	26	125
	49.6%	22%	20.6%	26.7%	68.4%	
Total	133	82	34	30	38	317

Tax rises and spending cuts on the wealthy

	Guardian	Telegraph	Sun	Mirror	BBC	Total
Endorsed	24	3	1	18	1	47
	20.2%	5%	6.3%	60%	3.2%	
Rejected	8	36	7	1	2	54
	6.7%	60%	43.8%	3.3%	6.5%	
Neutral	87	21	8	11	28	155
	73.1%	35%	50%	36.7%	90.3%	
Total	119	60	16	30	31	256

Government investment in economy

	Guardian	Telegraph	Sun	Mirror	BBC	Total
Endorsed	46	4	6	21	5	82
	40.4%	15.4%	40%	70%	15.2%	
Rejected	5	4	1	1	3	14
	4.4%	15.4%	6.7%	3.3%	9.1%	
Neutral	63	18	8	8	25	122
	55.3%	69.2%	53.3%	26.7%	75.8%	
Total	114	26	15	30	33	218

Tax cuts for general population

	Guardian	Telegraph	Sun	Mirror	BBC	Total
Endorsed	9	25	15	17	9	75
	11.5%	56.8%	75%	58.6%	23.1%	
Rejected	2	0	0	0	1	3
	2.6%	0%	0%	0%	2.6%	
Neutral	67	19	5	12	29	132
	85.9%	43.2%	25%	41.4%	74.4%	
Total	78	44	20	29	39	210

Table 2.2 shows the possible responses most frequently mentioned to the problem of the UK deficit, by outlet and stance. Table 2.3 shows the most frequently-mentioned possible responses to all the economic problems combined. In both cases austerity is by far the most frequently mentioned response. When it comes to the UK deficit, austerity accounted for 46.8 per cent of possible responses and was mentioned 2.5 times more frequently than the next most talked-about option, which was increasing taxes on the wealthy. In the context of all the economic problems combined, austerity accounted for 19.7 per cent of possible responses and was talked about 1.6 times more frequently than the next

most frequently-mentioned response, the bank bailouts. With regard to the deficit especially, other possible solutions did not get much of a look in. Given the way the problem was framed, this in some way 'makes sense'. If the deficit was caused by Labour overspending, it makes sense that cutting spending would be the focus of the debate over solutions. If, on the other hand, the deficit had been framed as the result of a banking crisis caused by financial misconduct, systemic problems in the sector and decades of neoliberal capitalism, cutting public spending might not have seemed like such a sensible focus of attention.

Even though, as we will see, austerity was controversial, the lack of discussion over alternatives helped to frame it as the 'common-sense' primary response. To the degree that tax rises on the wealthy and other options were mentioned, they were presented not as alternatives but as *supplements* to austerity. Other options for dealing with the deficit are discussed later. For now, we will concentrate on the contours of the austerity debate.

As seen in Tables 2.2 and 2.3, there was no media consensus over austerity. Overall, the *Telegraph* and the *Sun* showed more support for austerity than opposition to it. The *Guardian* and the *Mirror* showed more opposition than support, the *Mirror* being consistently opposed. The majority of coverage of austerity in the BBC news reported neutrally on cuts that were planned or taking place. However, the BBC did frequently endorse austerity. In the context of the UK deficit, the BBC news reported austerity neutrally 77.5 per cent of the time, endorsed austerity 20 per cent of the time and rejected it 2.2 per cent of the time.

At first glance, the press coverage of austerity seems to be quite balanced, with the right-wing sections more in support and the left-wing sections more opposed. However, there are many twists and turns behind these figures, and it is important to consider the quality and the parameters of the austerity debate as it evolved over time. As will be seen, even in the *Guardian*, some degree of austerity was accepted, and no outlet managed to reject austerity outright or give sustained attention to alternatives. Austerity may not have been framed as the *only* option for tackling the deficit but it was seen as the primary option, and a necessary and inevitable one at that.

Pre-austerity

The austerity frame really became established during the week of the budget in April 2009, when attention shifted to the public finances.

However, just as 'fiscal irresponsibility' was already given as an explanation for the problems, the possibility of tax rises and spending cuts was occasionally raised right from the beginning of the crisis. In March 2008, the financial meltdown was underway but was not yet at full throttle. Its impact on the economy was already being felt, however, and articles in the *Sun* were advocating public spending cuts (along with tax cuts) even then, reminding us that these kinds of demands were not new: 'What we desperately need is a sharp cut in the crippling burden of tax – now running at a mind- boggling £522 BILLION a year. And a reduction in state spending which sprays a shocking £589 BILLION at wasteful and inefficient public services' (Kavanagh 2008a).

After the bank bailouts, which pledged some £500 billion of public money to the banks, predictions of tax rises and spending cuts became more commonplace. In one item, the *Guardian* presented tax rises or spending cuts as inevitable: 'Whichever party forms the next government, it will have to raise taxes or cut spending or both to bring the public finances back into balance' (Seager 2008b). Pieces in the *Telegraph* expressed a similar idea, but with less equanimity: 'In the years ahead there will be unemployment, hardship and social dislocation. Borrowing will be higher, taxes will rocket, spending on services will fall, and it will have its origins not in the Thatcherite mid-1980s but in the past decade of the most reckless financial mismanagement' (Martin 2008). While *Telegraph* writers expressed annoyance at the idea of taxes going up, the *Mirror* insisted that public services mustn't suffer: 'Brown must ensure shoring up the banking system isn't funded by robbing public services. To short-change patients and pupils to prop up financial institutions would trigger a public backlash as nasty as the credit crunch' (Maguire 2008b).

From the beginning of the crisis, then, tax rises and spending cuts were predicted. They were not the main focus, however, and had not yet come to dominate the economic, political and social landscape as they would later on. The term austerity was not at that time being used – in relation to public finances, that is. One piece in the *Guardian* from October 2008 actually predicted 'a new age of austerity' for the banks (Treanor 2008)! That version of the concept was not the one that took off.

The age of austerity

After the bank bailouts, attention to public finances mounted, with David Cameron claiming in January 2009 that the UK might have to go to the IMF for a bailout. The Tories had been calling for cutbacks as early as autumn 2008, against the international consensus at that time, which was for Keynesian stimulus. However, it was during the week of the April 2009 budget that the austerity frame came into full force. The media latched on to the borrowing figures and wouldn't let go. Mike Berry (2018) shows that the media exaggerated the extent of the problem, using language like 'horror', 'horrific' and 'frightening'. Some reports gave inaccurate or questionable accounts of the deficit and the public debt. Berry argues that this media hysteria created the impression that something needed to be done urgently, and thereby helped justify austerity. In reality, even mainstream economists were saying that although borrowing had risen considerably due to the banking crisis and subsequent recession, there was no need for alarm. We have already seen that prior to the crash, the UK's debt burden was relatively low. In 2010, after the 'horrific' increase in borrowing, Robert Neild wrote in the newsletter of the Royal Economic Society: 'Today's ratio of debt to GDP does not look abnormal, let alone alarming… Our deficit – the one figure picked out by the Chancellor – is high, but our debt to GDP is average and our tax ratio is low' (quoted in Berry 2018).

When it came to austerity, there was rapid and major change during the course of that budget week. At the beginning of the week, the Labour government was emphasising spending, announcing investment in the housing market, jobs and green technologies – though it had already planned 'efficiency savings'. Its position was encapsulated in its Keynesian soundbite: 'You cannot cut your way out of the recession – you can only grow your way out of the recession.' The day after the budget statement, however, the Institute for Fiscal Studies (IFS) released its report on the government's budget figures, something the think tank does every year. The analysis revealed that, while Labour was emphasising fiscal stimulus, the 'efficiency savings' they had planned were actually cuts that would 'dwarf those imposed by Margaret Thatcher in the 1980s' (Watt 2009), including '17 per cent annual cuts in investment spending from 2011–12' (Seager and Wintour 2009). The IFS report, and especially the 'cuts worse than Thatcher' soundbite, were, understandably, splashed all over the news.

This helped the other parties commit wholeheartedly to the idea of cuts without fear of looking like the bad guys. If even the fiscally reckless Labour Party was planning cuts, the public could probably be persuaded to accept even deeper cuts, especially since now no major party could claim to be opposing them. By the end of the week the austerity narrative occupied centre stage. On 26 April, David Cameron took the plunge. In a speech that made the headlines, he promised a 'culture of thrift' and warned of a 'new age of austerity' ahead. Austerity would be the buzzword from then on.

As seen above, the right-wing press had already been calling for spending cuts. It amped up those demands. By the end of the week, even items in the *Guardian* and, to a lesser degree, the *Mirror* were accepting that some form of austerity would be 'required'. The following is from a report in the *Guardian*, and refers to the IFS analysis:

> The fiscal tightening now *required* meant that 'by 2017/18, the . . . impact of the crisis will be costing families in the UK around £2,840 a year each in today's money through a combination of tax increases and cuts in public spending', Chote said. Adam added that the budget only specified how half that money would be raised, so the next government *would have to* bring in further spending cuts and tax rises (Seager 2009, my italics).

This quote reports an IFS statement suggesting that spending cuts and tax rises were 'required'. However, it frames this claim more as a fact than an opinion. It certainly doesn't balance the claim by quoting a source with the opposing view – that cuts and tax rises were *not* required. This is despite the fact that deficit spending during recessions to boost growth was established economic theory, espoused by respected economists like Paul Krugman. This type of framing, which implies that austerity is objectively necessary rather than a political choice, quickly became commonplace, not only in the right-wing press but on the BBC news and in the *Guardian*.

A second fudge has to do with the question of *who* would be taxed more or have their spending cut, and with the definition of austerity. For the IFS, 'austerity' simply means cutting spending and/or raising taxes, the only means by which to balance the books. However, as Mark Blyth (2013: 14) puts it, 'austerity is first and foremost a political problem of distribution, and not an economic problem of accountancy'. There are huge variations in the kinds of cuts and taxes that could potentially be implemented, which could put the burden either on capital or labour – the 1 per cent or the 99 per cent.

Labour announced a 5 per cent rise in the top rate of income tax, which received extensive coverage. However, even at this early stage, taxing the well off was seen as a secondary measure – spending cuts were presented as the main story. By the end of the week, the *Guardian* was offering headlines like 'The party's over – cuts will wipe out decade of growth', 'Rise of the state under New Labour is over. Prepare for the fall, and it will be dramatic', and 'Living with cuts: "We'd cope – even if it meant selling the house"' – a human interest story about a part-time health-worker. Unlike the *Sun* and the *Telegraph*, items in the *Guardian* don't demand cuts. Cuts are presented negatively. However, they do present cuts as inevitable. And the talk about what the average family or worker will pay assumes that ordinary people will pay the debt – not the rich. In this way, through a series of omissions and displacements, austerity – meaning tax rises and spending cuts *for the general population* – quickly began to be framed as 'painful but necessary'. Cuts began routinely to be described as 'tough', 'painful' or a 'bitter economic pill', implying that austerity was unpleasant but necessary for the country to recover.

Election 2010

As momentum built towards the 2010 elections, the Tories shied away from a harsh position on austerity, and Labour used the idea of swingeing 'Tory cuts' as one of its main campaign weapons. Nevertheless, all parties were planning some degree of austerity, and the debate narrowed to being about the balance between cuts and taxes, and how quickly to wield the axe. The differences were minor. The IFS calculated that Labour planned £24 billion of tax increases and £47 billion of spending cuts, while the Conservatives planned £14 billion of tax increases and £57 billion in spending cuts (Pirie 2012: 356). Rather than being challenged on austerity itself, both parties were criticised for not spelling out what exactly they would cut. While it was right to push the parties to be honest with the electorate, in focusing on what would be cut, the media arguably neglected its duty to question the basic premises of the policies on offer.

The 2010 election resulted in the first hung parliament since 1974. The Conservatives and Liberal Democrats formed a coalition, with Conservative leader David Cameron as Prime Minister. In their 'emergency budget' in June, the coalition announced £99 billion in spending cuts and £29 billion in tax increases per year by 2014–15, including those already planned by Labour. The idea was to get the finances 'in balance' in one parliament. This retrenchment was much more radical than any party had suggested before the election. It would have surprised the 79 per cent of respondents in one survey who believed the savings could be made through efficiency savings alone (Ipsos Mori 2009).

The right-wing press supported these moves overall, though admitting they were 'blood curdling' (Johnston 2010). The *Telegraph*'s Edmund Conway (2010) wrote, '[The Chancellor's] plans are not merely brave, but inspiring; the maths is immaculate. By the end of this parliament, the yawning chasm in public finances will have been closed.' The *Telegraph* had long since shrugged off its irritation at the prospect of tax rises and spending cuts and had embraced austerity (weighted as it was in favour of spending cuts).

At this point, however, the *Guardian* began featuring pieces vigorously attacking austerity. There were two main criticisms: that the cuts would hit the poor hardest and therefore failed on grounds of fairness, and that they would further damage the economy and thus wouldn't work on their own terms (see also Fairclough 2016). Seumas Milne (2010), one of the strongest anti-austerity voices in the *Guardian*, called the cuts 'a programme of social regression' and began his piece with an apt image ridiculing Conservative claims that 'we're all in it together':

An iconic Labour movement cartoon from the early 30s, when another coalition came to power in the wake of a financial crisis and slump, shows four class stereotypes of the day on a ladder. A cloth-capped unemployed man is standing at the bottom, up to his neck in water. 'Equality of sacrifice – that's the big idea, friends!' says the silk-hatted figure at the top. 'Let's all step down one rung.'

Note that it was only *after* the election, when deep cuts were certain, that the *Guardian* began featuring items attacking austerity in earnest. At the crucial moment – from April 2009 until the 2010 elections, when the austerity frame was being established – the *Guardian* overall was actually slightly more supportive of austerity than it was opposed. Before the election, the *Guardian*'s content mix endorsed austerity 21.4 per cent of the time vs rejecting it 14.3 per cent of the time. It is true that journalists couldn't know how far the cuts would go, since no party was honest about them during the election campaigns. However, it is fair to speculate that the media's acceptance of some form and level of austerity prepped the ground both for a Conservative election win and the radical cuts that ensued.

Even in the midst of the outrage during the June 2010 emergency budget, *Guardian* commentators failed fully to reject austerity. Polly Toynbee (2010), in a piece savaging the budget, nevertheless conceded that 'frugality is undoubtedly necessary, but people will turn against all cuts if they go far further and deeper than absolutely essential'. Some cuts, it is assumed, are 'essential'. The same curious pattern of *Guardian* copy implicitly backing cuts before an election and then expressing outrage at those cuts after a Tory win can be discerned in 2015. In the budget week of March 2015, just before the election, it endorsed austerity 50 per cent of the time versus rejecting it 12.5 per cent of the time.

Some level of austerity was thus normalised, even though the emergency budget was controversial. By the time of the coalition's October 2010 Comprehensive Spending Review, the favourite game in town was choosing what to cut. Media scholars Jilly Boyce Kay and Lee Salter published a revealing analysis of the BBC news Online's special season on the spending review. One interactive feature was titled 'What would you cut?' Users were invited to choose which departments should have their budgets cut, using a sliding scale. The only tax increase included was VAT – widely accepted as the most regressive form of tax. In focusing on what to cut rather than the question of whether there should be any cuts in the first place, the feature 'closes down the space beyond the status quo' where alternative solutions might be explored. This feature began at the time of the June emergency budget, long before the spending review took place in October. The *Guardian*'s Aditya Chakrabortty described the BBC's coverage as a 'six-week long series of programmes softening up the public for [Cameron's] government's spending cuts' (Kay and Salter 2014: 760).

The amazing markets!

Why was there so much panic about increased borrowing and public debt? What would the – apparently dire – consequences be? The fear was that indebted countries would lose credibility with 'the markets', and would be punished by 'the markets' refusing to lend to them at manageable interest rates. The BBC, and especially then-economics editor Stephanie Flanders, were particularly attentive to the wishes of these 'markets'. In a segment from the day before the March 2010 budget – the last budget before the election – Flanders said: 'The Chancellor will want to please voters with his budget tomorrow, but he needs to speak to another audience as well: the City investors who are lending the government a quarter of what it needs to pay its bills.'

The segment cuts to talking heads first of a representative from Fitch, one of the credit ratings agencies (which had played a part in the banking meltdown), and then someone from Barclay's Capital. When asked about the possibility that positive economic figures might allow the government to spend a bit more on its citizens, the Fitch representative states that it 'would I think be taken quite negatively by, at least us as a ratings agency, and I think by investors'.

The Barclay's Capital figure chimes in: 'If the markets like what they're hearing, the interest rate may fall slightly, if it doesn't like what it's gonna hear, it will rise.'

Flanders concludes: 'The financial markets aren't expecting fireworks from the Chancellor tomorrow. He'll be hoping he doesn't get any from them either' (BBC 2010a).

What is extraordinary about this kind of coverage is not that it evokes the power of the 'markets' – which are indeed powerful, perhaps even more so since the banks were bailed out. It is that there is no interrogation of why these 'markets' should be in a position to be making demands over fiscal policy. Even stranger, hardly any of the news items recognise that 'the markets' are in many cases the very same financial institutions responsible for the crisis and resulting expansion of the deficit in the first place. There is almost total amnesia on this point. In the entire sample of 1,133 news items, only two acknowledge this fact. Both are in the *Guardian*. One is by Costas Lapavitsas (2010), and the other is by economist Jayati Ghosh (2011). Both are focused on the eurozone crisis as well as the UK deficit. Ghosh explains: 'Arguments that cuts are necessary to appease financial markets are specious. Fiscal imbalances were a result of the financial crisis, not a cause of it ... Governments have been spooked and even paralysed by the very financial markets that they have just saved.'

One question to ask here is whether the UK really was in danger from 'the markets'. Although some officials and economists expressed concern, many respected economists have shown that this was misplaced. As Simon Wren-Lewis (2015) explains, countries with their own central banks can never 'run out of money', even though the Conservatives and even Labour ministers used this phrase and the media frequently repeated it. If 'the markets' won't buy the debt, the central bank can always buy it, acting as lender of last resort. The problem with the eurozone countries was that their own central banks did not have control over monetary policy, and the European Central Bank (ECB) was at that time refusing to act as lender of last resort to the troubled countries. 'The markets' actually saw the UK as a safe haven for that reason and interest rates stayed low (Wren-Lewis 2015: 6).

But there is a deeper question to be asked than whether the UK was really likely to be punished by 'the markets'. Should governments supposedly accountable to their citizens allow the financial institutions that had caused the damage to demand policies that further hurt those citizens? Some news items implied that 'the markets' had actually managed to overthrow democratic process. One piece referred to the markets as 'gods of economic policy' (Jenkins 2012) and another claimed that 'the biggest and most powerful electorate is the money markets' (Kavanagh 2012). More than once were the words of former President Clinton adviser James Carville quoted:

> Back in the early 1990s, he saw the power the bond market had over the government, and observed that he no longer wanted to be reincarnated as the President or Pope: 'Now,' he revealed, 'I want to come back as the bond market. You can intimidate everybody' (Lambert 2010).

What is striking is not that such ideas are expressed. It may indeed be the case that the financial markets have become more powerful than governments. This is one feature of postdemocracy, in which states orient themselves increasingly to the interests of corporations rather than citizens (Crouch 2000). Andrew Sayer argues that instead of living in a democracy – the rule of the people – we are now living in a plutocracy – the rule of the rich. What is disturbing is that this apparent usurpation of democracy by plutocracy seems to be so readily acceded to by the media. There is no discussion of whether plutocracy is acceptable or how it should be removed. The discussion is instead focused on how best to obey its commands. There is a tautology at work: the assumption is that the markets should be in charge because they are in charge. As Sayer (2015: 128) points out, this is tantamount to saying 'might is right'.

Austerity post-2010

Predictably, austerity led to the notorious 'double dip' recession. The British economy was mired in 'the longest recovery on record' – discussed in Chapter 3. This led to discussion of whether the government should change course on austerity and adopt a 'plan B'. Even so, some degree of austerity continued to be framed as necessary. This was encapsulated in Labour's limp soundbite under its new leader, Ed Miliband, of 'too far too fast'.

As in other countries, the UK has seen strong opposition to austerity, from the unions and from grassroots campaigns such as the People's Assembly and UK Uncut. In a BBC segment on a big anti-cuts protest in 2011, the reporter said: 'One union leader said there should be no cuts at all. Labour's leader conceded that there had to be some, but said his party would cut the deficit more slowly.' Note the implication that the call for zero cuts is extreme, while Miliband's concession to some cuts is reasonable. This BBC report could actually be considered relatively open – most reporting didn't even recognise the existence of the zero cuts view.

If we consider the *Guardian* items from this period, they tended not to endorse austerity, even indirectly (as they sometimes did before the election, discussed above), and were often highly critical. However, they never explicitly rejected austerity wholesale. Arguably, given support in the *Guardian* early on for austerity, its failure to reject it outright from 2010 led implicitly to the continued message that some austerity was 'painful but necessary'. Even the *Mirror*, though it was the most consistently critical of austerity, failed to reject it *in totum*. The view that there should be no austerity in the UK at all was mentioned *twice* in total, and endorsed *zero* times. What is crucial to understand is that even the news outlets that were most critical of austerity based their commentary and reports on the assumption that some austerity was necessary. The implied alternative to austerity, then, was 'austerity lite'.

The twists in the austerity debate in the build-up to the 2015 election were mind-bending. As both Larry Elliott (2015a) and Seumas Milne (2014) pointed out in the *Guardian*, George Osborne's austerity plan had failed badly even on its own terms. Borrowing was set for £90 billion, two and a half times what the government had planned in 2010. They had had to extend their plan to 'balance the books' by almost another full parliament. What is more, because of the damage austerity was causing to the economy, the government had actually changed course and slowed the pace of cuts from 2012. For that reason, a technical 'recovery' began in 2014. However, as economist Simon Wren-Lewis (2015) shows, the Conservatives went into the election on the basis of more planned cuts. The party managed this by pretending that it hadn't changed course in its deficit reduction plan, then claiming that the 'recovery' was due to austerity, and that therefore austerity should be continued. With some notable exceptions, there was overall a media failure to challenge this line of reasoning.

Against all expectations, the Tories managed to win a majority in May 2015. In their July budget, the Conservative government announced a further £37 billion in spending cuts, including £12 billion from welfare and £20 billion from departmental budgets. But it had comprehensively failed to meet its deficit reduction targets, and spending to 2020 was set to be £83.3 billion higher than projected before the election. When Labour carried out the post mortem on its election loss, it concluded that, as well as Ed Miliband's lack of credibility as a leader, the main reason for its defeat was the public perception that it had crashed the economy by spending too much and was not sufficiently committed to austerity. In the words of politician Margaret Beckett, the party could not overcome 'the huge myth it was overspending by a Labour government that caused the crisis' (Islam 2016). It is likely that media amnesia had played a role in creating this public perception.

The lesson some Labour politicians chose to learn from their defeat was that the public wanted more austerity. This ignored the fact that the Scottish Nationalist Party had swept to victory in Scotland on an anti-austerity ticket. In September 2015, Jeremy Corbyn was elected as the new leader of the Labour Party on an explicitly anti-austerity agenda. The media treatment of Jeremy Corbyn is addressed in Chapter 5. Since 2015, the government has been forced to perform U-turns on some of its austerity policies, especially on tax credits and disability benefits. The landmark referendum of June 2016, in which the British people decided to leave the European Union, led to the government abandoning its deficit targets. Then, in 2017, new prime minister Theresa May called a snap election. The Tories were expected to win a landslide against the 'unelectable' Jeremy Corbyn. However, in the latest of a series of unprecedented international political events – like Donald Trump and Brexit – under Corbyn the Labour Party did not win but gained enough seats to undermine the Conservative majority. Labour pledged to increase public spending, paid for by raising taxes on the top 5 per cent.

'CLASS WAR'

Tables 2.2 and 2.3 show the coverage of austerity in the context of other possible responses to the problem of the UK deficit and to the crisis as a whole. In terms of the deficit, austerity was mentioned almost two and a half as many times as the next most commonly mentioned response, which was tax increases and spending cuts on the wealthy – 'austerity for the rich'. Other frequently-discussed policy options – 'business-friendly' measures, government investment in the economy, tax cuts for the general population, and tackling tax havens – are discussed in Chapters 3 and 5. These were some of the most widely covered responses not only to the deficit but to the economic downturn and the drop in living standards. For now we will concentrate on 'austerity for the rich'. This accounted for 18.9 per cent of possible responses to the deficit mentioned. Overall, in the context of both the deficit specifically and the crisis as a whole, 'austerity for the rich' was strongly opposed by the *Telegraph* and the *Sun*, strongly supported by the *Mirror*, more supported than opposed by the *Guardian* (which was nevertheless quite critical) and more or less neutrally reported by the BBC.

'Austerity for the rich' received most media attention in April 2009, when the Labour government increased the top rate of income tax from 45 per cent to 50 per cent. Unlike the coverage of the spending cuts, which often ignored class divisions, this policy was repeatedly described as 'class war' and faced outrage in the right-wing press. *Telegraph* headlines thundered: 'Return of class war; High earners hit by 50p tax rate; It's the death of New Labour, say Tories'; 'Labour reverts to type and raids wealth creators'; 'The taxman's taken all our dough, and our children's too'; 'Attack on the high earners is a desperate gamble; attempt to shore up support'; 'Blair's despair over 50p tax rate'. As the *Guardian*'s Polly Toynbee pointed out, the *Telegraph* tried to label it a 'tax on the middle classes', even though it only applied to those earning over £150,000 a year – the 1 per cent.

Even the *Guardian*, however, contained criticism of the tax, running headlines like: 'A return to class politics – but will Cameron dare to fight for the rich?' And '50p rate will create new brain drain, bosses warn'. The *Mirror* was the only outlet which fully supported the tax hike, hailing a 'Robin Hood' budget with headlines like: 'Robin good; he taxes rich to help the poor'; 'The robin hood chancellor aimed a few well-placed arrows at rich'; 'The truth about tax; 1 in 50 will pay top rate'.

It is interesting to note the extraordinary fuss made over raising income tax on the highest earners to 50 per cent – especially when we consider that, historically speaking, that is not very high. From the 1940s until the 1970s, when inequality was at its lowest and capitalism was booming, the top rate of tax was maintained at around 90 per cent (Sayer 2015: 8). In Germany, France and the US, the top rate likewise reached 90 per cent at different points during the same period. It is only in the context of the neoliberal era that 50 per cent seems high.

Many academics and campaigners advocate stronger tax measures targeted at the wealthy. Both Thomas Piketty and Oxfam, for example, advocate a tax not just on high incomes but on wealth. Others advocate a land tax. As Mark Blyth (2013: 243) points out, it is not only 'progressives' talking about these possibilities, but mainstream economists and officials. Economists in the US have calculated that raising income tax on top earners to 43.5 per cent from 22.4 per cent, the level in 2007, would raise revenue by 3 per cent of GDP, enough to close the US structural deficit while still leaving top earners with more after-tax income than they would have had under Nixon (243).

Polls have revealed public support for targeting taxes at the rich (Dahlgreen 2014). In focus groups, Mike Berry (2018: 11) found that virtually no one had heard of options like a land-value tax or a financial transactions tax. When they were explained, they were generally well received, and most participants thought that the media – and public service broadcasting in particular – should feature alternative ideas.

Blyth reminds us that 'there is plenty of room to tax at the top *because of the bailouts*' (243, original emphasis). After the 1929 crash, income inequality and financial-sector pay declined sharply relative to ordinary earnings, but this time they did not, so 'taxing now is simply taking the bailout back to the taxpayer' (243). Andrew Sayer proposes that instead of borrowing from 'the markets' to raise money, governments should be taxing financial investors more. This could kill two birds with one stone. It would remove the ability of the bondholders to dictate policy, by removing the political leverage gained by holding government debt. And it would also provide revenues for public services, eliminating the need for cuts.

It is true that the Labour government brought in a bank levy which the coalition extended, which did receive some attention in the media during coverage of each year's budget. It raised around £5 billion between 2011 and 2015. After aggressive lobbying by the banks and threats to move abroad, in July 2015 the new Conservative government replaced the levy with an 8 per cent surcharge on profits. It expects the surcharge to raise £1.7 billion over five years. This is not a large amount relative to the costs of the bailouts or the £34 billion a year the government pays in interest alone every year.

One option Blyth discusses to deal with public debt interest is the delightfully named 'financial repression'. Financial repression was used during the Second World War to help reduce the massive stocks of debt accumulated then. It is effectively a tax on the holders of government debt. Mainstream economists Reinhart and Sbrancia found that after the war, this tax, in the cases of the UK and the US, amounted to 3 to 4 per cent of GDP per year. The UK deficit of 2009–10 was around 12 per cent of GDP. Financial repression works best when you have the banks 'over a proverbial barrel – such as when they are losing money and are dependent on state funding, just like today' (Blyth 2013: 241). This is precisely the kind of condition that could have been attached to the bank bailouts discussed in Chapter 1 – but wasn't. Had the mainstream media remembered the role of both the financial sector and wider neoliberal policies in creating the crisis, these kinds of solutions – which target banks and those who have benefited most from financialisation – could have gained more traction. Depending on the way in which the crisis is framed, they make more practical and ethical sense than austerity.

One of the main arguments against taxing the rich is that they will move their money abroad. This claim is often made by the IFS and repeated in the media. The logic is this: the rich are good at avoiding tax, therefore they should not be taxed. Again, 'might is right'. Would it not be worth focusing attention on how plutocracy can be replaced by democracy? Being serious about tackling tax avoidance and evasion would be a start. As a response to the deficit, tackling tax avoidance and evasion was mentioned more than 18 times less frequently than austerity.

So much for taxing the rich. What about cutting public spending on them? That might seem an odd question, because it tends to be assumed that public spending is for the benefit of the less well off. We assume this because there is a black hole in the media coverage of government spending, in the shape of 'corporate welfare'. The *Guardian*'s Aditya Chakrabortty tried to fill that void by exposing the extent of corporate welfare in 2014 and 2015. Based on research by Kevin Farnsworth at York University, Chakrabortty's exposés claim that the UK pays out £93 billion a year in corporate welfare – meaning a combination of tax benefits (£44 billion a year), direct and indirect subsidies, and grants and insurance, advocacy and advice services. On top of that, Chakrabortty notes that businesses benefit from state-funded infrastructure.

This was an admirable attempt by Chakrabortty and the *Guardian*'s editorship, which put the story on its front page, to reframe the debate around the crisis and austerity. Unfortunately, it came too late to influence the debate on austerity in the formative months when the narrative was being established, and was not picked up enough by other media outlets to cause the necessary clamour. Corporate welfare certainly wasn't one of the areas of spending featured in the 'what would you cut?' BBC Online series on the 2010 spending review, discussed above. And it did not feature in opinion polls about what areas of government spending should be cut. Jeremy Corbyn tried to pick up on the issue after becoming Labour leader in 2015. While he has managed to put an anti-austerity position on the agenda, however, corporate welfare specifically has not become the hot topic it deserves to be.

THE MEDIA AND POLITICS

There are two crucial points to note about the options for tackling the deficit that attracted the most media attention. First, they were all policies either announced by the government or, to a lesser degree, proposed by the opposition. The debate around possibilities for tackling the deficit – and indeed the crisis as a whole – was almost entirely circumscribed by the main political parties. Secondly, as already noted, since the coverage was led by the main parties, and since all parties were planning cuts, the other options were all framed not as alternatives but as *supplements* to austerity.

Why was the debate around the deficit so contained? Some of the answers to this question will be different depending on which kinds of media we are talking about. As more than one *Guardian* journalist pointed out to me, it is hardly surprising that the right-wing press backed austerity.

The right-wing press

The UK is well known for having a press that is very skewed to the right. Unsurprising, given that it is mostly controlled by rich and powerful media barons like Rupert Murdoch (the *Sun* and *The Times*), the Barclay Brothers (*Telegraph*), Richard Desmond (the *Express*) and Lord Rothermere (*Daily Mail*). Theoretically, there is not necessarily a direct link between media ownership and the types or range of voices found in the media. However, it seems likely that there is at least an indirect link between the two. For Stuart Hall, analysis of media ownership is not 'a sufficient explanation of the way the ideological universe is structured, but it is a necessary starting point' (in Freedman 2014: 59).

Owen Jones (2015: 90) writes, in *The Establishment*, that UK media barons are politically motivated and that through their titles 'the terms of political debate are ruthlessly policed'. They push policies that benefit the rich and powerful and oppose ones that disadvantage them. The newspapers are aligned with political parties and editorially come out in support of one or other of the parties during elections. Owners and editors aren't necessarily wedded to a particular party but will make strategic decisions about who to support. In postdemocracy that can be any of the main parties, as famously illustrated when the *Sun* supported Tony Blair's New Labour in 1997. However, most of the news media continue to have an affinity with the Conservative Party. In the words of one *Guardian* columnist I spoke to:

> 85 per cent of the media in the country is passionately, devotedly committed to keeping a Conservative government in power ... It's a wild force, controlled by ... ultra right-wing non-British-tax-paying, very eccentric moguls with their own political agenda and whenever they can, they will do Labour down.

In 2010, the *Sun* and most other papers backed the Tories. The Labour leader, Gordon Brown, was deeply unpopular. The Tories' image had been given a makeover and they were looking fresh. They were standing for austerity – a smaller public sector and a more powerful private sector. What self-respecting media baron could resist? And so, the right-wing press pushed the Tory line on Labour overspending and austerity.

Owners have been known to intervene directly to make sure their journalists report in line with their interests. Rupert Murdoch is well known for taking a hands-on approach. Or editors will be appointed who have a particular worldview and who are certain to roll out that view. Owen Jones (2015) relays stories of the incredible pressure journalists come under to report in certain ways.

However, instances of direct censorship from owners and editors are comparatively rare. Far more common is self-censorship. Journalists, especially those lower down the hierarchy (the majority), want to please their employers. They know what kinds of stories to pitch and they know how to frame stories in ways that their managers will approve of. Thus, although newspapers are not monolithic and individual journalists do have agency, through self-censorship a particular way of framing politically important issues – such as austerity – will emerge. Several of the journalists I spoke to conceded that self-censorship was the norm among journalists, except perhaps at the most senior levels.

During the neoliberal era, viewing public spending on welfare and public services negatively became commonplace (spending on the military and 'law and order' was ok). But the right-wing media was tapping into a much longer tradition. Mark Blyth (2013: 100–1) explains that liberal economics (the 'liberal' in 'neoliberal') grew up in reaction to the state in the early stages of capitalist development in the seventeenth century. It set up an opposition between state and market, ignoring the fact that states make markets. This ideology existed long before states became large budgetary entities. That happened in the early twentieth century and it was then that the idea of shrinking the state became a distinct economic doctrine.

In the UK, the press has a history of supporting this doctrine. In 1976, when Britain was bailed out by an IMF loan, *The Times* pushed for £5 billion in spending cuts, supported by the *Telegraph* and the *Economist* (Needham 2015: 266). Even before the establishment of the welfare state, in 1931 during a currency crisis, an emergency budget slashed unemployment benefits and public sector pay by 10 per cent. This move was backed by *The Times* and the *Daily Mail*, and the *Economist* praised the government for curtailing national expenditure 'within its means' (Roberts 2015: 249). Strikes against the cuts were condemned. In the 1920s, the 'Geddes Axe', a government appointed committee to identify extensive cuts in government spending, was largely the outcome of a campaign waged by the conservative press (Roberts 2018).

Media support for austerity sits alongside widespread scapegoating of welfare recipients and the poor, which also has a long history – discussed in Chapter 5. Without these long traditions of opposing the state and scapegoating the poor that have laid ideological groundwork over many years – what we might call ideological 'terraforming' – it would be a lot more difficult to present public spending cuts as a logical solution to a problem first manifesting in the banking sector.

The right-wing orientation of the British press therefore has to do with ownership and profit orientation – the first of Herman and Chomsky's five filters by which news comes to serve the interests of elites. James Curran (2010a) shows that historically the highly concentrated ownership of British media was the result of market forces. During the eighteenth and nineteenth centuries, there was a popular radical press in Britain, run not by the wealthy but by members of the working class. The state and wealthy proprietors tried ruthlessly to put it down, through stamp duty and sedition laws. However, it was eventually extinguished not by state censorship but because of the rising costs of running a newspaper when the press was industrialised. By the early twentieth century, the media was dominated by press barons and reflected their interests.

The fact that news was increasingly funded through advertising also played a part in the eradication of the radical press and consolidation of the conservative press. Radical papers were unable to attract enough advertising revenue because they had the wrong sort of readership for advertisers – poor people (Curran 2010a). Advertising is the second of Herman and Chomsky's filters. It still has an influence on content. The 'wall' between advertising and editorial is sometimes breached. For example, in 2015, established journalist Peter Oborne blew the whistle on *Telegraph* executives censoring content to appease advertisers, notably the HSBC bank (Oborne 2015).

It's easy enough to explain media amnesia and the rewriting of the crisis by the right-wing press. That leaves us with the broadcasters, which are mandated to be 'impartial', and the sections of the press that are supposed to represent the left. Why did they not forcefully counter the Labour overspending narrative by foregrounding the real causes of the crisis? Why did they fail to reject austerity completely or give adequate attention to a wider range of alternatives?

The 'left-wing' press

When it came to the *Guardian* and the *Mirror*, an important reason is again the political affiliations of the press. Senior staff have strong personal and professional links to politicians in the main parties. Therefore, they tend to deploy the narratives of the party with whom they are connected. The Lib Dems were pro austerity. Prior to the 2010 election, there were divisions within the Labour Party between the prime minister and the chancellor on how to frame the crisis and how to respond (Schifferes and Knowles 2015). In the event, the party went into the 2010 election campaign with a deficit reduction plan. In 2015 it campaigned on a ticket of 'austerity lite'. Partly because the left-wing party failed fully to oppose austerity, the left-wing media failed likewise. And partly because the left-wing party failed to offer alternatives, so too did the left-wing press.

Labour also failed to challenge the overspending frame. Labour politicians, including Gordon Brown, Ed Balls and Ed Miliband, did deny that Labour overspending was the cause of the deficit. However, they failed to provide a clear, coherent narrative of their own. This was partly because the party was in disarray and partly because it was in the awkward position of having been in power for a decade when the crisis struck. Labour could not avoid taking the blame, but it did not want to point the finger at its own liberalisation of the economy. This would have jeopardised New Labour's legacy and would have antagonised the business community that it had been trying so hard to court. Furthermore, as noted, Labour was committed to some degree of austerity. It would have been tricky to frame spending cuts as the appropriate response to the deficit if it was simultaneously framing financial dereg- ulation and liberalisation as the cause. Meanwhile, the Tories had an effective media strategy revolving around repeating simple slogans about clearing up Labour's mess and fixing the roof.

Another problem for Labour was that there was a kernel of truth in the fiscal irresponsibility claim. As outlined above, though Labour's pre-crisis borrowing was nothing remarkable, it had entered the crisis with a deficit. According to the Washington Consensus that budgets should be balanced, it could be argued that Labour had overspent. The Tories made the argument that during the pre-crisis years of growth the government should have built up a budget surplus as a buffer should recession hit. This seemed to be the meaning of the 'fixing the roof' soundbite. And Labour *had* increased public spending using tax revenues accrued off the back of an unsustainable financial bubble.

In *News and News Sources*, Paul Manning identifies 'seven arts' of suc- cessful spin-doctoring, one of them being that information needs to be at least partially accurate (cited in Temple 2008: 153). Though spin doctors can be flexible with the truth, the best ones avoid outright lies when they can. The accusation that Labour mismanaged the public finances contained a kernel of truth and for that reason the charge stuck. Journalists I spoke to referred more than once to this kernel of truth, which was able to grow and flourish into the main explanation for the deficit.

The press doesn't only follow politics, however. It can also influence the political agenda. The importance placed by New Labour on courting the media moguls is testament to that. Influence between the media and politics is a two-way street (see Golding and Middleton 1982; Hall *et al.* 1978). Why didn't the left-wing press urge Labour to oppose austerity? The *Mirror* did feature the odd article urging the party to 'find its soul' (Goodman 2009). But the vast amount of its content focused on attacking the Tories rather than trying to shape the Labour approach to austerity. Much of the *Guardian*'s content did counter the 'state bad/ market good' formula and back government investment – discussed in the next chapter. However, many of its senior staff probably agreed with the 'too far, too fast' approach – that although the coalition government was taking austerity much too far, frugality was necessary.

Another issue that came up especially with journalists at the *Guardian* was the question of credibility, noted in Chapter 1. When I asked a columnist why so few opinion pieces endorsed the zero cuts option, she replied that opinion pieces needed to resonate with the (*Guardian*-reading) public. She felt that the zero austerity view would have been rejected by her readers and would have led people to disengage from her column. She pushed the anti-austerity argument as far as she felt she could without losing the interest of her readers.

This is a version of a position that is very common among journalists: that they reflect the views of the public. They rarely consider how they might help to *shape* the views of the public. Even columnists, whose job is to give their own opinion, seem to think they can't express views that are too divergent from those of their readership. As I listened to the *Guardian* columnist, I thought of a feedback loop, in which she was anticipating the views of her readers, trying to resonate with those views, and in the process helping to influence those views. This feedback loop process potentially helped create a 'common sense' around austerity at the paper: that the austerity the Tories were enforcing was unjust and counterproductive, but that some cuts were required. These kinds of feedback loops are never fully closed, because there is always a struggle around what is considered 'common sense', 'realistic' or 'credible'. Nevertheless they can help to preserve the *status quo* and the interests of the powerful. On the whole, journalists appear to be unaware of the feedback loops in which they operate.

The BBC

Public service broadcasters are different from newspaper brands. Far from being aligned with a political party, they are required to be impartial. However, research has found that they have a tendency to follow the news agendas of the papers (Cushion *et al.* 2016; Schlosberg 2016). Because the UK has a majority right-wing press, broadcasters tend to follow a right-wing agenda.

Another important issue is that the broadcasters, in the words of journalist Paul Mason, 'deify parliamentary politics' (Novarra Media 2017). They operate within a Westminster bubble, and so the views of those occupying that bubble dominate coverage. The BBC news coverage regularly implied that austerity was necessary not because it was biased towards or against one of the parties, but because all the main parties endorsed austerity as a policy. This is also partly why the BBC news neglected to cover proposals for dealing with the deficit that didn't come from one of the parties – they only covered proposals coming from within the bubble.

The BBC journalists I spoke to were of the opinion that their job was to cover the views of the main political parties equally. They did not think it was within their remit to seek out views beyond those of the main political parties. One former senior editor told me that even if he knew that austerity was 'completely wrong' he couldn't find a way to give voice to that view because it was not the role of the media to 'do the job of the opposition'. In fact, some BBC journalists thought that seeking out alternative views might be considered a *breach* of impartiality, because it could be interpreted as advocacy journalism and an abuse of their position. Thus it is possible that the interpretation of impartiality rules *actually leads to bias*, not towards a particular party but towards the baseline establishment view.

A TAXING QUESTION

Increasing taxes on the financial sector, wealthy individuals and corporations – discussed above – seems like a fairer way of reducing public deficits than cutting welfare and public services. These kinds of tax options certainly deserve a lot more attention in the media. However, it is worth questioning whether these moves are the most efficacious or desirable in the long run. A financial transaction tax, for example, relies on the continuation of the very kinds of financial operations that created the financial bomb that exploded in 2008. Much the same can be said of all the taxes targeted at capital or high earners.

Corporation tax, for example, taxes companies' profits. These profits are made by appropriating natural resources and by exploiting workers. In Karl Marx's analysis, exploitation has a specific meaning: workers do not control the surplus value that they create. This is taken by the capitalist and is the source of profit. John Smith (2016) shows that, in the era of the transnational corporation (TNC), profits are increasingly made through 'super exploitation': pushing wages down below the cost of living. Through outsourcing in particular, TNCs pay ultra low wages to workers in low-wage countries and sell their products to consumers in high-wage countries. Governments in rich countries accrue tax revenue from super exploitation by corporations in low wage countries. The tax revenue includes value added tax (VAT) and income tax paid by employees who provide advertising, security and other services to the company in the countries where its products are sold. Smith considers this kind of wealth extraction to be a modern form of imperialism.

Tony Norfield (2011) tells the story of a T-shirt made in Bangladesh and sold in Germany by the Swedish retailer H&M for €4.95. H&M pays the Bangladeshi manufacturer €1.35 per shirt. 40c of this covers the cost of importing the cotton from the US. Thus 95c of the final sale price remains in Bangladesh, to be shared between the factory owner, the workers, the suppliers of inputs and services and the Bangladeshi government, expanding Bangladesh's GDP by this amount. 6c is spent on shipping costs to Hamburg. The remaining €3.54 counts towards the GDP of the country where the shirt is consumed: Germany. €1.99 goes towards distribution costs in Germany, shop rent, sales force, marketing and administration in Germany. H&M makes 60c profit. The German state captures 79c of the sale price through VAT at 19 per cent. 16c covers sundry 'other items'. Therefore the German state actually captures more of the proceeds from the shirt than H&M. The German state will spend this money on its own citizens, the military and companies in the form of 'corporate welfare', and it will even give 'a few pennies to the poor countries in the form of "foreign aid"' (Smith 2016: 14).

Thus, though it makes sense to insist that governments raise revenue through taxing the wealthy, it is necessary to consider the labyrinthine ways in which resources are appropriated. Tax reform and tackling tax avoidance are important short- and medium-term goals. Global taxes of the kind proposed by Thomas Piketty and others, and international transfers, could go some way to confronting global inequality (discussed in Chapter 5). In the longer term it will be necessary to consider fundamental questions about how wealth is created, and how resources should be allocated. This will necessarily lead to questions about whether capitalism organised around nation states is inevitably imperialistic, and if so what could and should be done about that. Arguably, at a time of economic crisis, the media should be enabling discussion around precisely these kinds of basic questions. On the contrary, however, the superficiality and narrowness of the media coverage makes it impossible even to consider these questions.

GLOBAL DEBT

The absence of any discussion of the international implications of fiscal policy is related to all three of the major aspects of media amnesia: the lack of pluralism, the lack of historical context and the lack of global context. We saw in Chapter 1 that during the financial meltdown, journalists tried to explain the international dimensions of the crisis. The focus quickly shrank, however. The eurozone crisis was certainly in sight, but in reporting the UK deficit, coverage of the international dimension was usually superficial. Other European countries were often used as political footballs – for example, the narrative that 'we don't want to end up like Greece' was deployed to strengthen the hand of the pro-austerity establishment (see Schifferes and Knowles 2015).

Meanwhile, international factors such as the paradox of thrift were less emphasised. One person's debt is always another person's asset and income stream, and in order for someone to save, someone else must spend. According to Keynes' 'paradox of thrift', it may make sense for individual countries – Greece, say – to reduce their debts, but in order to do so, their trading partners cannot do the same thing at the same time. For one country to save, others must spend. Thus, *We cannot all cut our way to growth at the same time*' (Blyth 2013: 8, original emphasis). Between 2011 and 2013, when there were grave concerns about the global economy, there was some media discussion of the problems of all countries cutting at the same time – this was mentioned by Stephanie Flanders on the BBC, for example. However, this attention was minimal. When it comes to the economy, it does not make sense to think about individual countries in isolation from their international context. As we have seen, the economy is global.

Forgetting structural adjustment

While the eurozone problems were in the media eye, the wider global perspective seen during the financial crash in 2008 had largely receded. None of the news items found for this study had a primary focus on the public debts of non-Western countries. Of the items focusing on the UK deficit, 29.3 per cent also made reference to other countries, putting the UK deficit into some kind of international context. However, 93.2 per cent of the countries mentioned were Western countries. A further 4.8 per cent were Asian emerging and developed countries (mainly Japan and China). Developing nations barely got a mention. The media's persistent failure to provide global context is considered in Chapter 3.

Had journalists looked a little further afield and a little further back in time, they would have had an idea what to expect from austerity-type reforms directed at indebted countries. The introduction to this book describes how Western banks found themselves awash with dollars during the 1970s, and began lending them to other governments, often dictatorships, around the world. After the Volcker Shock sharply raised interest rates, these governments could not repay the loans, leading to the Third World debt crisis. The International Monetary Fund (IMF) stepped in to take on the loans. It insisted that, in order to obtain refinancing, these countries had to undergo 'structural adjustment': sell off public resources, end subsidies and cut public services.

These measures proved disastrous for the impacted countries. In the 15 years after 1975, per capita spending on healthcare in Africa was halved. By 2010, life expectancy had fallen by seventeen years on average in eight African countries: Kenya, South Africa, Mozambique, Zambia, Rwanda, Malawi, Zimbabwe and Namibia (McNally 2011: 129). Because of compound interest, these loans could never be repaid. Between 1980 and 2002, developing countries made $4.6 trillion in debt repayments. This represents about eight times what they owed at the beginning of the period ($580 billion in 1980). But, after making those payments, they still owed $2.4 trillion (McNally 2011: 127).

During the 1990s, the global justice movement demanded an end to structural adjustment. This led to around $130 billion worth of debt for 35 countries being cancelled through the Heavily Indebted Poor Countries Initiative (Stalker 2015: 75). The campaigns also succeeded in discrediting the IMF – at least for a while. By 2000, East Asian countries had begun a boycott of the IMF. Then in 2002, Argentina 'committed the ultimate sin: they defaulted – and got away with it' (Graeber 2014: 369). The debt jubilee campaigns and the havoc-wreaking IMF programmes received a substantial amount of media coverage at the time. By 2010, though, the media had forgotten its own past coverage. The IMF was given a new lease of life at the G20 summit in April 2009. World leaders agreed to bolster its fund by $1.1 trillion, purportedly to help economies worldwide cope with the crash. According to Varoufakis (2015: 164), however: 'those who looked more closely saw, in the fine print, a specific clause: the money would be used exclusively to assist the global financial sector. Indian farmers on the verge of suicide need not apply. Nor should capitalists interested in investing in the real economy.'

By 2011, twenty nations, including Greece, had been structurally adjusted by the IMF. Other governments, including that of the UK, were busy structurally adjusting themselves. Austerity post-2008 has not been solely a Western phenomenon, however. According to a report on 128 developing countries published in 2011 by UNICEF, despite an initial period of fiscal stimulus, 'premature expenditure contraction became widespread beginning in 2010 despite vulnerable populations' urgent and significant need of public assistance.' 70 developing countries (55 per cent of the sample) had reduced total expenditures by nearly 3 per cent of GDP, on average, during 2010, and 91 developing countries (more than 70 per cent of the sample) were expected to reduce annual expenditures in 2012. Nearly one quarter of the countries were undergoing 'excessive contraction', meaning they were cutting expenditures below pre-crisis levels as a proportion of GDP. Unsurprisingly, cost-cutting measures were found to threaten children and poor households (Ortiz *et al.* 2011).

What is important to remember is that debt has a strong precedent as a 'weapon of dispossession'. David Graeber's (2014) book on the history of debt for the past 5,000 years makes the key point that debt is not simply a question of a person or state failing to 'live within its means' but is a relation of power. This power relation has had an imperialist dimension, whereby businesses, institutions and wealthy individuals of the global north have been able to use debt to extract wealth from the global south.

US debt is another kettle of fish. It is unique, reflecting and reinforcing that country's role as the world's economic hegemon. The US's twin deficits – its budget and trade deficits – played a key role both in the establishment of the neoliberal phase of capitalism and in the crisis generated by it (see the Introduction and Chapter 1). According to Varoufakis (2015: 100–12), US policy-makers including Paul Volcker and Henry Kissinger deliberately expanded the nation's deficits. In fact, the twin deficits were at the core of the new post-Bretton Woods global system of trade and finance beginning in the 1970s and 1980s. After losing its status as a trade surplus country, rather than trying to regain its surplus status, the US deliberately began importing like there was no tomorrow. In this way, it remained the world's driver of growth, absorbing the exports of the rest of the world. It also jacked up its spending, especially on the military under Ronald Reagan. The trade surpluses that its trading partners – especially Germany, Japan and later China – were accumulating were then recycled straight back into the US. States and businesses either bought US treasury bonds – financing the national debt – or they invested in US companies. US businesses were attractive investments because of falling wages and increased profitability. These investments helped to balance out the trade deficit. In this analysis, America's massive deficits have actually been drivers of the world economy in the neoliberal era.

Thus, while the Washington Consensus is that national budgets should be balanced, and while the Washington-based IMF has been enforcing this dictum around the world, the US has retained its global hegemony *because* of its deficits. David Graeber points out that it is unlikely it will ever repay its debts, yet the shared fantasy that it will is what has kept the global economy going since the 1970s.

However, the US economy was gravely damaged by the 2008 crash. Its imports haven't recovered enough to absorb the world's exports. Regardless of the unique role played by the US deficits in the global economy, Republicans opposed Obama's 2009 stimulus package and demanded austerity measures (although the term austerity is not so prevalent as it is in Europe). By 2010, 36 states had cut higher education spending and 24 had cut services to the elderly and disabled (McNally 2011: 22–3). This may have further reduced the US's ability to absorb the world's surpluses. At the same time, it is uncertain whether another global hegemon will be able to take its place. Compared to its performance in the years preceding 2008, China is slowing down, its problems exacerbated by measures taken by world central banks and its own government and businesses to deal with the 2008 crisis. Its large fiscal stimulus and the availability of cheap credit have increased China's public and corporate debt dramatically.

Debt jubilees have been advocated in relation to the eurozone crisis and especially Greece, and will be addressed in Chapter 4. The key point is that, to understand public debt problems, it is important to consider the roles played by debt in the global economy. The media failed to inform the public about these global and historical dimensions to debt and austerity.

CONCLUSION

Thus austerity came to define an era, with the help of some convenient media amnesia and ultrafast revisioning. A media hysteria rose up around the deficit. But its origins were forgotten or misremembered. As the financial crisis and its root causes faded from memory, a new explanation – Labour overspending – occupied the explanatory void. Austerity was controversial in the mainstream media. The coverage followed a left-right split. However, even the leftwing sections of the press implicitly (and sometimes explicitly) endorsed some level of austerity – 'austerity lite'. Other options for reducing the deficit were (a) those offered by the establishment and (b) those presented as *supplements* rather than real *alternatives* to austerity. Meanwhile, the global journalism seen in Chapter 1 had vanished. The global role played by debt, and the devastation caused by austerity in other parts of the world, were missing from coverage.

At the time of writing, the age of austerity appears to be giving way to an age of nationalist populism that it helped create. Far-right figures are promising simultaneously to get national debts under control, invest in their own industries, and help their own people – struggling under austerity – by keeping foreigners out and erecting trade barriers. Austerity has arguably helped create a global economic slump that has lasted nearly a decade and has no end in sight. It is to the media coverage of this slump that we turn next.

3

Slump

The global financial crisis rapidly mutated into the Great Recession. Banks stopped lending to businesses and consumers, businesses laid off millions of employees, who reduced their spending, which in turn led to more lay-offs and less consumption and so on, in a vicious circle. By the Spring of 2009, the World Bank was predicting the first year of negative growth in the global economy since 1945 (Harvey 2011: 6). Although the Great Recession technically ended in 2009, the world has yet fully to recover pre-crash growth rates, leading to talk in economic circles of 'secular stagnation': a long-term slump. Global debt – of which about two-thirds is in the private sector – is, according to the IMF, at a record high, acting as a further drag on the economy (Roberts 2016d). Nationalist figures have risen to power across the globe partly in response to these economic conditions.

As we saw in the previous chapter, austerity was sold in two ways. First, it was presented as a necessary response to public debt, which had to be reduced to avoid punishment from the markets and unfairly burdening future generations. Secondly, austerity was presented as a solution to the economic slump. The theory was that a reduction in public spending would create more room for the private sector and would thus stimulate growth. Keynesian economist Paul Krugman refers to this idea that austerity will lead to growth as belief in the 'confidence fairy'.

Another of the major responses to the slump has been supply-side measures. These are reforms affecting the supply side of the economy – structures of production and ownership. They aim to attract business investment. They have included cuts in corporation tax and other tax cuts aimed at businesses and wealthy individuals, privatisation and the deregulation of labour and other markets. If we think back to Chapter 1 and the Introduction, we will recall that these kinds of measures are precisely those that have characterised the neoliberal period, which culminated in the 2008 crash. The measures brought in to deal with the crisis are versions of the same measures that helped create the crisis in the first place. As we will see, media amnesia has helped legitimise these responses.

In opposition to the responses of austerity and supply-side measures, which have escalated the inequality associated with the neoliberal era, the standard left position has been to advocate government investment to grow the economy: the Keynesian response. Public debate has come to be limited to these two positions, with little beyond. While Keynesianism has been important in countering the onward march of neoliberalism, it has its own limitations. Crucially, both sides of the debate take as given that growth is good, ignoring warnings that continued economic growth leads to depletion of natural resources and an increase in emissions of pollutants that jeopardise the survival of the human race. Neither position adequately addresses the problems of globalisation and the global division of labour within capitalism. The mainstream media has unfortunately failed yet again to provide a forum to discuss other possibilities.

OPEN FOR BUSINESS

Table 3.1 Mentions of top 5 possible responses to UK weak economy. Sample size: 282. Percentages show proportion endorsed, rejected or mentioned neutrally by outlet.

Solution	Outlet					Total
	Guardian	*Telegraph*	*Sun*	*Mirror*	*BBC*	
'Business-friendly' measures						
Endorsed	21	51	19	12	8	111
	24.4%	79.9%	82.6%	48%	33.3%	
Rejected	26	0	0	8	0	34
	30.2%	0%	0%	32%	0%	
Neutral	39	13	4	5	16	77
	40.7%	20.3%	17.4%	20%	66.7%	
Total	**86**	**64**	**23**	**25**	**24**	**222**
Austerity						
Endorsed	6	20	7	1	5	39
	6.3%	46.5%	46.7%	2.8%	17.2%	
Rejected	28	0	2	30	1	61
	29.5%	0%	13.3%	83.3%	3.4%	
Neutral	61	23	6	5	23	118
	64.2%	53.5%	40%	13.9%	79.3%	
Total	**95**	**43**	**15**	**36**	**29**	**218**

Solution	Outlet Guardian	Telegraph	Sun	Mirror	BBC	Total
Government investment in economy						
Endorsed	27	2	6	17	4	56
	37%	11.8%	54.5%	68%	18.2%	
Rejected	5	3	1	1	3	13
	6.8%	17.6%	9.1%	4%	13.6%	
Neutral	41	12	4	7	15	79
	56.2%	70.6%	36.4%	28%	68.2%	
Total	73	17	11	25	22	148
Tax cuts for general population						
Endorsed	4	15	8	14	8	49
	8%	57.7%	61.5%	63.6%	36.4%	
Rejected	1	0	0	0	1	2
	2%	0%	0%	0%	4.5%	
Neutral	45	11	5	8	13	82
	90%	42.3%	38.5%	36.4%	59.1%	
Total	50	26	13	22	22	133
Tax rises and spending cuts on the wealthy						
Endorsed	4	0	0	8	0	12
	8.9%	0%	0%	61.5%	0%	
Rejected	2	17	0	0	1	20
	4.4%	56.7%	0%	0%	7.7%	
Neutral	39	13	1	5	12	70
	86.7%	43.3%	100%	38.5%	92.3%	
Total	45	30	1	13	13	102

Table 3.1 shows the most frequently mentioned possible responses to the weakness of the UK economy in the sampled media. Table 2.3, in the previous chapter, shows the most frequently mentioned possible responses to *all* aspects of the crisis combined, including the financial crisis, the UK weak economy, the deficit, the eurozone crisis, and falling living standards and rising inequality. Both tables show that business-friendly or supply-side measures received a lot of attention. In the case of the UK economy, these were the most cited, accounting for 20.3 per cent of possible responses mentioned. In the case of the crisis overall, they were the third most cited after austerity and the bank bailouts, accounting for 8.8 per cent of possible responses.

In the context of the UK, the measures receiving media attention were predominantly those announced by the coalition government from 2011 onwards. After the newly-elected coalition had announced radical austerity measures in its 2010 'emergency budget', in 2011 it was keen to direct attention away from austerity and towards growth. The big idea was to restructure Britain's economy away from consumption and towards manufacturing. This was to be achieved through a raft of supply-side measures. Those announced in 2011 included a cut in corporation tax to 23 per cent, new and extended tax reliefs for small- and medium-size enterprises, the loosening of planning controls and the removal of £350 million of regulation on businesses, including the Equality Act's dual discrimination provisions. These kinds of measures have been extended in every budget thereafter. Notably, the 2012 budget saw a cut in the top rate of income tax, and corporation tax was cut further in 2012, 2013, 2015 and 2016.

Supply-side measures, associated with Ronald Reagan, are linked to 'trickle-down' economic theory – that incentives on the supply side encourage businesses to invest in production, thereby creating jobs and economic growth. The wealthy are therefore 'job creators' and 'wealth creators', and financial incentives given to them would eventually 'trickle down' to the rest of society. In reality, they have been shown to transfer wealth upwards and keep it there (Quiggin 2010: 137–75; Hudson 2017). Inequality and its media coverage are the subject of Chapter 5.

Despite this, Tables 3.1 and 2.3 show that overall these measures were received much more enthusiastically than austerity. They were whole-heartedly embraced by the right-wing press, as is perhaps unsurprising. The BBC news endorsed these measures 33.3 per cent of the time across the whole sample, and rejected them zero times. The *Mirror* contained mixed messages but overall showed much more support for supply-side moves than opposition. The *Guardian* is the only outlet in the sample that overall rejected these responses more frequently than it endorsed them. However, even the *Guardian* frequently contained supportive views, endorsing them 22.6 per cent of the time versus rejecting them 27.8 per cent of the time (Table 2.3).

The different kinds of supply-side measures – cuts in corporation tax and other business taxes, cuts in taxes on wealthy individuals, deregulation and privatisation – were bundled together in packages aiming to show, in the words of then-Chancellor George Osborne, that 'Britain is open for business.' The *Telegraph* and the *Sun* were unambiguously enthusiastic about these packages. They endorsed the view that tax cuts for corporations and the rich help to attract business investment to the country and embraced deregulation as 'cutting red tape'. The *Sun* gleefully reported that 'CHANCELLOR George Osborne is slashing corporation tax and red tape – to show that Britain is "open for business"' (Hawkes 2011), citing business executives who hinted that this might tempt them to move their businesses to the UK.

Commentators in the *Telegraph*, not satisfied with this 'shower' of neoliberal policies, repeatedly urged the government to go further on all fronts. When in 2012 the coalition reduced the rate of income tax for those earning over £150,000 from 50 per cent to 45 per cent, Jeremy Warner (2012) urged the government to go even further, despite acknowledging that British citizens supported a higher tax rate for the rich and that the measure was unfair:

> There is a danger that the compromise figure of 45p will mark the limits of the Chancellor's ambition … the political risks, given that opinion polls support soaking the rich, are all too obvious. A tax giveaway to the better off amounting to thousands of pounds a year does not look good against one to the lower paid worth just hundreds.

Another piece in the *Telegraph* welcomed the deregulatory measures, before quoting the Institute of Directors' Director General saying that the scale of deregulation in employment law was 'still very limited' (Winnett 2011). *Telegraph* items were also gung ho about the prospect of privatisation, once again urging the government to go further, to transfer resources as much as possible from the public to the private sector: 'the growth strategy we need requires a complete restructuring of our economy. It means dismantling large parts of the state apparatus and transferring resources to the private sector, where they would generate better value and enhance competitiveness' (Heffer 2011).

The support from right-wing sections of the press is perhaps to be expected, and they fulfil expectations with relentless consistency. Conversely, it might be expected that the left-leaning press opposed these measures with equivalent consistency, on the grounds that they widen inequality, transferring resources upwards to the wealthiest in society. However, the coverage of supply-side measures in the *Mirror* and the *Guardian* was inconsistent. In Chapter 2 we saw that these two papers rejected austerity more frequently than they endorsed it, but that both assumed that some degree of austerity was necessary, and the *Guardian* especially did contain pro-austerity views. When it came to business-friendly measures, the left-wing press showed even more support than for austerity. The *Mirror* overall actually supported them far more frequently than it rejected them. The *Guardian* overall was more critical, but nevertheless displayed substantial support.

The *Mirror* was very critical both of the cut in the top rate of income tax and of attacks on the public sector and privatisation. Its reports frequently highlighted the injustice of imposing austerity on the general population while giving tax breaks to the richest. In an item on a stealth tax on pensioners, dubbed the 'granny tax', Jason Beattie (2012) wrote, 'the Chancellor clobbered pensioners with a £3 billion "granny tax" to pay for the tax cut gifts to his rich cronies.'

However, the *Mirror* was contradictory when it came to business tax cuts. It generally styles itself as supporting polices for small businesses, while opposing those designed to support the rich (e.g. Roberts 2010). However, the line between helping small businesses and helping big business becomes blurred, and overall the *Mirror*'s content mix supported tax breaks benefitting large corporations as much as small businesses such as corporation tax cuts.

The *Guardian* displayed ambivalence when it came to tax breaks for business, cuts in the top rate of tax and deregulation. A report on the budget from 2011 repeated another of Chancellor Osborne's soundbites – that Britain would be 'carried aloft by the march of the makers' – and featured no less than five business representatives praising the measures, with no critical voices (Treanor 2011). The *Guardian* also featured opinion pieces from the neoliberal Adam Smith Institute and the City of London Corporation supporting the moves. The Adam Smith Institute's Eamon Butler (2011) proposed taking small businesses out of employment regulation entirely.

On the other hand, the *Guardian* also featured pieces vigorously attacking these policies, especially in opinion pieces by its most critical commentators, who often used the idea of a 'race to the bottom', whereby economic liberalisation has led to countries competing to have the worst employment and environmental standards and lowest tax regimes in order to attract business. Some commentators noted the redistributory nature of these regimes (though there were fewer accusations of class war than when Labour raised the top rate of tax to 50 per cent in 2009, discussed in Chapter 2). Zoe Williams, who also pointed out the measures' exacerbation of gender inequalities, wrote, 'This isn't really about sexism, still less regionalism, it's straight redistribution – taking from those at the bottom to mollify those in the middle' (Williams 2011).

The BBC news coverage demonstrated considerable support for supply-side measures (see Tables 3.1 and 2.3). The sampled segments were particularly positive about cuts in business taxes (the reporting of the cut in the top rate of income tax was more balanced, reflecting the stronger stance taken against it by the opposition party). The BBC has a business editor whose job it is to represent the voice of the business community. In the news coverage of each year's budget, an entire segment is devoted to doing this. There is no equivalent segment by a labour editor or a communities editor that might give opposing views. The business perspective is thus built into the structure of BBC news coverage of the budget – this will be explored in more detail later on. Its coverage of the 2011 budget, for example, contained a segment by the business editor featuring two endorsements by business representatives – with no critical voices. The endorsements promoted the message that helping business was tantamount to helping society. There was no mention of the incongruity between austerity measures for the general population – which were discussed at length – and tax cuts for business.

Think back to the Introduction and Chapter 1 of this book, where we saw that these same measures – tax cuts for the wealthiest, deregulation and privatisation – had helped to push profits up and wages down since the 1970s and, with the accompanying increase in personal debt to cope with low wages, created the conditions for the crisis in the first place. These post-2008 measures only escalate the same dynamics. We could say that, in response to the problems caused by neoliberalism, *hyper-neoliberal* policies have been brought in (Fuchs and Sandoval 2012: 44).

'Business-friendly' measures and media amnesia

These policies have been accompanied by a high degree of media amnesia. In the previous chapters, we saw that as time passed and the crisis progressed, the root causes of the 2008 financial crash were forgotten. Whereas at the start of the crisis its origins in economic liberalisation were sometimes mentioned, in 2009 this explanation had been abandoned and blame began to shift to government overspending. As time moved on and the crisis progressed and morphed, its timeline was being erased and reconfigured. Its history was being rewritten at extraordinary speed. In the context of the UK, the financial crisis remained the most frequently-cited cause of the weakness of the economy. This explanation accounted for 15 per cent of the explanations given. However, as with the reporting of the deficit, the causes of the financial crisis in turn were largely absent, with economic liberalisation and deregulation accounting for only 2.8 per cent of explanations given.

Yet again, in many cases no explanation at all was given for the problems. When it came to the weakness of the UK economy, in 47.5 per cent of the media items any attempt at explanation was missing altogether. In fact, from 2010, something astonishing started happening. The 2008 crash began to be talked about as if it was entirely unrelated to the ongoing economic problems! It began to be referred to as a comparison point rather than an explanation for the later economic problems. For example, in a piece for the *Telegraph* (2010), former Tory Chancellor Norman Lamont worried that a loss of market confidence in Britain's debt sustainability would trigger 'another financial crisis like that in 2008' and lead to a double-dip recession, without recalling that both the increased debt burden and the first recessionary 'dip' were the result of that financial crisis. Puzzlingly, even though business-friendly measures were explicitly intended to encourage business investment, the lack of business investment was almost never mentioned as a cause of the slump: it was referred to only three times in total. We will return to the question of business investment later on.

We could ask: had the neoliberal policies that helped to cause the financial crisis been remembered, would there have been such media support for further neoliberal moves? Or, perhaps conversely: had journalists and editors not supported neoliberal solutions, or at least taken them for granted, would they have forgotten neoliberalism's role in the crisis so quickly? This lack of reflection was identified only very rarely in the press. Seumas Milne, one of the most consistent critics of neoliberalism, wrote in the *Guardian* about the enthusiasm for more privatization: 'the solution to every problem turns out, like a broken record, to be privatisation. Nothing, it seems, has been learned from the failure of an economic model that brought us to the brink of breakdown' (Milne 2012).

Investment strike

Also in the *Guardian*, Nicolas Shaxson (2012), author of *Treasure Islands*, questioned not only the fairness but the effectiveness of tax breaks for the wealthy and privatisation:

George Osborne's tax giveaway to big corporations, with aggressive cuts to corporate tax rates and new corporate tax loopholes, is quack medicine built on economic fallacies. His cuts will take money away from a sector (government) that invests it directly in universities and roads, and give it to a sector (corporations) that will let it sit idle.

Jeremy Warner in the *Telegraph* actually endorsed these policies, despite acknowledging their ineffectiveness:

> The further cut in the headline rate of corporation tax and the big tax giveaway in raising the personal allowance would, just a little while back, also have been considered next to impossible, given the constraints of the five-year austerity programme ... Well done on that ...
>
> You might have thought that, with all the measures to help enterprise announced yesterday, business investment would become a rather more important element of growth. In fact, the Office for Budget Responsibility forecasts show the reverse, with it contributing less than previously hoped, while household and government consumption contribute more. So much for the holy grail of a more balanced UK economy (Warner 2012).

These accounts raise an important question: do these measures for business actually succeed in generating business investment and thereby stimulating the economy? The reverse appears to be happening. Rather than investing in plants and machinery, innovation or training, corporations are spending their profits on dividends to shareholders and buying back their own shares. Share buybacks are popular because those selling receive a handsome price and those who do not sell see their shares rise in value because buybacks concentrate ownership and magnify dividends. According to Bloomberg, in 2014, the top 500 US companies returned 95 per cent of their profits to shareholders in dividends and buybacks. In a piece for the *Financial Times*, David Bowers writes that 'Investment-to-gross-domestic-product ratios in the developed world are now close to the lowest levels in 60 years' (quoted in Smith 2016: 293).

Bowers also adds an important piece to the austerity puzzle, pointing to the link between budget deficits and business investment:

> Much has been written about how the developed world must tackle its budget deficits. But the link that remains to be properly recognised

is that the counterparts to those 'unsustainable' public-sector budget deficits are equally 'unsustainable' corporate-sector surpluses ... It is not that governments have been spending 'too much' that is the problem; it is that corporates have been spending 'too little'. Moreover, because this corporate saving is the main counterpart to the government's borrowing, until companies start to spend again, the burden of fiscal adjustment will have to fall on cutbacks in public services and higher personal taxation (quoted in Smith 2016: 292).

Bowers thus reminds us that one person's debt is another person's asset, and sheds some light on how money flows in today's economy. Given the enormous amount of attention given to public debt and austerity, it is striking that this part of the equation has received so little attention. The supply-side measures brought in since 2008, then, have succeeded in escalating inequality while failing to give much of a boost to the economy, which, though it is in 'recovery', is growing at a slower rate than before the crash.

The pro-business media

About the lack of business investment, political economist John Smith notes, 'this startling truth gets surprisingly little attention in the financial press and almost none beyond it'. He asks 'How can we understand the astonishing lack of attention to the capitalists' investment strike?' (Smith 2016: 293). More broadly, how can we understand the mainstream media's easy acceptance of the kinds of crisis response that helped cause the crisis in the first place? Smith gives two possible answers. The first is 'cognitive dissonance – when a mental conviction is contradicted by reality, the thinker remains blind to what should be blindingly obvious.' The second is 'more cynical – to protect capitalists from public criticism, by blaming instead their servants, the bankers, or governments for spending too much or too little, or indeed anyone except the real villains' (Smith 2016: 292).

It seems likely that journalists working for large corporations benefitting from business-friendly measures would indeed face direct or more likely indirect pressure from owners and editors to protect capitalists. This may help explain why the *Mirror*'s coverage tends to support these kinds of measures despite it styling itself as representing the workers' movement. Another reason relates to a trend explored in Chapter 2, that

British newspapers tend to be linked to political parties, and the Labour Party, backed by the *Mirror*, had become decidedly more pro-business since Tony Blair.

But cognitive dissonance may be a more probable explanation for why this kind of support is so widespread. As seen in the Introduction and Chapter 1, during the 1980s and 1990s, as capitalism was restructured, so too were media systems in many parts of the world. They were deregulated and marketised (see Hardy 2014). Business and finance news were prioritised at the expense of labour news. Business people came to be treated as objective experts on a wide range of issues, rather than as representatives of particular interests (Chakravartty and Schiller 2010). In this way, neoliberal ideology came to dominate news organisations, as it did all kinds of institutions (Bourdieu and Wacquant 2000). By the time of the 2008 crash, the view that what is best for business is best for everyone was so entrenched that it was taken as 'common sense', even in the face of blindingly obvious evidence to the contrary in the form of economic meltdown.

Thus, the very people who had played key roles in triggering the crash were summoned to give their views on how to fix it, while the part they played was forgotten. In news items focusing on Britain's poorly performing economy, business representatives, excluding those representing financial services, were the second most prominent sources after politicians and other officials. 10.5 per cent of all the sources cited came from this sector. When those representing financial companies are included, the figure is 18.4 per cent.

At the same time, politicians and other officials, comprising 47.1 per cent of sources cited, were keen to present themselves as 'pro-business'. In a major study during the economic crisis of the 1970s that precipitated the neoliberal restructuring of capitalism, the Glasgow Media Group found that the television news consistently framed that crisis as caused by workers' 'excessive' wage claims, again neglecting the role of business investment and other explanations. News reports that wage demands were the main cause of the 1970s crisis outnumbered by 8 to 1 reports rejecting that view (Philo 1995: 24). This explanation helped legitimise the government's project to impose wage restraint. As we have found throughout the present study, not only are official sources quoted more often, news content is also organised around their views, and their logic is built into the reporting (Philo 1995: 31).

The BBC is a good case in point when it comes to illustrating the reorientation of media towards business. Being a publicly-funded, largely non-commercial organisation, one might expect it to buck the trend. Tom Mills, in his history of the organisation, explains that during the postwar social democratic period, the BBC represented the social democratic perspective. John Birt, who came to the organisation in 1987 as deputy director general, wrote in his autobiography that it 'had not yet come to terms with Thatcherism', and that its journalism was 'still trapped in the old post-war Butskellite, Keynesian consensus' (as quoted in Mills 2016: 8).

However, as that phase of capitalism gave way to the neoliberal phase, the BBC too was restructured. According to Mills, John Birt, assisted by a 'small coterie of radical reformers ... worked tirelessly to put this to rights' (8). He introduced 'rigorous procedures' for monitoring programmes. Systems of newsgathering and editorial authority were centralised, and programme scripts were routinely vetted. High-ups at News and Current Affairs were forced out and eighty specialist journalists from the private sector were brought in. Reflecting his management style, Birt moved staff into shiny new buildings, 'designed for flexibility' (158), including the privately owned Millbank Studios opposite parliament. In the early 1990s, as director general, Birt introduced an internal market complete with an extensive neoliberal bureaucracy and a casualised workforce, which instituted buyer-seller relationships and competitive pressures, and integrated the BBC more fully into the private sector (8).

Birt's successor, the 'amiable millionaire Greg Dyke' (8), who was a close associate of Tony Blair until he was famously forced from office during the Iraq War, focused his energies on making the Corporation even more business friendly. In the early 2000s, he announced that the editorial team responsible for BBC Online's business coverage would be doubled, BBC News 24's business output would be expanded, the programme *Working Lunch* would be extended to one hour and a specialist business reporter would be appointed to the current affairs programme *Newsnight*. He also created the new post of business editor, and appointed the right-wing business journalist Jeff Randall (later a columnist for the *Telegraph*) to fill it (194). After a six-week review of the BBC's business and economics journalism headed by Randall and the deputy head of newsgathering, twenty new business and economics posts were announced (195).

Greg Dyke succeeded long term in making the BBC more business-friendly. Strangely, the 2008 financial collapse, rather than resulting in a more varied approach to economic issues, appears to have strengthened the influence of big business at the BBC. Content analysis commissioned by the BBC Trust found that in 2007, business representatives were more than five times more prevalent than representatives of labour. By 2012, the former outnumbered the latter by almost twenty times (204).

Thus we see the overlap of two of the major elements of media amnesia: the narrow range of (elite-dominated) perspectives; and the lack of historical context. The entrenchment of the business view helps explain why the BBC news did not emphasise the historical context of the economic slump, which would place the role played by corporations in the crisis under the spotlight, and why it tended to present business-friendly responses in a positive light. The factors explored in Chapters 1 and 2 explaining a chronic lack of historical context in journalism are also applicable here, including news values and the pressures of 'fast journalism'.

QE

During the budget week of March 2013, 'free marketeer' and editor of the *Spectator*, Fraser Nelson, wrote in the *Telegraph* that there were really two budgets being delivered: the official budget and the 'real budget'. The real budget was about quantitative easing (QE): 'the tricks that are being deployed by the Bank of England and its awesome money-printing machine'. The UK created £375 billion of new money in its QE programme between 2009 and 2012 (BBC 2016). Worldwide, central banks have created an estimated $12.3 trillion. The idea is that central banks create money to buy assets from financial institutions. This should reduce interest rates, leading consumers and businesses to borrow more, creating more consumer demand and business investment and thereby boosting the economy.

Fraser Nelson wrote that QE received little scrutiny from politicians, even though it was 'the most important part of British economic policy': 'There is a dangerous consensus at Westminster: that, if quantitative easing is the answer, it must have been a very long and boring question.' For the entire sample of media items in my survey, QE represented 0.8 per cent of the possible solutions to all of the economic problems mentioned. This might partly be because the sample is skewed towards the weeks of the budget, and budgets are not directly concerned with Bank of England activity. However, discussions around QE were by and large confined to the specialist sections of the newspapers, possibly because to understand it is indeed 'very long and boring'. Indeed, one might have expected that, at the time of the budget, which generates a large amount of coverage and much discussion about the state of the economy, news outlets might consider what the Bank of England as well as the Treasury is doing (as Fraser Nelson did). QE was endorsed in the *Sun* and the *Mirror*, and sometimes in the *Telegraph*. It was mentioned neutrally in the *Guardian* and BBC news on all occasions and in the *Telegraph* 80 per cent of the time. It was rejected zero times.

The effects of QE on the economy are difficult to gauge, since it is impossible to know what would have happened without it. Many economists agree that it probably helped economies escape the very worst possible effects of recession (Stalker 2015: 121; Varoufakis 2015: 235). However, it did little to boost productive investment or consumer spending (Roberts 2015). Indeed, many financial institutions used the money to 'deleverage' – pay off some of their debts and build up reserves (Sayer 2015: 230). Others used it to speculate on property, stocks or bonds (Stalker 2015: 121). Some of the money made it out of the financial sector to non-financial firms, some of whom then hoarded the cash (Roberts 2015).

In this way, QE can be seen as yet another measure whose effect has been to transfer wealth upwards. Some claim that 'helicopter money', deposited directly in people's bank accounts, or the 'People's QE' at one point considered by the Labour Party's new leadership, would have been both fairer and more effective (Roberts 2015). Fraser Nelson was one of the few to point out the redistributory effect of QE in the main news pages at the time, though his emphasis was on the negative impact on savers:

> Imagine, for example, if [Chancellor] Osborne had stood up on Wednesday and announced a trickle-down tax that would award £127,000 to the richest households while making the poorest about £310 worse off. Grim, he'd say, but sadly necessary for the recovery. There would be an outcry. [Shadow Chancellor] Ed Balls would be baying for blood. Yet this has been precisely the effect of all this

money printing, according to official Bank of England figures. No one has protested (Nelson 2013).

More recently, economists at the rating agency S&P (which played its own part in the financial crisis) have found that QE has 'exacerbated' the already widening gap between the rich and the poor in the UK, by boosting the price of financial assets and property, owned predominantly by the wealthy (*Financial Times* 2016). This important, redistributive economic measure has remained largely concealed from public scrutiny by the mainstream media's failure to give it sustained, in-depth attention.

DIGGING DITCHES

Apart from austerity and the business-friendly measures described above, one of the most frequently discussed sets of responses to the slump was government investment to boost the economy. This accounted for 13.6 per cent of possible responses mentioned to the weakness of the UK economy. As shown in Tables 3.1 and 2.3, this was popular in the left-leaning press. It became the standard alternative to the neoliberal responses that had by 2010 become dominant. The *Mirror* regularly featured Keynesian economist David Blanchflower, who was later briefly an economic adviser to Jeremy Corbyn, and also published the following, by economist John van Reenen (2013):

> The Budget's promised increase in infrastructure spending of £3billion a year is simply too small and won't start until 2015.
> It should be four times as big. We need to get moving on transport, energy and housing now, George, not in two years.
> Worse, the infrastructure financing is funded by yet another squeeze on spending. It would be better to take advantage of the rock- bottom interest rates and borrow to invest, as Vince Cable has argued. The markets are not scared of money being used to improve roads, power stations and our creaking transport system. Borrowing for a mortgage is not the same as borrowing to go to the Costa del Sol.

In the *Guardian*, a more detailed piece by Mariana Mazzucato (2013), author of *The Entrepreneurial State*, who was also briefly an economic adviser to Jeremy Corbyn, advocated far-reaching government investment, especially in green technologies:

So what must happen? First and foremost are ailing areas of infra-structure. But we must also remember that although Keynes talked about recessionary times as ones in which simply 'digging ditches and filling them up again' would spur growth, there is increasing evidence that the spending multiplier is almost three times higher when government investments are 'directed'.

In the 80s and 90s such investments were directed around IT – leading to what became decades of growth related to the internet revolution. Today, the government should be doing the same for green technologies – not only renewables but for all infrastructure spending. Indeed, those countries in Europe that have been growing after the crisis, like Germany, Finland and Denmark, all have a green strategy and are attracting international investments.

An opposition thus opened up between pro-austerity and pro-business neoliberals and pro-government-spending Keynesians. On the whole, the *Guardian* represents the Keynesian view, which tends to endorse government intervention in the economy in times of economic downturn. The resurgence of the left in the shape of Jeremy Corbyn in the UK, Syriza in Greece, Podemos in Spain and Bernie Sanders in the US, has been linked to these kinds of Keynesian and social-democratic policies, which aim to provide jobs and growth (though, as explored in Chapters 4 and 5, the *Guardian* has not consistently supported these movements). They reinvigorate ideas from the pre-neoliberal 'golden age' of capitalism of the post-Second World War period.

While the more social-democratic approach (emphasising government investment in the economy, better labour and environmental regulation, and a stronger role for the public sector) certainly seems fairer than the neoliberal norm (advocating austerity and a transfer of resources from the public to the private sector), it comes with limitations.

For a start, as seen in the Introduction, the reason that the Keynesian economic model gave way to neoliberalism in the 1980s in the first place was because it had eventually resulted in economic crisis and 'stagflation'. What would prevent it ending in crisis again? Moreover, according to Marxist economist Michael Roberts (2016e), a govern-ment-led investment programme would not be able to compensate for a lack of business investment, as such a programme would add just 1–2 per cent of GDP in investment when the capitalist sector invests over 15 per cent of GDP. In order for government-led investment to make a significant difference, the economy would have to be entirely restructured towards the public sector, which is not an option being proposed by the Labour Party or even being mentioned in the media.

Secondly, even if a more social-democratic form of capitalism was viable, would it be the most desirable option? The reader may have noticed that capitalist economies involve a lot of contradictory manoeuvres in order to resolve crises, which tend to result in further crises. The basic vicious circle of recession is businesses laying off workers, leading to less money spent on consumption, leading to even more unemployment, leading to even less consumption and so on. Thinking back to the 2008 crash, to avoid catastrophe, the authorities aimed to make sure that banks kept lending to businesses and households so that businesses could retain employees and households could keep spending. However, too much bank-lending, too much personal debt and consumption were precisely the problems in the first place. The sickness became the cure. Household debt in Britain has now returned to record highs, if student loans are included, leading economists to warn of future problems if Brexit causes the economy to take a dive (Milligan 2017).

Meanwhile, the loose monetary policies pursued to deal with the crisis have led to escalating levels of corporate debt. According to the IMF, non-financial sector (corporations, households and governments) debt worldwide has more than doubled since the turn of the century, reaching $152 trillion in 2015, and it's still rising. Including the banking sector, McKinsey finds that the total debt reaches $200 trillion. In emerging economies, investment bank J.P. Morgan finds that the debt of non-financial corporations has surged from about 73 per cent of GDP before the financial crisis to 106 per cent of GDP (Roberts 2016d). For those not steeped in the economics profession, this might appear to be an absurd system. In the wise words of Bill Leckie in the *Sun* on the 2008 bank bailouts, 'The country would borrow money to give to banks who'd already borrowed too much money so they could give it to the customers they'd cajoled into borrowing more money than they could ever pay back.' And remember, many corporations are not borrowing to invest in production but, as seen above, to buy back their own shares.

It is important to note that there are different kinds of Keynesian economics, with some closer to neoclassical, orthodox economics and others not far away from Marxist economics (Wolff and Resnick 2012: 125–31). However, the kinds of Keynesian economic perspective featured in the mainstream press in no way proposes an exit from these fundamental dynamics, only a set of theories for best keeping capitalism afloat and mitigating its worst effects. The focus of left-wing parliamentary politics on jobs and growth does not consider whether either jobs or growth contribute to anything other than keeping the system going. David Graeber (2013) has claimed that many jobs are 'bullshit jobs', that the people doing them do not find meaning in them or feel that they contribute to society. And growth, as we will see below, poses a danger to humanity itself. As has been remarked many times before, we appear to be in a situation where instead of the economy serving us, we are serving the economy (Sayer 2015: 352). It seems inadequate, therefore, not at least to have a public debate about how to extricate ourselves from what appears to be an endless cycle of meaningless work, consumption, debt and struggle.

Although they have come to represent the two poles on the spectrum of responses to the crisis, the proximity of neoliberal and the most prominent Keynesian solutions is revealed by the fact that they have become merged and blurred. In their (2015) book on the crisis and critical theory, Heiko Feldner and Fabio Vighi refer to policies pursued to tackle the crisis as an 'oxymoronic hybrid of *neo-liberal Keynesianism* as a lastditch response' (original italics). The response of austerity plus corporation tax cuts brought in by the coalition government and supported by the right-wing media is itself a combination of fiscal retrenchment and Keynesian fiscal stimulus – as fiscal stimulus encompasses both government spending and tax cuts, both of which are thought to boost demand. What has been called corporate welfare – supporting business through tax incentives and subsidies – can also be considered 'government investment', depending on how it is framed. Having U-turned away from austerity, in 2016 the head of the IMF, Christine Lagarde, advocated public spending on welfare and education *and* moving resources to the private sector through supply-side structural reforms simultaneously (Roberts 2016b). 'Trumponomics', the economic policies touted by US president Donald Trump, are the epitome of a neoliberal-Keynesian hybrid, promising government spending on infrastructure, cuts to the public sector, cuts in corporation tax, deregulation and de-liberalisation of the economy all at the same time. Thus, the economic ideas on either side of the debate are not necessarily poles apart. Again we are confronted by one of the key problems with journalism: the inclusion of only a narrow range of perspectives.

THIS CHANGES EVERYTHING

One thing that all the remedies to the slump receiving media attention have in common is that they all take as given that economic growth is good. These days, growth is assessed in terms of GDP: gross domestic product. GDP attempts to measure economic activity in a nation or region, adding up consumer expenditure, government expenditure, gross investment in fixed capital and net exports. Growth in GDP is not only assumed to be good, it is the measure on which economic health is assessed. All of the different economic policies brought in to tackle the crisis are aimed at increasing GDP growth. The debate is not about whether growth is good, but how best to achieve it.

This is in one sense understandable. Capitalist economies do indeed depend on infinite growth. Ecological economist Tim Jackson does a good job of explaining why. Due to capitalism's profit motive, emphasis is placed on the 'efficiency' with which inputs to production (labour, capital, resources) are used. Companies strive to ensure that more output can be produced for any given input, often by investing in labour-saving technology. This drives down costs and stimulates demand, thus contributing to a virtuous circle of expansion. However, it also means that fewer people are needed to produce the same goods. As long as the economy grows fast enough to offset this increase in labour productivity there is no problem. But if not, then the increase in labour productivity leads to unemployment. This in turn leads to decreased spending power and consumer demand, which leads to further unemployment, and we are back at the recessionary vicious circle described earlier. The recession means lower tax revenues, hitting public finances; governments might decide to impose austerity measures as a result, which, as we have seen, can weaken the economy further, thereby increasing government debt even more. Thus, under capitalism, there is no 'steady state': the economy is either growing or shrinking; 'its natural dynamics push it towards one of two states: expansion or collapse' (Jackson 2011: 64).

There are several problems with this state of affairs. One of them is that more and more jobs need to be created, even if these are 'bullshit jobs'. Another is that infinite growth, according to ecological economists, is simply not viable if humanity is to survive on planet earth. This is the fundamental point made by Naomi Klein in her seminal (2014) book, *This Changes Everything*. The levels of production and consumption required for continual growth entail the destruction of natural resources and the emission of pollutants at unsustainable levels.

Even the 'green growth' advocated by the likes of Mariana Mazzucato, is unlikely to be able to reduce carbon emissions and preserve natural resources sufficiently to be sustainable. For those advocating green growth, the aim is usually to 'decouple' growth in economic terms from growth in natural resources depleted and pollutants emitted. Especially in the developed countries, there is some evidence of 'relative decoupling': more economic activity with less environmental damage (Jackson 2011: 69). However, what is needed in order for humanity to remain within its ecological limits is not relative but *absolute* decoupling, where environmental impacts decline in absolute terms.

If relative decoupling occurs at a fast enough rate, it will eventually become absolute decoupling, but this is nowhere near happening. In order to avoid dangerous anthropogenic climate change, the Intergovernmental Panel on Climate Change argues that carbon emissions in the atmosphere need to be stabilised at 450 parts per million. This means reducing global emissions by between 50 per cent and 85 per cent from 1990 levels by 2050 (Jackson 2011: 13). However, if carbon intensities needed per unit of economic activity keep declining at current rates, by 2050 carbon dioxide emissions will be 80 per cent *higher* than they are today.

It seems unlikely that there will be any conceivable growth package green enough to deliver the sort of decoupling needed to avoid dangerous climate change. Meanwhile, the British government has been accused of overseeing a string of attacks on green policies, including scrapping subsidies for onshore wind and solar, selling off the Green Investment Bank set up in 2012, and promoting fracking (Vaughan and Macalister 2015). President Trump has denied that human-made climate change exists.

Media scholars Justin Lewis and Richard Thomas (2015) conducted a study on press coverage of economic growth in the US and UK. They found that the idea that 'growth is good' remains deeply embedded and that economic, social and environmental critiques of growth are generally ignored. Overall, 94.5 per cent of the sampled news items stated or assumed that growth was unambiguously positive; 5 per cent adopted a neutral position; and only 0.5 per cent (3 out of 591 articles) gave voice to more critical positions. Similar results were found on both sides of the Atlantic, with the US media slightly more inclined to be overtly pro-growth.

The findings of the study for this book were even more extreme. Of the sample of 1,133 news items, only one challenged the growth paradigm. This was a comments piece by George Monbiot (2008), the *Guardian*'s resident 'green' columnist, during the height of the crisis in 2008. He writes, 'If fish in a depleted ecosystem grow by 5 per cent a year and the catch expands by 10 per cent a year, the fishery will collapse. If the global economy keeps growing at 3 per cent a year (or 1,700 per cent a century), it too will hit the wall.' He suggests policy-makers read Herman Daly's book *Steady-state Economics*. A steady-state economy has a constant stock of capital that is maintained by a rate of throughput no higher than the ecosystem can absorb, while poverty is addressed through the redistribution of wealth. Banks can only lend the amount of money they possess.

Tim Jackson, who was influenced by Herman Daly, also puts forward some recommendations for restructuring societies in more sustainable ways. These include 'ecological tax reform' and expanding resource-transfer mechanisms, like carbon levies, that allow developing countries to continue to grow while rich countries focus on reducing consumption (Jackson 2011: 174–5). Working time should be reduced and more evenly distributed. Correspondingly, consumption in the rich countries would have to fall significantly, which could involve stronger regulation on advertising and trading standards.

New macroeconomic models would need to be developed that take ecological limits into account. Here Jackson comes as close as he dares to suggesting moving beyond capitalism. Ecological macroeconomics would need to rethink the idea of 'labour productivity' to better value activities that are socially useful – such as care work – but have low 'productivity' because they are by their nature labour intensive and therefore can't be made more 'efficient'. It would also need to rethink 'capital productivity'. This means that instead of prioritisng profit, investment should be geared towards long-term sustainability. Because this is unlikely to produce short-term financial rewards, this kind of investment would probably need to be carried out by the public sector. This means rebalancing the roles of the public and private sectors in the opposite direction to the one in which we are currently heading. And, as Jackson indicates, 'ultimately, this will also mean raising tough questions about the ownership of assets, and control over the surpluses from those assets. The nature and role of property rights lies at the heart of these questions' (178).

Finally, there is a well-established case for ditching GDP as the measure of economic well-being. According to ecological economists, it fails to account for the costs of long-term environmental damage. It also fails to account for the real welfare losses of economic inequality, for social costs such as crime and family breakdown, or the value of non-market services such as domestic labour and voluntary care.

Whether or not we agree with Jackson's proposals, it is of urgent importance that a vigorous public debate take place on the desirability of economic growth, and how best to design a system to replace it. The mainstream media, which in their economic coverage take it as 'common sense' that growth is good, are failing to ask the right questions.

THE GLOBALISATION QUESTION

The matter of planetary ecological destruction brings jarringly to light a fact that has come up repeatedly through this book: that the economy – and the crisis – are inescapably global. As we have seen, the large-scale relocation of production to emerging economies and the accompanying increased flows of capital around the world created financial global imbalances along with increased consumer debt in the rich world, culminating in the 2008 crash. The Great Recession affected people around the world, with some export-dominated countries seeing their exports fall by 20 per cent in just two months in early 2009 (Harvey 2011: 6).

When the Great Recession broke, the Chinese government launched a $584 billion spending programme to build bridges, cities, roads and railways (Stalker 2015: 120). Interest rates were slashed and local authorities were allowed to borrow in order to spend on housing and other projects. Although this kept the Chinese economy going, growth has nevertheless slowed from double-digit increases back in 2010–11 to under 7 per cent on official estimates in 2015 (many think the figure is in reality more like 4 per cent). Meanwhile, Chinese non-financial debt has risen from about 100 per cent to about 250 per cent of GDP (Roberts 2016a). In early 2016 this credit bubble looked as if it were about to explode into what the Bank of England's Andrew Haldane called 'part three' of the crisis, after the 2008 financial meltdown and the eurozone crisis. A snap currency devaluation in late 2015 was followed by freefall in China's stock markets in January 2016. 'Part three' did not ultimately occur, but high debt and slower growth in the emerging economies continues to cause concern for the future of global capitalism.

Similarly to the coverage of public debt discussed in Chapter 2, and unlike during the financial crisis, this global dimension to the economic slump was only rarely discussed in the media except in the financial pages. During 2011 and 2012, when things were looking particularly bleak, the 'global economic crisis' did sometimes make the headlines, usually in the context of a G20 meeting. However, this usually referred to the eurozone plus the US, and other countries were rarely the focus of attention. Surprisingly, even the Chinese stock market crash of early 2016 mostly failed to make it out of the specialist finance sections of the newspapers (it rarely even got into the 'world news' sections) or onto the BBC news.

In items focusing on the poorly-performing UK economy, international context was given 40.4 per cent of the time. However, this most often took the form of political manoeuvring, such as Chancellor George Osborne blaming poor growth figures on problems in the eurozone. Arguments in favour of corporation tax cuts, deregulation and privatisation often have an implicit international dimension, because they aim at making a country more 'competitive' *vis-a-vis* other countries and encouraging investment from abroad. But the implications of this international competition are rarely if ever explored. International competition is simply taken as given. In Chapter 1 we encountered Peter Berglez's (2008) concept of 'global journalism', which illuminates global interconnections and sees the world as 'a single place'. Unfortunately, this kind of journalism is largely absent when it comes to the coverage of the slump in the non-specialist news pages.

However, more recently, the globalisation project itself has been in the spotlight. Stagnating world trade has led to concern that globalisation is in jeopardy. Treaties such as the Transatlantic Trade and Investment Partnership (TTIP), the Comprehensive Economic and Trade Agreement (CETA) and the Trans-Pacific Partnership (TPP) were designed to keep flows of money and goods around the world going in the wake of the Great Recession. Popular opposition to TTIP, TTP and CETA, the success of political parties promising protectionist measures, Brexit, and especially the election of Donald Trump as US President, have turned fears for the future of globalisation into panic among elites, including media elites. Following Trump's election victory, a horrified *Financial Times* editorial declared that 'the free movement of capital, goods, and labour is one of the great achievements of the postwar era ... Mr Trump's victory, coming after the Brexit referendum vote in Britain, looks like another grievous blow to the liberal international order' (*Financial Times* 2016).

Supporters of globalisation argue that it is the best way of improving well-being for all. It has enabled emerging economies to engage in spectacular export-led growth, and the share of people living on less than $1 a day (in inflation-adjusted terms) has dropped to 14 per cent from 42 per cent in 1981 (Roberts 2016c). It appears that the problems with globalisation are being forgotten by those opposing protectionism, and rewritten by those supporting it.

Globalisation in its existing form has been criticised, by those living in the global south, the Global Justice Movement, heterodox economists and even some mainstream economists, since its early days (Bello 2013: 32–3). They argue that globalisation has amounted to a new form of imperialism, benefitting transnational corporations (TNCs) and rich countries (Ampuja 2012).

The main political institutions of globalisation are the World Trade Organisation (WTO), the World Bank (WB) and the IMF. The WTO established rules to foster the expansion of free trade. These included the National Treatment clause – which obliges governments to extend the same terms offered to national firms, including state-owned ones, to foreign firms – and the Market Access clause, which prohibits governments from hindering the entrance of multinational firms. The Trade-Related Investment Measures (TRIMs) serve to disarm attempts made by states to implement industrial and commercial policies for the benefit of their local populations. The General Agreement on Trade in Services (GATS), prepared by Anglo-American financial lobbies, forces signatory states to dismantle public-sector control of resources: 'It seeks to commodify public goods, public utilities, and commons, and to privatise natural monopolies' (Screpanti 2014: 111).

However, the Trade-Related Aspects of Intellectual Property Rights (TRIPs), also drawn up with the help of corporations, are another matter. These seek to protect patents, which are mainly registered in the rich countries. Patented products – such as seeds – cannot be used by developing countries without paying royalties to the multinational companies that own the patents. Thus, while all the other WTO agreements formally aim to promote free trade and competition, 'the TRIPS agreement takes the form of protectionist regulation. It explicitly seeks to protect monopoly positions and the monopoly profits provided by scientific and technological research, an activity in which the big multinationals of the North excel' (Screpanti 2014: 110).

According to Marxist economist Ernesto Screpanti, 'The WTO has become a partial substitute for gunboats in imperial governance' (111). The WTO establishes the principles and rules of economic liberalisation. Then, 'when a serious crisis arises and leaves a country in need of help from the IMF and the WB, the government is forced to sell off state-owned companies and commons to the multinationals' (111) through the 'structural adjustment programs' discussed in Chapters 2 and 4. As well as privatisation, the IMF has forced developing countries to remove agricultural subsidies, while rich countries continue to pay $300 billion every year in such subsidies to their agribusinesses (McNally 2011: 136).

While the number of people living on less than $1 a day has decreased, the number living on less than $2 is actually increasing. Furthermore, the progress made in lifting people out of extreme poverty has been largely confined to China, a country that has flouted free trade rules. While globalisation has spurred growth in some countries, it has failed to do so in others. According to the World Bank, the world's 35 low-income countries – 26 of which are in Africa – registered 103 million more extremely poor people in the twenty-first century than three decades ago (Roberts 2016c). Moreover, just because some countries have experienced economic growth, that doesn't mean all citizens have benefitted equally from that growth. In China, between 1990 and 2005, labour income, the total earnings of Chinese working people, plunged from 50 per cent of GDP to 37 per cent; 0.4 per cent of the population controls 70 per cent of the country's wealth (McNally 2011: 57). Globalisation produces winners and losers – and many believe there have been more losers than winners.

Donald Trump has managed to rewrite the problems of globalisation to turn the richest country in the world, the US, into the victim. However, while he complains that NAFTA, the North American Free Trade Agreement, was 'the worst trade deal the US ever signed', it has been worse for Mexico. Since its implementation, the minimum wage in Mexico has fallen by 40 per cent, the best-paid workers have faced an 18 per cent cut in income, 80 million people now live below the poverty line and 0.3 per cent of the population controls 50 per cent of Mexico's wealth (McNally 2011: 129).

Trump, though, has a point. The working classes of imperialist countries have also suffered unemployment, underemployment and wage stagnation due to the processes of globalisation. According to Branko Milanovic, the working classes of the rich countries have been among the losers in the age of globalisation (in Stiglitz 2016). The middle classes of emerging countries have been among the winners. But the main beneficiaries of globalisation have been corporations, headquartered mainly in Europe, the US, Japan and increasingly China. According to the United Nations Conference on Trade and Development (UNCTAD), 67 per cent of the total value-added generated in global value chains is captured by firms based in rich nations (quoted in Smith 2016: 49). Those opposing further free trade treaties such as TTIP and CETA often do so on the grounds that they enshrine the rights of corporations over states and populations even further, for example by instituting private courts in which corporations can sue governments for potential loss of profits incurred from regulation.

A central characteristic of globalisation, then, has been the empowerment of TNCs (transnational corporations). This led to crisis in 2008, as TNCs had relocated production to emerging countries, leading to great global financial imbalances, and wage stagnation and debt in rich countries, as we have seen. State responses to the crisis have been to empower TNCs even further, through cuts in corporation tax, further deregulation and further privatisation, explored above. This is despite the fact that, according to John Smith, one of the primary reasons for the refusal of businesses to invest in innovation, new equipment and training – thereby bringing the world out of economic slump – has been the deregulated global conditions that allow wages and standards to remain low. There is less incentive to invest in boosting productivity to increase revenues when labour costs are so low.

As sociologist Colin Crouch (2000) has argued, the rise of TNCs in the neoliberal period is linked to the political condition of postdemocracy, in which power is transferred away from elected governments towards corporations. Post-2008 measures look set to escalate this transfer.

Global media flows

It has taken extreme political crisis in the richest countries on earth for globalisation to come under scrutiny. Why has its role in the economic crisis largely been forgotten in coverage of the slump? Here we come to the third major element of media amnesia: lack of global context. We can start with the link between journalism and the transnational corporations at the heart of globalisation. Communication and information technology played a key role in globalisation. It enabled both financial innovation and the just-in-time supply chains central to the development of TNCs. In turn, media TNCs are some of the biggest in the world. In 2016's Fortune 500 list of the biggest companies, Apple, AT&T, Verizon and Amazon were in the top twenty. Alphabet (Google) was at number 36, while Facebook had jumped 85 spots to 157. These are the companies that enable the delivery of media content, and there is evidence that news content providers are gearing their content increasingly towards these corporations as they battle for online advertising revenues dominated by Google, Facebook, Baidu, Yahoo and Microsoft (O'Reilly 2016).

News content is also dominated by large corporations. Rupert Murdoch's 21st Century Fox and News Corp are both listed among the top ten media companies worldwide in terms of market capitalisation (Seth 2015). Among the biggest news providers are News Corp, Gannett Co. Inc., owning USA Today, Tribune Media Co, owning 42 TV stations, the Daily Mail and General Trust plc, which owns the *Daily Mail*, and the New York Times Company.

The priority of media corporations is not accurate and in-depth news but, like all corporations, profit. Getting to grips with the global dynamics of the economy is no easy task and journalists do not often have the opportunity or incentive to do this. Instead, 'infotainment' has come to dominate news. This trend has been observed in the UK, US, China, Japan, Mexico, Australia, Germany, Hungary and Scandinavia (Allan 2004: 206). Many scholars have argued that increased media marketisation during the neoliberal period has led to 'tabloidisation' and 'dumbing down' (Franklin 1997; McNair 1999: 44–50). While many of us have a place in our hearts for the frivolous, the danger is when it comes at the expense of understanding – or even attempting to understand – global processes affecting all our lives. For Colin Crouch, the commercial imperatives behind infotainment mean that the media occupy a special place in postdemocracy (Crouch 2000: 46), as citizens are not properly served by the extreme simplification of attention-grabbing headlines and sensationalist stories. Journalists working for multinationals may also self-censor to avoid criticism of big business.

At the same time, cost-cutting has affected foreign news particularly severely. Nick Davies writes that 'media outlets have succumbed to a crude commercial calculation: as a commodity, foreign news is high-cost and low-return. Why invest big money in covering the world, when consumers are happy with local news?' (Davies 2009: 99). Gannett, mentioned above, sells more US papers than any other news company and owns 300 local UK titles. Out of roughly 200 countries in the world, it gathers news from six. Foreign bureaux used to be backed up by a global network of freelance stringers. But this network too has disintegrated because media outlets will not pay (Davies 2009: 100).

This has two implications in terms of understanding the global dimensions of the crisis. First, people are less likely to be exposed to stories about economic issues facing other countries, especially if these countries are not 'elite' or culturally or geographically close to their own (according to 'news values', see Chapter 1). A survey by the Newspaper Advertising Bureau found that, by 2002, US newspapers were devoting only 2 per cent of their news coverage to foreign stories. Thirty years earlier, it was five times that amount. Secondly, the depletion of journalistic resources leads to a 'consensus – and conservative account of the world' (Davies 2009: 100). The foreign reporting that does happen increasingly takes place in bubbles. Foreign correspondents rely for their information on three sources: official PR, local media and each other. This means the same stories about the same places from the same angles are recycled over and over again. For this reason, we are unlikely to get a thorough or pluralistic understanding of the global flows of money behind the slump.

Moreover, flows of information inversely reflect these flows of money. Whereas money tends to flow from the global south into corporations based in the global north, information travels in the other direction. Journalists congregate in the capitals of the richest countries, creating 'news centres' and 'news peripheries'. News travels more from centres to peripheries than vice versa. One study found that more than 80 per cent of material found in news media worldwide emanates from agencies based in four of the world's major capitals – all of them in the West (Hachten 1993 cited in Horvit 2004: 73). Agencies based in China and Russia are gaining influence. But again this reflects the relative positions these regions occupy in the global pecking order.

In the Western world, newspapers, broadcasters and news websites rely for most of their international news on just two wire agencies:

Associated Press (based in the US) and Reuters (based in the UK). The agencies have been cutting costs, just like news outlets. Reuters cut 3,000 jobs in 2002 then another 2,000 by 2006. Its reporters now file an average of five stories a day. In TNC style, Reuters outsources some of its journalism to a centre in Bangalore India, where business news and data is recycled by staff who do not necessarily know the background to the stories they are writing. According to Davies, some 80 countries, around 40 per cent of the world's nations, have no print bureau from either agency. 130 countries have no TV bureau from either agency (Davies 2009: 104). Where there are bureaux, they are often staffed by just one or two people. This does not make either for proper coverage of economic issues around the world or for a grasp of the global interconnectedness of the economy and the economic crisis.

Deglobalisation?

One public reaction to decades of postdemocracy and a decade of slump has been to elect politicians promising to roll back 'free trade' and investment. Is the solution to the harms of globalisation the protectionism that is being offered by Trump and Brexit? Economists disagree as to how far protectionism is likely to affect the economy. Several institutions, including the IMF and the OECD, predicted that Brexit's impact on free trade would be damaging for Britain's economy. However, Keynesian economist Paul Krugman (2016), historically an advocate of free trade, denies that protectionist policies necessarily lead to recession. Nevertheless, they may lead to trade wars and increased antagonism between nations. Moreover, despite the nationalist rhetoric of Trump, UKIP and the Brexit wing of Britain's Conservative Party, the economic policies they offer would continue to empower transnational corporations. In fact, especially in the case of the UK and US, the priority of politicians representing both sides of the globalisation/ protectionism debate is assisting TNCs through tax cuts, privatisations and deregulation, as we have seen.

Some Keynesians and social democrats call not for isolationism but a better-regulated, 'tamed' kind of globalisation that assists those it disadvantages by providing a strong social security system (Stiglitz 2016). This is consistent with the Keynesian approach to capitalism overall, which is that a social-democratic form, which protects people from the worst ravages of the market system, is the best we can hope for. However, we can ask, while the world remains organised in such a way that not just individuals but nation-states compete with each other for resources, is it really possible to avoid imperialism – where stronger global players appropriate resources from weaker ones – in one form or another? Will all countries be able to provide an adequate safety net? If capitalism is inherently imperialist, is it acceptable even in a 'tamed' form?

There is a 'deglobalisation' movement that proposes a different alternative, first put forward by the organisation Focus on the Global South in 2000. It emphasises production for the domestic market over production for export. It is protectionist, in that it supports subsidies, quotas and tariffs in trade and industrial policies designed to serve local communities. However, it is not based on competition for resources but rather on cooperation. Crucially, the aim of production is not private profit but serving the needs of the community. Influenced by the writings of economic historian Karl Polanyi, it calls for a re-embedding of market relations in society, so that the market no longer reigns supreme but is subordinated to values of community, solidarity and equality.

It envisages a mixed economy including private enterprises, cooperatives and state-run ventures, but transnational corporations are excluded. Economic decisions are not to be left to the markets or technocrats but become subject to democratic discussion and choice. Income and land redistribution is to be implemented and growth is to be de-emphasised. Centralised global institutions like the IMF and World Bank would be replaced by regional institutions built not on principles of free trade and capital mobility but of cooperation (Bello 2013: 274). One of its proponents, Walden Bello, writes that this version of deglobalisation, though allowing a role for markets, 'transcends the logic of capitalism'. It offers a way of undoing the harms of globalisation without descending into the hostility of the protectionist politics offered by today's demagogues.

How exactly this kind of arrangement would work in different contexts, and how to transition to it, are matters for public deliberation. One question that needs addressing is whether a world organised on the basis of nation-states would ever really be able to avoid competition and conflict over resources. Arguably, popular news media should be providing the forum for precisely this kind of discussion during a time of crisis. However, as we have seen, the narrow framing of the debate over economic issues limits the potential to ask important questions about how to organise society.

CONCLUSION

Despite optimistic official growth figures and forecasts, the Great Recession has been followed by 'the longest recovery on record' in the UK, and the world's economic problems are far from being resolved. Media amnesia has helped legitimise policies that further empower transnational corporations over anything else, policies promoting the form of global capitalism that produced the crisis in the first place. In opposition to austerity, deregulation, privatisation and tax cuts for the richest, social-democratic Keynesianism has come to represent the other side of the public debate. But neither approach addresses the most critical issues to do with the environment and the global division of labour. Paradoxically, in reaction against the harm done by neoliberal globalisation to workers of rich countries, many have put their faith in those who would empower those corporations even further. In continental Europe, as we will see, the crisis there has spurred a kind of 'nationalist social-democracy', arguably assisted by the media as they rewrite accounts of the eurozone crisis.

4

Eurocrisis

During the 2008 financial meltdown, eurozone countries propped up their banks and plunged into recession, which led their public finances to deteriorate. European banks were very exposed to the toxic assets created out of US mortgage debt. They were also very highly leveraged, relied on short-term loans to fund their operations, and had loaded up on the sovereign debt of Greece, Italy and other peripheral euro-members. In short, they were very vulnerable and much too big for their sovereigns – the governments of the individual countries that had responsibility for them – to bail.

Then, in October 2009, the Greek government revealed that its budget deficit was almost 13 per cent of national income, double what it had previously projected. Almost immediately, it became subject to speculative attacks on its sovereign debt, which quickly spread to other peripheral eurozone countries. The speculators focused on countries with high debt-to-GDP ratios, low growth, trade deficits, and which, because of the euro, did not have central banks that could function as lenders of last resort (unlike the Bank of England in the UK) (Screpanti 2014: 143). Speculation drove up interest rates on the sovereign debt of the countries in question, pushing them closer to default. At the same time, eurozone banks became locked out of the money markets they depended on for their functioning, in another iteration of the 'credit crunch' of 2008. The eurozone crisis has bounced back and forth ever since in a 'death embrace' between banks and their sovereigns (Varoufakis 2015).

After months of inaction on the part of the European authorities, in May 2010, Greece received a €110 billion loan from the so-called Troika: the European Central Bank (ECB), the European Commission and the IMF, in exchange for a 20 per cent cut in public sector pay, a 10 per cent pension cut and tax increases. In November 2010, Ireland received €675 billion in return for a 26 per cent cut in public spending. In March 2011, Portugal received €78 billion for similar reforms (Blyth 2013: 71). Far from being stabilised from the first bailout, Greece had to take on another €110 billion of debt, which became €130 billion in October 2011, in exchange for another 20 per cent wage cut, more public spending cuts and tax increases (72). In March 2013, Cyprus received €10 billion in return for cuts in civil service salaries, social benefits, pensions, increases in indirect taxes and higher public health-care charges, as well as a controversial savings levy. In 2015, a third bailout of €86 billion was agreed for Greece, in exchange for further tax increases, cuts to social welfare and an increase in the retirement age.

Instead of solving the problems, the economies on which austerity was imposed weakened further following the bailouts. Greece lost 25 per cent of its GDP, the largest fall in modern history not linked to war or revolution. Spain's youth unemployment rate soared to 50 per cent. In another vicious circle, this meant yet lower tax revenues and higher social security expenditures, leading public debt to rise even further. Greece's debt reached 179 per cent of GDP in 2017, 1.79 times the size of its total economic output. The IMF predicts this will reach 275 per cent by 2060.

The eurozone crisis has been accompanied by an extraordinary bout of media amnesia. In a ramped up version of the way the UK deficit was covered, the 2008 crash was almost entirely forgotten as the immediate cause of the eurozone troubles. The majority of coverage gave no explanation for the problems. When explanations were given, they often focused on public profligacy and corruption, regularly using cultural stereotypes and accusing the citizens of the peripheral countries of being lazy and corrupt. The ongoing problems with the banks, though noted in the coverage, were subordinated to the public debt problems, which were often framed as both the source and the cause of the trouble, rather than its effect. On the other hand, in the broadsheets, a minority of reports did pay attention to longer-term structural problems with the eurozone.

The short-term responses of the bailouts and the accompanying austerity measures dominated the coverage. The coverage of austerity in the eurozone was less politicised than that of austerity in the UK, with the tabloids covering the measures fairly neutrally. The *Guardian*'s copy was quite critical of austerity in the eurozone, as it was of UK austerity. The *Telegraph* endorsed it overall, though less strongly than with the UK. The BBC regularly endorsed establishment narratives about the crisis, including the need for austerity. Overall, the assumption that some level of austerity was 'painful but necessary' was accepted. A minority of news articles did discuss longer-term solutions, such as deeper integration within the EU and, conversely, restructuring the EU into a more loosely-knit grouping. The possibility of Grexit was widely aired, and provoked debate over the desirability of Brexit, anticipating the Brexit referendum of June 2016.

MEDIA BLACKOUT

The first point to make is that the *Guardian* covered the eurozone crisis in its main news and opinion pages much more than the other outlets. Of the sample as a whole, 194 of the media items focused primarily on the eurozone crisis, of which 94 were from the *Guardian*, 41 from the *Telegraph*, 30 from the BBC, and only 15 from the *Mirror* and 14 from the *Sun*. Almost half, then, were from the *Guardian*. The coverage of the different outlets, in terms of the way they allocated blame for the problems or promoted certain responses, did not always conform to their treatment of the UK problems. Perhaps unsurprisingly, it was less politically charged. However, partly through media amnesia and misre-membering, it nevertheless tended to frame the eurozone crisis as located in and caused by the public sector, cut off discussion of viable long-term solutions, and failed to scrutinise the austerity measures sweeping the continent.

The coverage of the eurozone crisis came with an astonishing degree of media amnesia. Of the 194 items focusing primarily on the eurozone crisis, 70.1 per cent offered no explanation at all. This number is substan-tially higher than with journalism focusing mainly on the 2008 financial crisis, the recession or the UK deficit, which was already strikingly bereft of explanation. On top of that, the 2008 financial crash was almost completely forgotten as a cause of the euro crisis. It represented only 5 per cent of the causes mentioned. It was almost as if the eurozone crisis was an entirely unconnected crisis. Meanwhile, deeper structural causes of the financial crisis in turn – the dynamics of neoliberal capitalism, explored in previous chapters – made up only 1.7 per cent of explana-tions given.

If we think back to Chapter 1, we can recall that at the time – only about a year previously – the serious impact of the financial meltdown on the eurozone was high profile. In fact, over 70 per cent of the special purpose vehicles created to deal in the US asset-backed commercial paper that triggered the crunch were set up by European banks (Blyth 2013: 85). Between 2008 and 2012, the UK committed 40.3 per cent of its GDP to save its banks, Germany 25.1 per cent, Greece 59.9 per cent, Spain 53.6 per cent and Ireland 365.2 per cent (European Commission 2012: 30).

As we have seen, the lack of even a few months' worth of historical context resulted in an erasure of the timeline of the crisis: the media were in effect erasing their *own coverage* of the very recent past. This amnesia has played a major role in the framing of the eurozone crisis as a public-sector problem, which in turn has helped justify austerity and curtail serious discussion of other solutions. It has received indispensable help from journalists framing the eurozone crisis as caused by profligacy, laziness and corruption.

'FOREIGN WASTERS'

Profligacy, laziness and corruption, when taken together, made up the largest category of explanations for the eurozone crisis. They represented 25.6 per cent of the explanations given. The peripheral euro countries were referred to as 'fiscal miscreants', 'fiscal sinners', 'profligate member states', 'spendthrift econom[ies]' and even, in the *Sun*, as 'foreign wasters' and 'cheats and scroungers' (Kavanagh 2012). This does two things. It lumps together all the periphery countries (as does the commonly used acronym PIIGS – Portugal, Ireland, Italy, Greece, Spain), and allocates blame to the public sector.

In fact, the public-spending records of the different countries were very varied. All countries saw their public debts rise dramatically after the 2008 financial crisis, partly because they bailed out their banks and partly because the subsequent recession damaged public finances. Greece's debt-to-GDP was around 105 per cent before 2008 and leapt to 165 per cent in late 2011 (Blyth 2013: 62). Italy's public debt was also reasonably high at 87 per cent of GDP in 2007, but 'the markets' weren't worried until after the crash, when it rose to around 100 per cent (70). Ireland and Spain's debt-to-GDP were at 12 per cent and 26 per cent respectively before 2008, lower than Germany's 50 per cent (65). Mark Blyth writes that 'only in the case of Greece is the profligacy story plausible' (51).

In coverage that focused specifically on peripheral countries other than Greece, the immediate causes of their problems were often stated. Take the cases of Spain and Ireland and their property bubbles. Ireland had seen a 160 per cent increase in house prices between 1997 and 2007 and Spain a 115 per cent increase (Blyth 2013: 66–7). The three main Irish banks' combined assets at the time of the 2008 crash were around 400 per cent of GDP. The Irish government issued a blanket guarantee for the entire banking system's liabilities, and that bank debt 'very suddenly became the Irish public's problem' (Blyth 2013: 66). Public debt increased by 320 per cent to over 110 per cent of GDP. Spain also had a huge property bubble. Loans to developers alone constituted nearly 50 per cent of GDP by 2007.

Articles from the *Guardian* went into some depth on these collapsed property bubbles, and the BBC also (briefly) mentioned property bubbles as the cause of those countries' woes. Cyprus's overblown banking sector was also mentioned. However, the majority of coverage was not so specific. The other PIIGS countries were most often discussed either in items focusing mainly on Greece, or in reports on the eurozone crisis in general. In this coverage, the private-sector causes of the problems, even the most immediate ones like the property bubbles in Spain and Ireland, were not mentioned. Instead there is either no explanation at all, or all the countries are lumped together with Greece and the public sector framed as the source of the troubles.

This happened explicitly – such as calling the peripheral countries 'fiscal miscreants' – or more subtly, through vague language, as we saw in the case of the UK deficit. One good example is an opinion piece in the *Telegraph* that contrasted Ireland with Greece. The contrast, however, was not in terms of the different origins of their problems but the reactions of their people to austerity: while the Irish were taking their punishment on the chin, the Greeks were rioting like children. For this commentator, 'Both countries are living through a ghastly, prolonged, morning-after-the-night-before financial crisis after years of sunny self-indulgence' (McDonagh 2010). What is this 'sunny self-indulgence'? State profligacy is not directly mentioned here but seems to be implied, especially since this piece was published during the middle of the first Greek bailout in May 2010, when 'sunny' Greece was frequently being accused of profligacy.

Another linguistic fudge that has been central in the framing of the eurozone crisis is that it has repeatedly been termed a 'debt crisis'. Like the use of the soundbite 'Labour's decade of debt' in the coverage of Britain's deficit, discussed in Chapter 2, 'debt crisis' does not specify what kind of debt is at issue – public or private. However, given that most of the coverage focuses on Greece, which is directly accused of state profligacy, and given that the vast majority of items give no explanation for the problems, the implication seems to be that the 'debt' in 'debt crisis' means public debt. Other items refer to the peripheral countries as 'debt-laden', 'debt-riddled' or 'debt-stricken', which similarly suggests public debt. There is no doubt that these countries were facing sovereign debt crises. But in all cases except for maybe Greece, these debts originated in the private sector and not the public sector. Because explanations were not usually given, and because public debt and profligacy were mentioned more frequently than private-sector problems, the public sector was framed not only as the site of the crisis – which it was – but also the origin of the crisis – which it wasn't.

Even to the extent that public borrowing was the problem, the missing part of the news framing of public borrowing is private lending (and borrowing). The story of eurozone sovereign debt has to do with the joining of the 17 member states' currencies in the euro in the 1990s, and the reactions to this of the sovereign bond markets. Banks began swapping out their German and Dutch debt for as much PIIGS debt as they could find. They considered PIIGS debt to have become less risky now these countries had joined the euro, but yields (returns) were still slightly higher than the yields on northern European sovereign debt. They then 'turbocharged' the sovereign debt they had bought with leverage ratios as high as 40:1 – higher than their US counterparts – in order to boost profits.

On top of that, European banks were using this risky periphery debt as collateral for their borrowing. In 2011, the top three French banks had a combined asset footprint of 245 per cent of France's GDP. The top two German banks had assets equal to 117 per cent of German GDP. In Blyth's words: 'the respective sovereign debts of these countries pale into insignificance' (Blyth 2013: 83). In comparison, in the third quarter of 2008, the combined assets of the top six US banks came to about 61 per cent of GDP. No sovereign can bail out a financial sector with exposures of the European banks' magnitude. However, while lending and borrowing were cross-border in the eurozone, bank resolution and bailout implementation were still national responsibilities. According to Blyth, while US banks were 'too big to fail', the European banks were 'too big to bail', but were posing such a risk to the entire system that they could not be allowed to collapse (Blyth 2013: 82). For Blyth, blaming the crisis on profligate public sectors is 'the greatest bait and switch in modern history' (73).

A minority of news items dismissed profligacy and corruption as the causes of the eurozone crisis, and some identified the financial crisis, bailouts and subsequent recession as the cause. The *Guardian* featured multiple comment pieces by Costas Lapavitsas, economist at SOAS and former Syriza MP, which consistently gave alternative explanations and creative solutions. In an early piece, before the 2010 Greek bailout, he wrote:

> During the 2007–09 crisis, European banks faced big problems because of speculative investments in mortgage-backed securities. The European Central Bank (ECB) provided abundant liquidity to banks and kept interest rates very low. But when countries faced heavy borrowing needs, it behaved very differently.
>
> Public debt rose in 2009 mostly because states rescued the financial system and tax revenue collapsed as the recession unfolded. Profligacy and public inefficiency had little to do with it. But, unlike banks, countries were left to fend for themselves. The ECB simply watched as financiers proceeded to bite their saviour by speculating on public debt (Lapavitsas 2010).

Those financial institutions that were speculating on sovereign debt were in many cases the very same institutions that had caused that debt in the first place. They were using the public money given to rescue them to speculate on public debt. To do this, they used CDSs, the insurance policies that pay out when someone else defaults, which pushed up the interest rates that the victims of the speculative attacks had to pay to borrow, driving them further into the red and towards default in a self-fulfilling prophecy (Varoufakis 2015: 207). The ratings agencies, who had played their own part in the 2008 crash, downgraded the sovereigns, making it harder still to borrow. Because the countries in question were members of the eurozone, their central banks could not act as lenders of last resort, buying their debt to prevent them from defaulting, and the European Central Bank (ECB) was refusing to act in this capacity. The role of the markets in creating high levels of sovereign debt in the first place was almost completely forgotten in the media coverage. Out of the 1,133 news items analysed for this study, it was mentioned in only two. The role of the credit ratings agencies was likewise blacked out.

CORRUPTION

The other side of the state profligacy coin, according to the media, was corruption, especially when it came to Greece. One illustrative opinion piece in the *Telegraph*, during mass protests in May 2010, states, 'Beyond the barricades there is widespread anger in Greece that the entire country will have to bear the burden after decades of corruption and mismanagement by the political elite' (McElroy and Anast 2010). According to this narrative, state profligacy and corruption had gone hand in hand to cause a catastrophic debt crisis. Its epicentre was the particularly profligate and corrupt Greece and it had spread to other countries that had indulged in similar practices.

There is little doubt that the Greek political system was corrupt. But, as with profligacy, there are two sides to corruption. While the state was accepting bribes, the private sector was offering those bribes. To give just two examples, an investigation into money laundering found that the German company Siemens had a €10 million slush fund it used to bribe individuals in the Greek Ministry of Defence and the army. Greece bought 170 Leopard II tanks from the German company Krauss-Maffei Wegmann for €1.6 billion on credit. One man was bribed €600,000 to keep quiet about the fact that the ministry had bought no ammunition for them. Another official received €1.7 million from the company (Corporate Watch 2014: 49). One estimate links 10 per cent of Greece's public debt to bribes from foreign multinationals (47). And it was the investment bank Goldman Sachs, for which so many officials, including ECB chief Mario Draghi, formerly worked, that helped the Greek government conceal the state of its finances. Christina Laskaridis writes that 'there has been a long-standing symbiotic relationship between foreign corporate bribery and the Greek political establishment' (Corporate Watch 2014: 49). This relationship went virtually unnoticed in the news coverage.

In the case of Spain, there were articles in the *Guardian* that did go into some detail about the corruption involved in that country's banking crisis, looking at the dynamic of corruption between banks and politicians. One piece describes 'multi-million euro payoffs taken by some senior executives shortly before their banks collapsed and decisions taken by unqualified board members who admit they were incapable of analysing the banks' books', and claims that 'Boards were stuffed with political placements or people who had little idea about banking –

including, in one case, a supermarket checkout worker' (Tremlett 2012). However, these more in-depth analyses of the role of corruption in the crisis were few and far between. Overall, corruption served to 'frame' the public sector as the culprit.

'CHEATS AND SCROUNGERS'

A particularly insidious aspect of the profligacy and corruption narrative is that it frequently slips from blaming the state to blaming the people themselves. Again, this happens both explicitly and implicitly. One piece in the *Guardian* claimed,

> It's a non-transparent system that has been protected for decades by politicians and civil servants alike since it provides cover for corruption and patronage. The problem is that the average Greek voter was content with this system as long as it provided jobs and permanent status as a public employee (Papahelas 2010).

Similarly, in the *Telegraph*:

> Those tens of thousands ripping up Athens may be calling for heads to roll and venting what seems to be a bottomless supply of fury at their politicians, but the truth is that the vast majority of them are certain to have conspired, at some level, with the system of deceit and corruption that has now brought Greece to its knees (de Quetteville 2010).

Thus it is not just the state but the people who are profligate and corrupt. This goes hand in hand with the cultural stereotypes deployed in the tabloids and even the right-wing 'quality press'. The *Sun*'s Trevor Kavanagh contrasts Germany's 'hard work' and 'thrift' with its EU partners, who 'prefer a siesta to hard work', and refers to 'greedy Greeks and feckless French who insist on retiring at 60' (Kavanagh 2012). A piece in the *Mirror* compared the periphery countries to 'tramps asking the price of a cup of tea' and quips, 'When Italy demands the next bail-out maybe Angela Merkel should throw a pile of coins into the Trevi Fountain and make a wish – that she could send the entire population of Southern Europe to Dignitas' (Reade 2012). The piece from the *Telegraph* mentioned above, comparing the Irish to the Greeks, does not explicitly call Greek and Irish people lazy, but its claim that their crises are a result of 'years of sunny self-indulgence' seems to apply at least as much to the people themselves as the state. This indirect slippage between the state and the people is not uncommon.

There's no doubt that the Greek state had engaged in corruption and had squandered considerable amounts of public money in the process. However, how far the Greek people benefitted from either corruption or state profligacy is very much up for debate. OECD statistics show that Greek, Italian and Spanish workers all worked more hours between 2000 and 2010 than German workers (OECD.Stat). Eurostat figures show that, in 2005, the retirement age in Greece, Spain, Ireland, Portugal and Cyprus was higher than in Germany and the EU average. The Greek retirement age has risen from 61.7 years to 67 years under austerity. OECD data suggests that social spending in Greece, Ireland, Portugal, Spain and Italy is lower as a percentage of GDP than in Germany (Corporate Watch 2014: 35).

Several studies of media coverage of the eurozone crisis have found that media outlets in different countries have been guilty of 'Greek bashing'. Bickes *et al.* (2014) compared the coverage of Greece, Spain and Italy in three magazines: the UK's *Economist*, Germany's *der Speigel* and the US's *Time*. They found a large amount of 'Greek bashing' in the early part of the crisis, with articles presenting Greeks as enjoying siestas and early retirement, especially in the German publication. The crisis was often portrayed as a disease, with Spain and Italy its victims and Greece its locus. James F. Tracy studied the framing of the Greek crisis in a range of mainstream US media. He similarly found an 'incorrigible Greeks' framing, portraying Greeks as 'spendthrift, unruly, irredeemable, and thus perpetrators of the event' (Tracy 2011: 517).

Interestingly, Yiannis Mylonas, in his (2012) study of the coverage of the Greek crisis by Germany's most popular newspaper *Bild-Zeitung*, found that touristic stereotypes were deployed, whereby the image of tourists holidaying in Greece – complete with sun, sea, sand and relaxation – was projected onto the Greek people themselves, as if they enjoyed this kind of lifestyle all the time. This kind of framing was also to be found in the British tabloids and the *Telegraph*. More broadly, puns around 'Greek tragedy' and evocations of the decline of an ancient civilisation were commonplace.

The dominant narrative about the causes of the eurozone crisis – that it was caused by the profligacy and corruption of the peripheral states and their people – reflects the fact that the coverage contains a narrow range of elite perspectives which, as we have seen, is one of the main elements of media amnesia. As both Blyth and Corporate Watch show, these were the narratives being disseminated by officials in the EU institutions, the IMF, the German government and even the governments of the bailed-out countries.

'EURO LAGGARDS'

After profligacy and corruption, the next largest category of explanations given for the eurozone crisis stressed deeper political and economic problems with the structure of the eurozone. These accounted for 17.4 per cent of the causes mentioned. Some of the deepest explanations focused on the structure of the monetary union and its effects on national current accounts. These were featured both in the (europhile) *Guardian* and the (eurosceptic) *Telegraph*. They were entirely absent from the BBC news and the tabloids. In his column for the *Telegraph*, Peter Oborne explained,

> The experiment of imposing a single currency and a single monetary policy upon economies as divergent as those of Germany and Greece has gone tragically wrong. Germany, bolstered by an artificially low exchange rate and rock-bottom interest rates, is enjoying a boom. But the economies of Ireland, Portugal, Greece and others are being destroyed.

Oborne continues,

> It cannot be emphasised too strongly that were these countries outside the eurozone, there would be no real problem. The IMF could intervene, reschedule their debts and allow the national currencies to float until they reached a competitive level. In the case of Greece, this level would be well under half where it stands today as a member of the euro (Oborne 2011).

When the currencies of European member-states were joined together in the euro, there was a group of countries with persistent trade surpluses – notably Germany – and a group with persistent trade deficits – such as the southern, peripheral countries. The euro served to deepen these imbalances. With floating currencies, when a country runs a trade surplus, the value of its currency tends to increase. This makes exports more expensive and thus helps to drive exports down again. Inversely, countries running trade deficits see their currency lose value, boosting exports by making them cheaper and thus helping to rebalance their accounts. However, because all the euro countries share a currency, currency fluctuations could not help balance intra-European trade and instead trade imbalances became more entrenched. As Screpanti puts it, the euro is a structurally undervalued deutsche mark and an overvalued lira (or drachma etc.) (Screpanti 2014: 164). Thus, although part of the reason for Germany's trade surplus is that it makes innovative and desirable industrial products, it is also because the euro makes its economy competitive at the expense of its neighbours. A dynamic evolved whereby the peripheral countries would import from the European core, which would then finance the deficits of the periphery, creating more demand (and debt) in the periphery, which was used to buy more exports from the core.

The structure of the euro thus benefits Germany at the expense of the southern countries. Keynesian economist Joseph Stiglitz, who was a high-profile critic of the way international organisations and Germany handled the eurozone crisis, reframed the problem as lying with Germany in a piece in the *Guardian*:

Germany (like China) views its high savings and export prowess as virtues. But John Maynard Keynes pointed out that surpluses lead to weak global aggregate demand – countries running surpluses exert a 'negative externality' on trading partners. Indeed, Keynes believed it was surplus countries, far more than those in deficit, that posed a threat to global prosperity; he went so far as to advocate a tax on surplus countries (Stiglitz 2010a).

Stiglitz thus brings us closer to the role of international power relationships within the eurozone. A piece in the *Guardian* headlined 'Germany: a euro laggard', again by Costas Lapavitsas, explores the political economic background to the euro crisis in most depth, including both international and class dynamics. He digs into the imbalances caused by the monetary union, Germany's low GDP growth and its squeeze on workers, in another effort to provide a counter framing of the euro crisis. It is one of the most interesting analyses and is worth quoting at length:

The crisis facing the eurozone looks at first sight as German efficiency clashing with Portuguese, Irish, Greek and Spanish sloppiness. But in many respects Germany has performed worse than the 'peripheral' countries in the last decade. The largest economy of the eurozone has been marked by slow growth, poor domestic demand, weak investment, high unemployment, and minuscule productivity gains.

The only area in which Germany has excelled is exports, where it has chalked up large surpluses, while peripheral nations have had large deficits. But this imbalance is due to the skewed nature of the European monetary union. The eurozone has imposed a single monetary policy and tight fiscal policy. Member countries have applied systematic pressure on wages and working conditions across the zone; in Germany, wages have barely risen in real terms for 15 years, helped by the absence of unions in the old East Germany and easy access to the labour markets of other eastern countries (Lapavitsas 2010).

This piece comes as close as it gets to placing the eurozone crisis within the context of the neoliberal phase of capitalism, including both the imperialist nature of globalisation and the transfer of resources from labour to capital. According to Ernesto Screpanti, Germany's strategy in the post-Bretton Woods era has been to create 'a mercantilist imperial dominion'. As the quote from Lapavitsas suggests, with the creation of the eurozone, not only was a single monetary policy imposed, but public spending, though remaining the responsibility of the member-states, was restrained through a cap on budget deficits of 3 per cent of GDP and debt-to-GDP ratios below 60 per cent. This meant that governments were not allowed to use fiscal policy freely to support their citizens. For Screpanti, this combination led to a situation in which 'a new division of labour is being established, in which the southern (and eastern) countries specialise in low-cost and low-tech production, while Germany takes on the role of lead innovator and its firms seize half of Europe's capital' (Screpanti 2014:162; see also Streeck 2016: 131).

In this analysis, part of the German strategy was to shift resources away from workers and towards German capital, a redistributory process characteristic of neoliberalism that we have been exploring through this book. Screpanti writes that 'German beggar-my-neighbour policies are based on a beggar-my-worker strategy' (161). Between 2002 and 2005, the 'Hartz reforms' compelled unemployed Germans to accept 'mini jobs' and 'midi jobs' that paid less than €450 a month, and even jobs paying €1 an hour, under threat of having their benefits cut. Firms do not have to pay payroll taxes on these wages, so that labour costs shrink while labour flexibility rises. In 1974, the share of national income going to wages was 71 per cent (149). In 2007 it was 61 per cent (164). This reduction of labour costs made German exports cheaper, helping to maintain trade surpluses. The reunification of Germany had also meant that 'dirt-cheap labour became available to German companies' (Varoufakis 2015: 202), not only from East Germany but from across the former Soviet Union. Once the euro was introduced, its gains from wage decreases became permanent (202). As we have seen, the wider neoliberal restructuring of capitalism occurred in response to a crisis in the previous, Keynesian, social-democratic phase of capitalism, reminding us of David Harvey's (2011) point that capitalism never resolves its crises, it only moves them around.

'A FOURTH REICH'

The explanations foregrounding structural problems with the monetary union are given by both the left- and right-wing press. Often, these structural explanations are wedded to portrayals of the EU as anti-democratic, especially by eurosceptic commentators. Simon Jenkins' portrait in the *Guardian* is exemplary:

> I regard myself as a 'good' European, but as far as the EU was concerned, that idealism was dented as each advance of Brussels power took ever greater liberties with Europe's taxpayers and legislators: regulating, subsidising and corrupting all it touched ...
>
> Not for the first time in Europe's history, a centralised superstate stalks the continent with a retinue of uncritical appeasers unable to see the wood for the tax-free salaries (Jenkins 2011).

The *Sun* more concisely refers to: 'the fascist regime of European banks. They are a Fourth Reich' (2015).

There are two things to say about the *Sun's* scanty coverage of the euro crisis. First, it is interesting to note how it veers between painting the peripheral eurozone countries as 'foreign wasters' in such a way as to justify austerity, and portraying those countries as victims of a European elitist bureaucracy, in such a way as to promote euroscepticism. It thereby serves two not entirely compatible political agendas at the same time.

The same is true for the *Telegraph's* coverage. In addition, however, and not for the first time, the *Sun* here is also a source of wisdom. This quote simultaneously evokes the power financial institutions have over politics, hints at the lack of democratic process within the European Union, and links states and banks together in two snappy sentences.

The lack of democracy within the eurozone – the dominance of financial institutions and the centralised bureaucracy taking the place of elected national representatives – is part of the wider neoliberal restructuring of capitalism described earlier. Financialisation – the growing dominance of finance relative to the rest of the economy – is one of the defining features of this phase of capitalism. The rules governing eurozone membership set out in the Maastricht Treaty are aligned with neoliberal, Washington Consensus ideas of balanced budgets and lower social spending, removing responsibility for economic policy from the hands of elected politicians and giving it to 'independent' technocrats. The idea is that politicians should not be able to intervene in their economies on behalf of their citizens, because markets are efficient and should be left to themselves. Political meddling in the markets in this view leads to disaster. In the ideology of ordoliberalism, the German version of neoliberalism, markets are to be managed but only in such a way as to provide a stable institutional framework for their optimal functioning, based on free competition (Dardot and Laval 2017: 83). Thus free-market capitalism has coincided with less, not more, democracy. It is perhaps ironic, then, that it is often the pro-free market papers – the *Sun* and especially the *Telegraph* – that are so annoyed about the lack of democracy within the EU.

Criticisms in the press of the democratic deficit within the EU, particularly by eurosceptics, became more scathing as time wore on. They might have had good reason. If they were paying attention, they would have seen Memoranda of Understandings (the austerity packages) signed without being ratified in the usual way in parliament, and the installation of unelected governments by the Troika to implement the 'reforms'.

In 2011, the unelected Lukas Papademos – ex vice-president of the ECB and former governor of the Bank of Greece – was appointed as Greece's prime minister. In the words of one activist organisation: '[the Troika] described his government as "technocratic", even though its members were distinguished for their lack of political legitimacy rather than their technical expertise' (Corporate Watch 2014: 71). After the anti-austerity Syriza Party won the election in January 2015, and its leader Alexis Tsipras became prime minister, the Troika was accused of trying to engineer regime change by inflicting further damage on the economy. When the Syriza government announced it would hold a referendum on Greece's bailout conditions in the summer of 2015, its partners refused to continue negotiating and the ECB restricted emergency funding, causing banks to close. It eventually succeeded first in the resignation of Finance Minister Yanis Varoufakis and then in the capitulation of Tsipras to more austerity and the splintering of the Syriza Party.

'HANDING OUT THE BEGGING BOWL'

The short-term solutions of the bailouts and the accompanying austerity measures were by far the most frequently discussed responses to the eurozone crisis, accounting for 18.7 per cent and 20.1 per cent of the possible solutions mentioned respectively. Mark Blyth believes that the ideal solution to Greece's crisis back in 2009 would have cost around €50 billion: 'It would have required either the ECB, or Germany as its major creditor, to buy the secondary-market Greek debt that was subject to near-term rollover risk, bury it somewhere deep in its balance sheet, and walk away' (Blyth 2013: 64).

This didn't happen partly because of German politics and partly because the Maastricht Treaty contains a 'no transfers' clause, meaning that eurozone countries were prohibited from assisting each other in times of fiscal crisis. At the same time, the ECB was not mandated to act as lender of last resort to stop the peripheral countries from going bankrupt. There were no crisis resolution mechanisms put in place when the eurozone was formed, and the institutions did not know what to do when the markets went berserk. Ever since then, the EU institutions have been muddling through.

The bailouts have come from a combination of sources, raised through the European Financial Stability Facility (EFSF), the European Financial Stabilisation Mechanism (EFSM), and later the permanent European Stability Mechanism (ESM) – facilities that raise money on behalf of the eurozone to lend to members in difficulty – the Greek Loan Facility, containing bilateral loans to Greece when it was initially bailed out, and the International Monetary Fund (IMF). The bailouts are administered by the Troika – the European Commission, the ECB and the IMF.

Although the bailouts dominated the coverage, there was very little scrutiny of the bailouts themselves outside the specialist pages, though the view that they were unsustainable was deftly captured in the *Mirror* in the piece comparing indebted countries to tramps, mentioned earlier:

> I'm no economist but surely lending hundreds of billions of euros to countries whose problem is being hundreds of billions of euros in debt is like saying to a tramp asking for the price of a cup of tea 'no I won't give you that but I've just arranged for you to have an unlimited tab at Bargain Booze. Pester me again if it doesn't make your liver pack in' (Reade 2012).

The piece was right to question the economic 'logic' of the bailouts, and Greece's debt has now been deemed unsustainable by the IMF. The stability of the bailout mechanisms was also dubious. The EFSF used financial structures similar to those that triggered the 2008 meltdown (a special-purpose vehicle, and its bonds were structured in the same way as the CDOs discussed in the Introduction), and their credit worthiness was dependent on the main contributors. The EFSF bonds were downgraded by credit ratings agencies because one of the main contributors, France, was downgraded. On top of this, the amount that the EFSF could lend was revised upwards from €250 billion to €440 billion. This was done by leveraging the fund – borrowing. Thus, 'the very mechanism to shore up confidence in the financial markets was therefore to be made, at least in part, dependent on the confidence of the financial markets' (Aufheben, quoted in Corporate Watch 2014: 60).

An important point to note about the media coverage of the bailouts is that, just as the crisis was framed as a 'debt crisis', the bailouts were almost always framed as *sovereign* bailouts. The one exception to this was Spain, whose bailout was officially and publicly differentiated from the others in being specifically aimed at its banks. Many critics claim, however, that not only Spain's but the other peripheral countries' bailouts would better be understood as bank bailouts. Although they were officially loans to sovereigns, showing up on the public balance sheets, it is questionable how much of the money stayed in the countries in question, never mind their public sectors. An investigation by the Jubilee Debt Campaign from 2015 found that over 90 per cent of Greece's bailout money had gone to financial institutions – both Greek banks and banks of the core European countries, especially Germany and France.

Thus, a large proportion of the bailouts was going to the sector that had triggered the sovereign debt crisis in the first place.

Relatedly, a large part of the coverage across outlets presents the bailouts as 'helping' the bailed-out countries. One *Sun* article described countries requesting bailouts as 'handing out the begging bowl'. A BBC segment on the Greek crisis after Greece's July 2015 referendum quoted a German politician saying 'you can't rescue a country against its will, and you can't give solidarity without the readiness to accept solidarity.' The BBC correspondent continued, 'elsewhere in Europe other leaders will take some convincing that they can continue helping the Greeks' (BBC 2015). Given the effects of the bailouts and the conditions imposed on the 'beneficiary' countries, media scholar Yiannis Mylonas (2012) describes this language as 'Orwellian'. It could be argued that framing the bailouts as public-sector assistance rather than bank bailouts helps justify the conditions of those bailouts, namely austerity. If the loans are to help the people, it may seem fair that the people should pay for them by taking cuts to their services and wages. If the loans are for banks, what justification can there be for those cuts?

The ECB's crisis responses have also favoured the financial sector. As well as using 'conventional' monetary policy (lowering the interest rate at which banks can borrow) it has pursued 'unconventional' policies. Its 'open market operations' buy government and private debt securities to provide liquidity to banks. Liquidity provision was ramped up in late 2011, under its 'long-term refinancing operations'. In March 2015, the ECB started its quantitative easing programme, buying assets from commercial banks. By February 2017, the ECB held more than €1.5 trillion of assets (Hale 2017). These ECB interventions have been criticised for lending to banks at low interest rates (as low as 1 per cent) with no strings attached, while public sectors were initially left with no support at all. When states were loaned money, this came with higher interest rates and harsh austerity conditions attached. Initially, banks receiving cheap money from the ECB sometimes then loaned to sovereigns at higher rates (up to 5 per cent or higher).

Later the Troika took on the majority of the debt, and in the case of Greece, institutions within the Troika now own close to 80 per cent of its loans. This means that the financial institutions are no longer bearing the risks they initially took on the loans, and that the Troika is loaning Greece money that it then uses to pay itself back. In 2012, the ECB finally announced that it would undertake 'outright monetary transactions', that is, buying government securities without limits, thereby acting as lender of last resort to stricken states. Unlike with the banks, these loans would be subject to strict conditionalities, discussed in the next section. Astonishingly, given what we know about the financial sector's role in this crisis, banking regulation made up no more than 1.1 per cent of the possible responses to the eurozone crisis mentioned in the media coverage sampled in this study.

Rather than scrutinising the details of the bailouts and assessing their desirability, the media frequently framed them as necessary to avert catastrophe – a point developed in the next section. In this way they were implicitly endorsed, especially during the early stages of the eurozone crisis. It could be said that this framing also served subtly to endorse the austerity conditions attached: if the bailouts are necessary to avoid disaster, so, it might seem, are the accompanying conditions. Over time, the bailouts themselves faded into the background, and were mentioned as things set in stone that were simply happening rather than being debated. Their conditions, however, especially austerity, were much more conspicuous.

AUSTERITY EUROPE

In return for the sovereign bailouts – which, as we have seen, can be considered largely bank bailouts – the Troika imposed deep spending cuts and tax increases on the populations of the bailed-out states, leading to social unrest, recession, rising not falling public debt and, in some cases, humanitarian crises. Despite this, in 2013, the Fiscal Compact came into force for all the eurozone countries plus certain other EU states that had opted in. It strengthens the rules over public budget deficits, stipulating that any country exceeding the 3 per cent limit must follow a structural adjustment programme. Former BBC economics editor Paul Mason (2011) said of the compact, 'enshrining in national and international law the need for balanced budgets and near-zero structural deficits, the eurozone has outlawed expansionary fiscal policy'. These targets are widely considered unreachable. However, in order for a country to make use of the ECB's 'outright monetary transactions', mentioned above, it must sign up to the compact. These governments are banned from using fiscal policy to support their economies during recessions, placing the burden of adjustment on citizens.

Table 4.1 Mentions of austerity as possible response to the eurozone crisis. Sample size: 194. Percentages show proportion endorsed, rejected or mentioned neutrally by outlet.

		Guardian	Telegraph	Sun	Mirror	BBC	Total
Austerity	Endorsed	8	3	1	0	5	17
		10.4%	11.1%	20%	0%	20.8%	
	Rejected	20	1	0	0	0	21
		26%	3.7%	0%	0%	0%	
	Neutral	49	23	4	10	19	105
		63.6%	85.2%	80%	100%	79.2%	
	Total	77	27	5	10	24	143

The coverage of austerity in the eurozone was somewhat different to the coverage of austerity in the UK (see Chapter 2). As shown in Table 4.1, the *Guardian* rejected austerity in the eurozone more frequently than endorsing it, similar to its stance on austerity in the UK. The *Telegraph* endorsed austerity in the eurozone more frequently than rejecting it, though less frequently than it endorsed austerity in the UK. The *Sun* was much less strongly supportive and the *Mirror* was much less strongly opposed to austerity in the eurozone than in the UK (the *Mirror* covered austerity in the eurozone entirely neutrally). The BBC endorsed austerity in the eurozone on a number of occasions, reflecting its reporting of austerity in the UK.

Austerity was endorsed most strongly early on, during Greece's May 2010 bailout. The need for austerity was expressed using metaphors of cleaning up, growing up and atoning for past sins. A Greek journalist wrote in the *Guardian*: 'This is clearly the time to put our house in order, restore our credibility in the world, and regain the optimistic and extrovert attitude that characterised our country during the Athens Olympic Games of 2004' (Papahelas 2010). This longer section from a piece in the *Telegraph* is rich with metaphors in support of austerity:

> In this apparently gloomy conclusion, however, lies the key to Greece's redemption. Deep down, most Greeks accept that it is not just the politicians who have sinned. They, too, are to blame and must now repent.
>
> 'The majority of Greeks are clear that things will have to change,' says Ms Iatrou. 'They understand that everyone will have to pay, that Greece will just have to grow up.'

... Yesterday the Greek government said it would press ahead with austerity reforms despite their deep unpopularity ...

And if Greece's politicians – long derided, now despised – can suddenly find it within themselves to do the right thing, surely it is not beyond the Greek people? (de Quetteville 2010).

Alongside ideas of guilt, sin, repentance and redemption, we also have the idea that Greece needs to 'grow up' and accept austerity. This framing of the Greek people as childish, and that accepting austerity is 'grown up' is not uncommon, and will be explored later in this chapter.

Though there was explicit support for austerity in opinion pages, endorsement of austerity was usually more implicit. As with UK austerity, it was regularly framed as 'painful but necessary', as in this comment from a BBC report on looming spending cuts and tax rises: 'The government here has made it clear there are no alternatives. Otherwise Greece will be bankrupt' (BBC 2010b). Austerity, like the bailouts, was therefore framed as needed to prevent something even more catastrophic from occurring, evoking Margaret Thatcher's TINA ('there is no alternative').

Yiannis Mylonas, in his study of the German media coverage of the Greek crisis mentioned above, finds a similar pattern of the crisis being depicted as armageddon. He argues that this kind of media framing has played a role in the application of the 'shock doctrine' to Greece. Naomi Klein (2008) argues that crises are often used as opportunities to impose radical neoliberal restructuring on the afflicted region. Crises disrupt the normal functioning of society, and under these conditions reforms that would in other circumstances be unthinkable have a chance of getting through. For Mylonas and others, austerity and the accompanying structural reforms (see below) imposed on Greece are instances of this process, and the media have played a key role in preparing the way.

On the other hand, the *Guardian* did criticise austerity in the eurozone, rejecting it 2.5 times more frequently than it endorsed it. Criticism mounted over time, as the damage to Greece's economy and the suffering it was causing became clear. Another piece by Costas Lapavitsas in the *Guardian*, from September 2011, when financial speculation on the periphery countries' debts was causing grave concerns for the global economy, explains:

In early 2010 Greece was effectively bankrupt. In its wisdom, the troika imposed policies of severe austerity and deregulation consistent with the neoliberal ideology of the EU. Quite predictably, demand collapsed and banking credit became scarce, with the result that the core of the Greek economy was crushed.

The social implications have been catastrophic. Entire communities have been devastated by unemployment, losing the means to live as well as the norms, customs and respect of regular work. Barter has appeared among the poor and the not so poor. Medical services in working-class areas are running low on basic provisions. Schools and transport are disintegrating. People are abandoning cities to return to agriculture, a sure sign of social retrogression (Lapavitsas 2011).

However, even in items sceptical of austerity, the *logic* of austerity was often still accepted. For example, in an article on Spain, the *Guardian*'s economics editor Larry Elliott made the case for Keynesian growth measures as opposed to more austerity – a view less common in the coverage of the eurozone than in coverage of Britain's own economic problems:

[Prime Minister] Rajoy's argument is that he already has IMF-style structural reforms in place, so a further package of austerity would amount to overkill. He is absolutely right about that. What's more, any attempt to accelerate the pace of Spain's structural reform would almost certainly backfire, leading not just to widespread popular unrest but precisely the sort of adverse reaction in the markets that Europe's policymakers are seeking to avoid (Elliott 2012).

Note that Elliott is opposed to more austerity measures but endorses the argument that Spain already has an austerity package in place so doesn't need any more austerity. As we have seen, Spain had a very low debt-to-GDP ratio prior to the 2008 financial crisis. Its problems were squarely located in the private sector, in a property bubble. And its bailout was explicitly differentiated from the others by being a bank bailout not a sovereign bailout. Why, then, would any austerity at all be appropriate? The acceptance of the *logic* of austerity was widespread in the mainstream media. This, alongside forgetting the origins of the crisis, framing it as a public sector crisis, blaming state profligacy and corruption, and using cultural stereotypes to blame the people of the crisis-countries themselves, serves to obscure a deeper understanding of the problems and prevent sustained public discussion of long-term, viable alternatives to austerity.

On top of that, even though the *Guardian*'s content mix tended to be critical of the extreme austerity being imposed across Europe, as in the case of the UK deficit, some form and level of austerity was implicitly framed as being necessary. The popular Syriza Party in Greece was publicly advocating a zero austerity approach, pledging to undo the reforms that had been put in place. This view did get some attention in the UK media, especially as Syriza became more powerful. However, though the possibility of completely reversing austerity was mentioned more frequently than in the context of the UK, it only made it into the coverage eight times. It was endorsed *zero* times.

As with the explanations given for the crisis, the acceptance of the bailouts and austerity as inevitable and necessary reflects the fact that a narrow range of elite views tends to dominate media coverage. Again, these were the messages being communicated by officials. This changed somewhat when Syriza gained power in Greece – the media treatment of Syriza is analysed later.

STRUCTURAL REFORMS

Interestingly, although business-friendly supply-side measures were widely discussed in relation to the UK economy (see Chapter 3), their equivalent, 'structural reforms', were rarely discussed in the non-specialist UK coverage of the euro crisis. They accounted for only 2.7 per cent of the possible responses mentioned, despite the fact that they were arguably as radical as the austerity measures. In Greece, as well as spending cuts and tax increases, bailout conditions included the privatisation of all major public companies and infrastructure, including ports, airports, roads, public utilities including water and electricity, public buildings and real estate, mining rights, the lottery and railways (Corporate Watch 2014: 114). In addition, labour-market reforms have replaced full-time permanent contracts with flexible forms, made work-shifts more flexible, and made the termination of contracts easier. The minimum wage has been lowered by 22 per cent – 32 per cent for young people (Corporate Watch 2014: 74). As a result, in 2013, waged workers on average earned 18 per cent less and paid 52 per cent more tax than in 2012. Privatisations and labour-market deregulation were also part of the economic adjustment programmes for Ireland, Portugal and Cyprus.

Spain took it upon itself to implement these measures, as did several other European countries.

When it came to the eurozone crisis, business-friendly policies did not make it at all into the tabloids. They were reported entirely neutrally by the BBC, almost neutrally by the *Guardian* (rejected once) and more frequently endorsed than rejected in the *Telegraph* (though only twice). Most often there is no detail about what kinds of policies are being implemented or proposed: structural reforms or simply 'reforms' are mentioned in passing, as in the following examples:

> Across southern Europe, governments such as those in Italy and Spain are making brave efforts to enact long overdue reforms (Hague 2015).

> The crisis of 2010 meant that Greece could not remain a member of the eurozone without opening up its economy and fixing its deep social injustices. Such reforms required trust, but there was none to be had (Eleftheriadis 2015).

> Experts said Rajoy's attempts to wriggle out of external control of Spain's economy were doomed to failure. 'The terms and conditions are going to want to see a clear path to restore growth and structural budget balance. That will include structural reforms and fiscal measures,' said Luis Garicano, of the London School of Economics (Tremlett and Traynor 2012).

It is unclear what is meant by 'reforms'. Sometimes the term seems to be a catch-all for austerity and supply-side measures. The language of 'opening up' the economy suggests privatisation and deregulation, recalling IMF's 'structural adjustment', discussed in Chapter 2. We might ask, had the effects of these programmes been remembered in the coverage of the eurozone crisis, would their European incarnations have been passed over so breezily in the UK media? As we have seen, the lack of global context is a key element of media amnesia.

In Chapters 2 and 3, we saw that forgetting the causes of the ever-changing economic crisis helped legitimise the escalation of the kinds of neoliberal policies – austerity and business-friendly supply-side reforms – that helped cause the crisis in the first place. In the case of the euro-crisis coverage, a similar dynamic emerges. Forgetting the causes of the eurozone crisis has helped entrench the logic of austerity, enable structural reforms to go unscrutinised and short circuited deliberation about more viable solutions.

GREXIT AND BREXIT

The possibility of one or more member-states leaving the eurozone, or even the European Union, was widely canvassed. It comprised the third biggest category of possible responses to the eurozone crisis mentioned after austerity and the bailouts – 12.8 per cent. The discussion about the possible break-up of the EU was more polarised than that of the other response options. Overall, the idea was opposed almost twice as often as it was endorsed. As shown in Table 4.2, it was rejected much more frequently than it was endorsed in the *Guardian* and endorsed more frequently than rejected in the *Telegraph* and the *Sun*, in alignment with their later stances on the Brexit referendum in June 2016. In the *Mirror*, the possibility was covered only neutrally, when at all. The BBC was very negative about the idea. It endorsed it zero times, and rejected it as frequently as reporting it neutrally.

Table 4.2 Mentions of country leaving the euro/EU as possible response to the eurozone crisis. Sample size: 194. Percentages show proportion endorsed, rejected or mentioned neutrally by outlet.

	Guardian	*Telegraph*	*Sun*	*Mirror*	*BBC*	*Total*
Country leaving euro/EU						
Endorsed	4	6	3	0	0	13
	9.8%	25%	37.5%	0%	0%	
Rejected	16	2	0	0	7	25
	39%	8.3%	0%	0%	50%	
Neutral	21	16	5	4	7	53
	51.2%	66.7%	62.5%	100%	50%	
Total	41	24	8	4	14	91

Often, the possibility of a peripheral euro country exiting the eurozone or the EU was not portrayed as an active response to the crisis but as a disastrous consequence that would just 'happen' if the bailouts – with all the conditions attached – were not agreed. This quote from the *Guardian* gives an example:

Creditors made it clear that if Athens rescinds the structural reforms seen as vital to kickstarting its moribund economy, further injections of cash will stop. Without the money, Greece will have to default, declare bankruptcy and leave the eurozone, sending the 17-nation bloc into a tailspin from which the global economy might take decades to recover (Smith 2012).

Or this one on the controversial case of Cyprus: 'Cyprus approved legislation to restructure its banking sector and create a national solidarity fund that could save the island from crashing out of the eurozone' (Treanor 2013). If we think back to the framing of the bailouts and austerity as necessary to avert an unthinkable catastrophe, it turns out that that catastrophe was leaving the eurozone.

On the other hand, there was some support for Grexit, especially as it became clear over the years how damaging the loan arrangements were for Greece, and especially in the *Telegraph*. In an opinion piece for the *Telegraph*, Conservative politician and Brexiteer William Hague laid out the structural problems with the euro described above. He concludes: 'In such circumstances, it is better to be able to leave sooner, with some generous support, than leave later with even greater resentment and failure' (Hague 2015). Anger over the Cyprus savings levy led to claims that Cyprus too would be better off leaving the monetary union.

Although *Guardian* copy often framed the possibility of Grexit as catastrophic, one of the pieces it featured by Costas Lapavitsas, discussed above in relation to wage suppression in Germany, advocates a people-led Grexit. It is a rare example of such an idea in the mainstream media. It goes into some detail as to what would be required:

> This more radical approach would involve devaluation, restructuring of foreign debt, and capital controls. The productive sector would benefit but the initial shock would be substantial. To protect the economy there would have to be public control of banks and other key areas of the economy, including transport, energy and telecommunications. Peripheral economies might then be shifted in a more productive direction – for example, supporting the transition to low-carbon activities.
>
> Finally, exit by the periphery might also help German workers appreciate the extent to which the eurozone has been tormenting them, leading to much-needed corrective action at the core (Lapavitsas 2010).

The prospect of one of the southern countries exiting the euro also provoked discussion of the UK's place within the EU. In 2010 the Lib Dems had pledged an in-out referendum in its election manifesto (something which also now tends to be forgotten). This was taken over by the Conservative Party shortly after. The idea of the UK leaving the EU found support in the *Telegraph* and the *Sun*. A column by Charles Moore in the *Telegraph* (Moore 2012) supported negotiating a withdrawal from the EU and a referendum on the end result. Interestingly, the *Sun*'s Trevor Kavanagh argued for Britain distancing itself from the EU, especially the European Court of Human Rights, but did not support a simple in-out referendum, because he was concerned for UK business and finance (and perhaps, as the quote suggests, because he was worried voters might choose to stay in):

Our firms need free access to European markets. We must safeguard the financial industry which is so crucial to our economy.

We must cut loose from incessant meddling by Brussels bureaucrats and, above all, from the European Court of Human Rights.

These are landmark decisions. If we are to have a referendum, ministers must start talking to us and each other about The Question.

It must not be a simple IN or OUT – although that may come.

With all party leaders campaigning for continued membership, worried voters could be frightened into sticking with an irrevocable mistake (Kavanagh 2012).

The Brexit referendum was thus anticipated and the eurozone crisis used to marshal support to leave several years before the referendum took place.

INTEGRATION AND DISINTEGRATION

Several of the eurosceptic voices, especially in the *Telegraph*, floated ideas for a different, less tightly-integrated EU. This formed one vision for long-term reform to solve the continent's economic problems. The other vision for long-term reform proposed just the opposite: more EU integration. In the *Telegraph*, Charles Moore advocated a smaller eurozone and a wider collection of loosely-associated countries, evoking the idea of the EU as bureaucratic and anti-democratic:

For most Continental leaders and bureaucrats, European integration is their life's work, not to mention their salary, meal ticket and startlingly attractive pension. They will now try yet again, harder than ever and presumably very soon, to rescue it. To the sceptic, this looks no more sensible, and scarcely more moral, than the Soviet Union trying to hold its empire together by making Poland impose martial law in 1981. But if some countries wish to do this – as Mrs Merkel, talking across David Cameron, said on Thursday that she did – then we cannot prevent them.

What we can do is insist that this is a parting of the ways. The most likely eventual result is some sort of euro in a much smaller, fiscally united zone, centred on Germany, with France agonising about whether it can fit inside. Beyond it will be a wider ring, including ourselves, of non euro countries no longer agonising at all. We could fairly happily be part of a loose association of more than 30 countries called, say, the European Community, but we, and most others, would be out of any Union (Moore 2012).

Conversely, the *Guardian* featured voices promoting closer integration, including the ideas of a banking union and a fiscal union. Joseph Stiglitz, in a column mentioned earlier, outlined three possible solutions to the eurozone problems. The first was to engineer a decrease in wages in the peripheral countries to make their economies more competitive (the solution that had been implemented in the form of austerity and structural reforms) – an idea he rejected as being unfair and non-viable. The second was the division of the eurozone into two sub-regions. The third, the one he advocated, involved further integration: 'implement the institutional reforms, including the necessary fiscal framework, that should have been made when the euro was launched. It is not too late for Europe to implement these reforms and thus live up to the ideals, based on solidarity, that underlay the euro's creation' (Stiglitz 2010a).

The vision here is both a more successful, less crisis-prone Europe, and a more social Europe based on solidarity. Costas Lapavitsas evokes an even more social vision of Europe, though seeing the chances of attaining it as more remote than a people's Grexit, discussed above. This would aim for a 'good euro':

Several steps could be taken, for example, restoring some fiscal freedom to member states, expanding the European budget, instituting fiscal transfers from rich to poor, and introducing a minimum wage and unemployment insurance. The ECB might also be allowed to buy state debt. The 'good euro' relies on creating a radical cross-European political alliance, the prospects of which are slim. And it would probably weaken the international role of the euro (Lapavitsas 2010).

Both Stiglitz and Lapavitsas call for a reformed, social-democratic Europe, as opposed to the more radically neoliberal or ordoliberal one brought about by austerity and structural reforms. Lapavitsas proposes what might be termed a radical social-democratic vision, emphasising transfers of wealth from capital to labour (as opposed to the current transfers, which are flowing in the opposite direction) and more public control of certain industries, more democratic control over financial flows, and 'green growth'.

It should be remembered, though, that these kinds of discussions were extremely rare in the mainstream media, limited to Lapavitsas and a handful of other commentators in the *Guardian*. Most of the time, longer-term solutions are not debated at all. Long-term reform of the EU, be it through more or less integration, accounts for only 4.3 per cent of the possible solutions to the eurozone crisis mentioned. And of that 4.3 per cent, almost none of the discussions of EU reform includes reducing inequality. Bearing in mind the discussion of economic growth in Chapter 3, none of the eurozone reform options covered addresses the ecological limits of economic growth.

THINKING THE UNTHINKABLE: DEFAULT

The possibility of a country exiting the euro was inextricably tied to the idea of that country defaulting on its national debt. The news reports and opinion pieces that frame dropping out of the euro as a disaster to be avoided at all costs paint default in the same light. The following *Guardian* report on the bailout plan for Cyprus – which included a levy on people's bank deposits as well as austerity measures – is illustrative of this kind of narrative. It repeated the Cypriot president's view without providing a counterbalance:

President Nicos Anastasiades, only in his first weeks in office, warned of a catastrophe if the plan was not accepted as he came under intense pressure from the eurozone and European Central Bank to ensure the levy was enacted.

In a nationally televised speech, he said he was trying to amend a key provision of the bailout plan but he urged lawmakers to approve the tax in today's vote, saying it was essential to save the country from bankruptcy (Traynor 2013).

Of the coverage citing default as a possible response to the eurozone crisis, it was framed negatively, if not presented as catastrophic, 61 per cent of the time. Default was mentioned more or less neutrally 31.7 per cent of the time, and was only framed positively 7.3 per cent of the time – on three occasions, all in the *Guardian*. In September 2011, for example, Simon Jenkins, self-styled conservative voice of the *Guardian*, wrote:

Greece's bluffing of the high priests of the eurozone may, after all, be called. The unthinkable may be unavoidable. The priests are suddenly talking of 'when, not if,' Greece defaults. Greeks themselves seem to regard devaluation as a less painful discipline than state-imposed austerity, and are probably right (Jenkins 2011).

One of the comment pieces by Costas Lapavitsas advocates a controlled default, managed in such a way as to benefit the Greek people. It complements his idea of a 'people-led Grexit':

With the best interests of its people in mind, what should a government do? The first step would be to default, but without entrusting the process to bankers, the EU and the IMF ...

If default is to secure a deep cancellation of debt, it must be driven by Greece and it should be coercive as far as the banks are concerned. But it must also be democratic, based on an independent auditing of debt to ascertain how much might be illegitimate (Lapavitsas 2011).

This idea of a debt audit to determine whether some foreign debt is illegitimate suggests that, instead of complete default, some of the debt could be written off. The option of debt restructuring and partial debt relief got very little traction in the media, comprising only 4.9 per cent of the possible solutions mentioned to the eurozone crisis. Even then, it got virtually no attention until Syriza's referendum in July 2015 – very late in the day. Greek debt did actually undergo a major restructuring in March 2012. In fact, according to former Greek Finance Minister Yanis Varoufakis, it was the largest restructuring in the history of sovereign defaults (Greece was officially in default at this point but nobody wanted to mention it). Unfortunately, in the words of Varoufakis (2015), it 'was unique in economic history in that it left the indebted nation with a heavier debt burden at the end of 2012 than that which it was shouldering at the end of 2011!' (239).

In July 2015, with the anti-austerity Syriza Party leading the government, Greece called a referendum on its bailout conditions. It won a resounding victory, with 61 per cent voting no to more austerity. Syriza had hoped that this would push the creditors to renegotiate the terms of the bailout, and wanted debt-restructuring to be part of the negotiation. This option found support in the *Guardian*, especially from its economics editor, Larry Elliiott. It was covered entirely neutrally – simply as something Prime Minister Alexis Tsipras was demanding – in the other media, when at all. Just three days after winning the vote, Tsipras formally requested a new bailout and agreed terms more onerous than those rejected in the referendum, with debt relief off the table. Soon after, the IMF diverged from its EU partners and itself started advocating debt relief.

Lapavitsas' proposal in the quote above was much stronger than the debt relief requested by Tsipras. It did not centre on debt forgiveness, but on refusing to pay debts found to be illegitimate by a debt audit. Campaigns for a debt audit began after Greece was bailed out the first time, and in April 2015 the speaker of the Hellenic parliament launched the Truth Committee on Public Debt. It investigated to what extent Greece's debts were not only unsustainable, but illegal, illegitimate or odious – meaning that:

the lender knew or ought to have known that the debt was incurred in violation of democratic principles (including consent, participation, transparency and accountability), used against the best interests of the population of the borrower State, or is unconscionable and whose effect is to deny people their fundamental civil, political, economic, social and cultural rights (Lumina 2015).

The committee published its preliminary findings in 2015, concluding that:

Debt to the IMF should be considered illegal since its concession breached the IMF's own statutes, and its conditions breached the Greek Constitution, international customary law, and treaties to which Greece is a party. It is also illegitimate, since conditions included policy prescriptions that infringed human rights obligations. Finally, it is odious since the IMF knew that the imposed measures were undemocratic, ineffective, and would lead to serious violations of socio-economic rights.

Debts to the ECB should be considered illegal since the ECB over-stepped its mandate by imposing the application of macroeconomic adjustment programmes (e.g. labour market deregulation) via its participation in the Troika. Debts to the ECB are also illegitimate and odious, since the principal raison d'etre of the Securities Market Programme (SMP) was to serve the interests of the financial institutions, allowing the major European and Greek private banks to dispose of their Greek bonds (Truth Committee 2015: 4–5).

Overall, it found that the loans breached domestic and international law, their conditions infringed human rights, and that they were used against the interests of Greek citizens to benefit financial institutions. Moreover, the committee considered that 'Greece has been and still is the victim of an attack premeditated and organized by the International Monetary Fund, the European Central Bank, and the European Commission … aimed exclusively at shifting private debt onto the public sector' (5). The report concluded that Greece met conditions under which a sovereign state can exercise the right to a unilateral act of repudiation or suspension of the payment of debt under international law.

The Greek debt-repudiation campaigns have links with and draw heavily from earlier campaigns to abolish debt incurred by developing countries, often with the involvement of the IMF. Debt audits have been commissioned in Rwanda, the Democratic Republic of Congo, Brazil and Paraguay – albeit with little success (as is the case to date with the Greek audit). A more successful debt audit in Ecuador in 2008 encouraged President Correa to oblige creditors to accept a 70 per cent reduction of the debts concerned, which enabled an increase in social spending beginning in 2009–10 (Toussaint 2016).

There have been comparisons between Greece and Argentina in this regard. Between the beginning of its dictatorship in 1976 and 2001, Argentina repaid approximately $200 billion, nearly 25 times what it had owed in 1976. Under the auspices of the IMF, the Argentine government had imposed round after round of austerity measures, and had sought debt forgiveness from its creditors. Then, in 2001, amid mass social unrest, the Argentine authorities unilaterally suspended debt repayments amounting to $80 billion to private creditors and the Paris Club. Between 2003 and 2009, Argentina's annual economic growth was between 7 per cent and 9 per cent. This was in large part due to a rise in the prices of Argentina's raw-materials exports. However, the default allowed the increased income from exports to be used to aid the unemployed, raise pensions and extend retirement rights to everyone, and to stimulate economic activity in areas other than the export sector, rather than going to debt repayments. Between 2002 and 2005 the Argentine authorities negotiated a debt write-down, eventually leading to a reduction in the stock of debt of between 50 and 60 per cent (Toussaint 2016).

There have been debates about whether Greece could have successfully followed Argentina's path, for example between Paul Krugman (in the 'yes' camp) and Yanis Varoufakis (in the 'no' camp). Whichever side is right on this particular point, the discussions about debt and unilateral defaults are welcome. While on the surface they focus only on solving the immediate debt problems, they also provide an alternative way of viewing debt – as being relations of power between unequal people and entities – and grasp the historical and global dimensions of debt. These discussions occasionally make it into the *Guardian*. However, they remain peripheral and do not form part of the core media narratives on the crisis. Once again, the lack of historical and global context surface as key elements in the amnesiac coverage of the crisis.

RESISTANCE

There was widescale public resistance to the conditions attached to the bailouts, including strikes and mass street protests, in Greece and in the other eurozone countries affected by the bailout conditions. These were widely covered. Images of public demonstrations and confrontations with the police are a lot more exciting than those of charts representing economic statistics or officials in suits at summits. However, the coverage of resistance was almost entirely superficial. The BBC and the *Telegraph* could be accused of focusing disproportionately on violence – perpetrated by the protesters, that is, not the police. One piece warned that 'the spectre of something altogether more sinister than just the usual run of riots hovered over Greece – class war' (de Quetteville 2010). A *Telegraph* news report reassured readers that 'The violent protesters were eventually contained by police' (McElroy and Anast 2010). The *Guardian*, which was the only outlet to feature voices supportive of collective action, also contained pieces portraying the protesters as almost hysterically angry. One article talks of public-sector demonstrators 'screaming' slogans, and quotes one particularly angry participant:

> 'All of us are angry, very, very angry,' bellowed Stella Stamou, a civil servant standing on a street corner, screaming herself hoarse, a block away from where the bank had been set alight.
> 'You write that – angry, angry, angry, angry' (Smith 2010).

As well as being violent, another framing of Greek strikers was as juvenile. In the *Telegraph*, one commentator opined:

> Every conceivable ethnic stereotype has had a revival, some of them not very far from the truth. The Greeks really owe 40 billion euros in unpaid taxes, and despite this scandal, Greek tax collectors really are on strike. The firesale of Greek assets will run into the minor obstacle of, say, an overmanned and heavily unionised electricity industry threatening to switch off all the lights. No wonder a senior German politician has compared sorting out Greece with telling a recalcitrant child to tidy its bedroom (Burleigh 2011).

This kind of narrative presents collective action as part of the 'incorrigible Greeks' frame mentioned earlier, locating their tendency to strike as part of what makes the Greek people 'problematic'. Protest is thus framed as part of the problem rather than part of the solution.

Collective action was thus condemned occasionally – especially in the *Telegraph*. The *Guardian* did contain some supportive voices – featuring pro and anti views in about equal measure. Most often, however, protests and strikes were featured as a kind of constant background noise to the crisis, without explicit positive or negative views being given. Strikes and protests were thereby turned into spectacle. When protesters were quoted, it was mainly to demonstrate the extent of their anger, and not to explore their ideas in any depth.

In this way, the coverage of the protests fits into what media scholars have called the 'protest paradigm' (Chan and Lee 1984; Gitlin 1980; McLeod and Hertog 1999), whereby journalists focus on spectacle, tactics and drama, rather than exploring the underlying reasons for the protest or proposals for alternative policies advocated by the participants. Through turning resistance against austerity in the eurozone into a kind of spectacular background wallpaper, this kind of action was delegitimised. Other actions – such as workers taking over and running workplaces, community-run clinics, social movements linking farmers directly to urban consumers, education movements helping children driven into poverty continue to attend school, and student occupations (Corporate Watch 2014: 122–3) – received much less media attention.

The resistance of the Greek people to austerity and 'reform' was translated into increasing electoral success for Syriza, a political party that began as a coalition on the left. It promised to reverse austerity, resist privatisations and provide for those living in poverty. The UK media reacted to this with a mixture of concern and ridicule. Items in the *Telegraph* referred to them as 'far left', 'extreme left', 'radical elements' and 'neo Marxist oddballs', and described the 'idiocies of an extreme left-wing policy agenda'. A BBC reporter described Tsipras as a 'left-wing radical'. Even the *Guardian* contained items describing them as 'radical leftists' and 'leftist radicals' and fretted over the 'dangers posed by Syriza'. One piece expressing anxiety about the rise of populism even referred in the same breath to the 'far right' and the 'far left', turning parties promoting social democracy and parties promoting racial division into equivalents. This is all the more perplexing when we consider that in Greece the far right is represented by the neo-nazi Golden Dawn.

From the beginning, Syriza was depicted as threatening stability – and stability was uniformly assumed to be a good thing. The following view was contained in a *Guardian* news report without being balanced by an opposing view:

'If Syriza comes first, Europe should be very afraid . . . we would have chaos,' says Prof Kevin Featherstone, of the London School of Economics. 'There would be huge instability and uncertainty on international financial markets and frenzy (among EU leaders) with a government that is a loose coalition and lacking clarity of purpose being forced to make decisions' (Smith 2012).

Maria Kyriakidou and Iñaki Garcia-Blanco (2018) studied the coverage of Syriza in Greek newspapers and of Podemos – another left-wing anti-austerity party that had been gaining considerable electoral success in Spain – in Spanish papers. They found, in both cases, that the media drew on anti-populist discourses to present the parties as threats to domestic stability. In addition, particularly in the case of Podemos, they delegitimised the political agendas of the parties, by neglecting their policy proposals and by 'presenting both parties' discourses as purely emotional, vague, utopian, unrealistic, or impracticable'. The authors argue that by delegitimising these popular anti-austerity parties the media implicitly delegitimised anti-austerity views, and helped safeguard the status quo.

This goes for the UK coverage too. Interestingly, the *Guardian*'s coverage of Syriza foreshadows its treatment of Labour leader Jeremy Corbyn, discussed in the next chapter. The *Guardian* projects an image of representing a social-democratic agenda, but when social democrats begin to attain positions of power, the paper closes ranks.

EXPLAINING THE COVERAGE

The pattern of the coverage of the eurozone crisis was a large core of quite homogeneous, highly superficial, amnesiac content, with a handful of outliers offering alternative perspectives and in-depth analysis. This pattern is not dissimilar from that of the coverage of UK problems, but is more pronounced in the case of the eurozone. Why is this?

We can begin with the usual suspects of news values and the financial pressures on news organisations, explored in previous chapters. The causes of the eurozone crisis and the issues involved with its resolution are highly complex, in direct conflict with the news value of simplicity (Allan 2004: 206). Blaming profligacy and corruption, or simply not dealing with causes at all, is easier. Likewise, focusing on austerity and the social crisis it has created is both simpler and more dramatic than discussing complex possible long-term solutions. Most journalists probably did not themselves understand the crisis.

As we saw in Chapter 3, media critics have shown that news content has become more simplified during the past decades, due to the free-market restructuring of media industries in the neoliberal era. The crisis has itself had an impact on journalism, leading to more budget cuts and more precarious work. In Greece this has taken on an extreme form. In June 2013, the government shut down the public broadcaster in a voluntary act to please its creditors. Six months of 'pirate' broadcasting followed as the airwaves were taken over by media workers, who were eventually evicted by riot police. This led to Greece losing 17 points in press freedom rankings compiled by independent watchdog Freedom House (Corporate Watch 2014: 69).

Another key point is that most reporting relied on official sources – German politicians, officials from EU institutions, and politicians from other countries as well as UK politicians. Of all sources cited, 54.5 per cent were politicians or other officials when it came to the coverage of the euro crisis. This is a slightly higher percentage than for the sample as a whole (50.9 per cent). Until Syriza and Podemos came along, they were all saying similar things, and the media simply 'retweeted' their narratives. When Syriza and Podemos did start succeeding in challenging the status quo, the full might of the establishment came down on them, and the mainstream media reproduced messages about the threat these parties posed to stability.

US media scholar Daniel Hallin (1986; 1994) argues that when mainstream media do offer multiple perspectives, it is usually because there is disagreement within the political establishment, and that is reflected in the coverage. When there is little dissent among the political establishment, a unified elite viewpoint will dominate the coverage. Hallin theorises three media 'spheres': the sphere of consensus, the sphere of legitimate dissent, and the sphere of deviance. Fascinatingly, Syriza, even when it was leading the Greek government, was still framed as deviant. According to Greek media scholars, while Syriza was holding out against austerity – even after it had come to power – the Greek media, which is owned by oligarchs, ran a smear campaign against it. Once the party capitulated to austerity in July 2015, the Greek media stopped giving it flak. There is thus a two-way dynamic between the media and politics – the media will amplify the messages of politicians, but can also punish and discipline them if they are seen as too 'deviant'.

The reliance on official sources helps explain all three elements of media amnesia. It means a narrow range of elite views dominates the coverage. These sources deliberately omit reference to the causes of the crisis to aid their own (austerity and reform) agendas. And they certainly don't want to remember the use of debt and the imposition of austerity on developing countries by one of the Troika institutions, or the struggles of those countries to repudiate that debt.

A related issue is the political nature of the media. While British media and politics are deeply interwoven, British journalists are not so embroiled in eurozone politics. On the one hand, this probably added to the homogeneity of much of the content, since there was less political side-taking from the press, and, because there was little meaningful dissent within the European establishment, less need for balance from the BBC. This would help explain, for example, why the *Mirror* defended the public sector in the UK but not in the eurozone. On the other hand, it could be that the distance between UK journalism and the eurozone crisis was also behind the outlying pieces that did give alternative perspectives. Journalists and editors may have felt freer to feature ideas that did not come from mainstream politicians and were not usually found in the media – such as those of heterodox economists Costas Lapavitsas and Jayati Ghosh, for example.

One of the most politicised aspects of the eurozone crisis in the UK coverage revolved around euroscepticism versus europhilia. In the case of the *Telegraph* especially, the eurosceptic position can be linked to some coverage that is less amnesiac, and that remembers the origins of the crisis in the structure of the monetary union and the undemocratic nature of the European Union. Interestingly there are two contradictory thrusts of the right-wing press, one that paints the peripheral countries as victims of a dictatorial European regime and one that paints them as lazy cheats and scroungers, and supports austerity. Thus, we find again that it is the economic and political contexts in which media outlets operate, and the everyday routines of news production, that are behind both media amnesia and its opposite, in-depth and pluralistic coverage.

CONCLUSION

The media's coverage of the eurozone crisis was highly amnesiac, forgetting its origins in the financial crash just months previously, and their own prolific coverage of those events. In most cases, causation was omitted altogether. In other cases, blame was shifted on to profligate and corrupt states, using cultural stereotypes about their citizens. With coverage such as this, at a time when 'fake news' is in the limelight, we can ask where the line is drawn between 'fake news' and 'real news'. Although support for austerity in the right-wing press was less gung-ho than in the UK, and the *Guardian* featured a substantial amount of criticism, the logic of austerity was mostly accepted across the board and some degree of austerity was framed as being 'painful but necessary'. Discussion of solutions was mostly confined to the bailouts and austerity, cutting off reflection about possible alternative social arrangements that would not involve structural crises and suffering. On the other hand, a minority of pieces did remember the immediate and deeper causes of the euro crisis and did explore other possible responses. Elite disagreement about Britain's place in the EU led to debates around Grexit and Brexit, and deeper integration or the possible disintegration of the EU. These, however, tended not to reflect too deeply on what reformed European societies would or should look like. A tiny minority of pieces did situate the crisis within the wider neoliberal context, offering 'people-led' solutions.

The Greek crisis goes on and on. European banks continue to threaten financial stability. The eurozone crisis, in combination with the refugee crisis, has led to political turmoil across Europe and the rise of extreme-right political parties. Immigrants are being blamed for low wages and the squeeze on resources, and globalisation is being reframed as victimising the white populations of rich countries – with the help of some serious media amnesia (see Chapter 3). Britain has voted in a referendum to leave the EU, on a largely anti-immigration ticket. At the time of writing, far-right parties, though not winning the electoral success they had hoped for, are increasingly setting the political agenda in the Netherlands, France, Germany and other core European countries. Meanwhile, the ultra-conservative governments of Hungary and Poland have been accused of eroding media and political freedoms. Again, 'fake news' is being blamed for their successes. We must also ask what role 'real', mainstream news is playing – as we do in the next chapter, on the coverage of rising inequality and poverty in the UK.

5
Inequality

Inequality has been making a comeback lately. Thomas Piketty's book on inequality, *Capital in the Twenty-first Century*, was a *New York Times* bestseller, with the dubious distinction of being one of the most bought and least read books on Amazon in 2014 (Wile 2014). In recent years, the IMF, the OECD and the World Economic Forum (WEF) have all put inequality high on their agendas. Some might find this ironic, as these organisations are associated by many with the neoliberal reforms that created a trend of rising inequality of both wealth and income within countries and globally since the 1970s.

As we have seen, the financial crisis of 2008 was in many ways a crisis of neoliberalism. The reforms that national and international authorities had pursued – cutting back social spending, privatising resources, attacking labour unions, deregulating financial, labour and other markets, opening up national economies to foreign investment – led to a situation of falling real wages, rising debt, 'global imbalances', ballooning finance sectors and complex financial products and, eventually, crisis. This restructuring of capitalism resulted in rising inequality. Inequality graphs often follow u-shaped curves, with inequality falling from very high levels at the start of the twentieth century and then rising again from the 1970s (see Sayer 2015: 3–4). Indeed, for many scholars of political economy, the restructuring was precisely *intended* to have this effect, to transfer resources from labour to capital and restore profitability.

Since the onset of the crisis, rather than trying to row back on these trends, many governments and international bodies have escalated neoliberal reforms, through austerity and business-friendly supply-side measures such as tax cuts for corporations and the wealthy, further deregulation and privatisation. Accordingly, inequality is growing apace. In 2017, Oxfam reported that eight men owned as much wealth as the poorest 50 per cent of the global population. In the UK, the Resolution Foundation think tank projects that the poorest quarter of working-age households will be around 5–15 per cent worse off in 2020–21 than in

2017. In contrast, the highest income quarter is predicted to rise by 4–5 per cent (Corlett and Clarke 2017).

Before the crisis, rising inequality had been accompanied by the idea that inequality was nothing to worry about, as long as there was economic growth – that 'a rising tide carries all boats'. This was famously encapsulated in Britain by New Labour politician Peter Mandelson's statement that he was 'intensely relaxed about people getting filthy rich as long as they pay their taxes'. However, when, after 2008, people saw their living standards fall while those responsible for the crisis appeared to be faring no worse – indeed, even benefitting – inequality reappeared on the agenda, along with the related issues of living standards and poverty. According to the Resolution Foundation, the UK has seen 'one of the longest and deepest squeezes on household incomes in living memory' (Whittaker *et al.* 2016). A report published in 2016 by the Institute for Fiscal Studies (IFS) showed that living standards, measured in terms of household income, had finally passed their pre-recession levels. However, average gross employment income was still lower than prior to the recession, and living standards had still not recovered for 22–30-year-olds (Belfried *et al.* 2016).

These circumstances have driven some into poverty. More than a million people now use food banks in the UK (Trussell Trust 2017). There has also been an important shift in the composition of poverty, with an increase in in-work poverty. The IFS projects that by 2020 as many as one in four children in the UK will be living in poverty (Hood and Waters 2017).

Once again, news coverage of living standards, poverty and inequality has been characterised by acute media amnesia. Explanations, though rightly paying attention to the role of austerity and low wages, rarely stretch back to the financial crisis, never mind to the longer-term causes of the crisis – the dynamics that have given rise to higher inequality levels and falling real wages since the 1970s. Solutions canvassed tend to revolve around tax cuts on the one hand and progressive tax rises and closing tax havens on the other. Raising wages through the 'living wage' and controlling energy prices are also mentioned. The problems of living standards, poverty and inequality are addressed far more frequently in the left-leaning press than the BBC news or the conservative papers. The right-wing press, when they do cover these issues, sometimes blame those living in poverty for their problems, following a long media tradition of scapegoating the poor. Meanwhile, Jeremy Corbyn, who won the Labour leadership contest in 2015 after putting inequality at the heart of his campaign, has received continual flak from media across the board.

MEDIA AMNESIA, AGAIN

Falling living standards, poverty and inequality began to attract attention in the media from 2011, as UK household incomes fell steeply in the wake of the financial crisis. If we think back to Chapter 1, the soup kitchens that were evoked during the 2008 crash as a dystopian fantasy by the likes of former mayor of London Boris Johnson had become a reality for many. It is striking, though, that these issues received far less attention than other aspects of the crisis, and that attention was overwhelmingly from the *Guardian* and the *Mirror*. Only 53 media items out of the sample of 1,133 focused primarily on living standards, poverty or inequality (though those focusing mainly on Britain's weak economic growth did also sometimes discuss living standards as well). Of these, 21 were from the *Guardian*, 18 from the *Mirror*, 9 from the *Telegraph* and only 3 each from the *Sun* and the BBC. Other studies have also found a relative lack of media attention to these issues (Golding and Middleton 1982; Redden 2011). Possible reasons for this will be explored later in this chapter.

Unlike other aspects of the crisis, for which explanations were often entirely absent, explanations for the problems of falling living standards, poverty and inequality were given in 83.3 per cent of the 53 media items – which is a relief. However, these explanations tended to be highly superficial. A trio of causes was most frequently cited for all three issues: a combination of austerity, falling or low wages and rising prices. In one of a series of articles on 'real Britain' in the *Mirror*, following individuals suffering under austerity, the reporter explains,

> As Tory-led spending cuts combine with rising food prices, fuel bills and record increases in public transport fares, tales like Linda's are increasingly common ... The jobless rate now stands at 7.9 per cent of the workforce. And many of those in work are enduring wage freezes, so poverty is claiming new victims daily who are both employed and unemployed (*Mirror* 2011).

A later article in the *Guardian* on an Oxfam report on UK poverty and inequality – which highlights the fact that the majority of those in poverty are in work – gives similar reasons:

> Oxfam said that for the first time more working households were in poverty than non-working ones, and predicted that the number of children living below the poverty line could increase by 800,000 by 2020. It said cuts to social security and public services were meshing with falling real incomes and a rising cost of living to create a 'deeply damaging situation' in which millions were struggling to get by (Elliott 2014).

The *Telegraph*, meanwhile, tellingly left austerity out in this report on falling living standards:

> HOUSEHOLDS face falling standards of living for at least another two years as rising prices outstrip wage increases, the Government's official economic forecaster has warned. Inflation will exceed expected salary increases until the middle of 2013, more than five years after the onset of the recession, figures from the independent Office for Budget Responsibility (OBR) suggest (Winnet *et al.* 2011).

BBC news, in one of its three segments on these issues, stated explicitly that austerity was *not* a cause of falling living standards.

In terms of the top end of wealth distribution, explanations are very oblique indeed. The *Guardian* piece on UK wealth inequality reports that five individuals own as much as the poorest 20 per cent. We are told that 'Since the mid-1990s, the incomes of the top 0.1 per cent have grown by £461 a week or £24,000 a year. By contrast, the bottom 90 per cent have seen a real terms increase of only £2.82 a week or £147 a year.' As to why the 0.1 per cent have seen such gains, we are simply told that it is due to 'the ability of the better off to capture the lion's share of the proceeds of growth' (Elliott 2014).

These explanations seem eerily superficial, often failing even to reach back a few years to the 2008 financial crisis, never mind getting to the deeper causes. Again, we see that the timeline of the crisis is being erased. Austerity is the most frequently-cited explanation for the problems of living standards, poverty and inequality, making up 27.6 per cent of all the causes mentioned. But why are we living in an age of austerity? The downturn is the fourth most cited explanation (after austerity, falling wages and rising prices), comprising 8.6 per cent of the explanations. And why is the economy so weak? The financial crisis accounts for only 3.8 per cent of the explanations. And as for the causes of the financial crisis in turn, the bankers-behaving-badly narrative represents only 2.9 per cent of the explanations, the systemic problems with the financial sector are not mentioned at all, and the deeper explanations situating the problems within the context of the neoliberal era comprise only 1.9 per cent of explanations – cited on only two occasions.

HYPER-AMNESIA

Not only does the coverage fail to contextualise the problems in terms of the financial crisis and its origins, it often neglects to contextualise them in terms of policies governments have been pursuing *since* the crisis. News reports rightly identify austerity as impacting living standards. Austerity is a serious business. According to 2015 figures, the UK government has implemented £35 billion of spending cuts so far (Gentleman 2015). Real spending on public services has fallen by 10 per cent since 2009–10 – by far the longest and biggest fall in public service spending on record (Emmerson *et al.* 2017). Councils have seen 40 per cent reductions in their funding. Changes to the benefit system mean spending in 2015–16 was £16.7 billion (7 per cent) lower than it would otherwise have been (Hood and Phillips 2015). The government is planning a further £12 billion reduction in working-age benefits. A further £12 billion is expected to be cut from day-to-day spending by central government on the delivery and administration of public services by 2020 (Emmerson *et al.* 2017).

While focusing on austerity, media coverage fails to identify the other policies that Britain and other states have pursued to tackle the crisis – such as bank bailouts, quantitative easing and business-friendly supply-side measures. Andrew Sayer writes that *'The bailout is itself a huge transfer of wealth from the majority of society to those at the top'* (Sayer 2015: 231, original italics). He shows that executive pay and bonuses have continued to rise – 'indeed soar' – since the 2008 crash. In 2011–12 the pay and benefits of business executives in the top FTSE 100 companies rose by 27 per cent to an average of £4 million each. Bank bonuses, briefly a tabloid bugbear but now fading from memory, also rose after the crash (Sayer 2015: 219–20). Meanwhile, quantitative easing (QE), pursued by the major central banks, has pumped vast sums of money into the financial sector – $12.3 trillion globally, according to a CNBC report (Cox 2016). Economists at the ratings agency S&P have found that QE has 'exacerbated' the already widening gap between the rich and the poor in the UK (*Financial Times* 2016a), boosting the value of financial assets, which are owned predominantly by the wealthiest 10 per cent of UK households, and house prices themselves, increasing the gap between those who own property and those who don't.

The pro-business supply-side measures that have been adopted around the world, ostensibly to stimulate the flagging economy (see Chapter 3), are barely mentioned as an explanation for increasing inequality in the sampled media items, though they are occasionally referred to in passing. However, Oxfam (2014b) has identified what it calls 'market fundamentalism' as one of the primary drivers of global inequality, citing deregulation, privatisation and reducing taxes on the rich, as well as cutting social spending, as contributing to inequality. The British Labour Party have calculated that by 2022, the government's planned tax changes will have handed the richest more than £70 billion (Labour Press 2017). Thus, apart from the (important) factor of austerity, media amnesia has led to the obfuscation of even the most immediate contributors to inequality – the policies pursued to deal with the economic crisis since 2008 – never mind the deeper causes.

There are rare occasions where longer-term explanations are given. Kevin Maguire writes in the *Mirror*: 'Dismantling public services is shrinking permanently a state – hospitals, schools, prisons, armed forces – we rely on under political cover of reducing a deficit created by greedy banksters' (Maguire 2014), recalling the deficit, the banking crisis and the 'greedy banksters' responsible for it. Other items – a minority – gesture towards different aspects of neoliberalism. For instance, Polly Toynbee, in one of her *Guardian* columns, alludes to Thatcherism: 'Britain never recovered from the social damage done by the Thatcher years. Now yet again, wealth and income is syphoned up from the have-nots to the already-haves, with fortunes more segregated by gender, age, race, region and above all by social class at birth' (Toynbee 2012a).

Other pieces mention labour-market deregulation and the dismantling of workers' movements that have been central to neoliberalisation and its attendant low wages. The *Guardian*'s economics editor Larry Elliott quotes an Oxfam report mentioning that the UK has weaker worker protection than Mexico. An item in the *Mirror* refers to recent attacks on unions as well as public-sector pay cuts: 'He [Chancellor George Osborne] weakens workers' ability to secure higher pay to compensate for lost tax credits by shackling trade unions. Instead of improving pay for nurses, teachers and council staff he freezes or reduces the value of earnings. If you ever hear Osborne tell the time it would be best to look at your own watch' (Maguire 2015). Maguire here is referring to the Trade Union Act, which became law in 2016 and limits the right of unions to take industrial action, building on the restrictions imposed on trade unions in Britain under Margaret Thatcher.

If we piece together bits and pieces from the different media items, we can therefore begin to get a picture of rising inequality and falling living standards caused by crisis policies – austerity, deregulation, attacks on unions – that stretch back to the 1980s and Thatcher. As we have seen, post-2008 crisis policies can be seen as escalating the trends associated with neoliberalism – cutting the social state, deregulation, privatisation, attacks on workers' movements, tax cuts for the wealthiest – that helped cause the crisis in the first place. They have been legitimised partly through media amnesia. Now we see that their effects have been to continue the transfer of resources upwards that began with the onset of the neoliberal era. However, media amnesia has meant that the role of most of these policies in the transfer has gone largely unacknowledged. The shallowness of the explanations is linked to two of the three main features of media amnesia explored throughout this book: the lack of historical context, and the narrow range of (usually elite) views shaping media coverage.

INEQUALITY IS A CLASS ISSUE

Formulating rising inequality as a redistribution of wealth from 'the have-nots to the already-haves' in Polly Toynbee's words, reveals that inequality is a class issue. This might seem too obvious to mention, but the degree to which media reporting fails to mention class in its coverage of inequality makes it necessary to point this out. Indeed, in some ways, talking about inequality seems to be a substitute for talking about class. Andrew Sayer (2015) notes that for the past 35 years, wealth and power have shifted towards the rich, who through their increasing control of resources are able to 'siphon off wealth that others produce' (20).

John Smith foregrounds the class dimension by showing what share of national income goes to labour in the form of wages and what share goes to the owners of capital. The wage share has steadily declined over the past decades in rich and poor countries alike. Correspondingly, the share going to capital has increased. In its *Global Wage Report 2008–9*, the International Labour Organisation (ILO) found that, since the 1970s, 'in Europe, the change is enormous: labor's share of aggregate income has declined as much as ten percentage points of GDP' (quoted in Smith 2016: 149). And these figures mask another important fact: that income inequality has also increased, especially in the US and the UK. The wage share includes 'super wages' like the CEO remuneration and bankers' bonuses discussed above. One study in the US found that between 1980 and 2011, a decline of 3.9 per cent in the share of national income of all employees became a 10 per cent decline when the highest-paid 1 per cent of employees was excluded and a 14 per cent decline when the highest-paid 10 per cent was excluded (quoted in Smith 2016: 148).

This brings us back to the struggles waged against workers during the neoliberal period, and resulting precarity of work and falling or stagnating wages. In the UK, according to a report in the *Guardian*, 22.2 per cent of workers were subject to precarious employment in 2016, up from 18.1 per cent in 2006. 750,000 more people were on zero-hours contracts (Booth 2016). Smith writes:

> Nothing could be less mysterious or surprising than the fall in labor's share of income in the neoliberal era. This dramatic trend reflects the change in the balance of class forces to the detriment of the producers of wealth resulting from neoliberalism, the economic/political counter-revolution that eviscerated labor unions, drove the informalization and flexibalization of labor, mobilized armies of police and soldiers to restrict the international mobility of workers as it removed obstacles to the international mobility of capital (Smith 2016: 152).

Coverage of inequality rarely discusses the wage share or foregrounds the class nature of inequality, though certain columnists in the *Guardian* such as Zoe Williams and Seumas Milne make the important point that rising inequality has involved a *transfer* of wealth upwards. Certain pieces in the *Mirror* (particularly those by Kevin Maguire) also adopt the tone and language of class struggle. They frequently refer to how wealthy members of the government are, in order to paint the Conservative Party as the party of millionaires: 'Osborne's capitalism is the language of priorities. This Trust Fund Tory – the personal beneficiary of a fortune he never earned, with the title of "Sir George" to come – looks after his own at the cost of the overwhelming majority' (Maguire 2015).

The *Telegraph*, meanwhile, interestingly both reveals and conceals its class allegiances by focusing its coverage not on inequality but on the 'squeezed middle':

> The predicted squeeze is far worse than ministers had previously signalled. A typical middle class family will see their disposable income fall by more than £1,500 this year ...
>
> From next month, anyone earning more than £45,000 also faces tax rises as National Insurance is increased and higher earners will see more of their salaries being taxed at the higher rate (Winnett *et al.* 2011).

As the *Guardian*'s Polly Toynbee regularly points out, the labelling of those earning over £45,000 as 'middle class' is misleading, since the median income for the UK is £26,000. This is a distortion of the picture of class, attempting to turn the concerns of the wealthy into those of people in the middle of the social spectrum. For cultural theorist Stuart Hall, this glossing over of class divisions had been a common feature of journalism in recent decades. 'The nation' is presented as a unified entity, with the interests of national capital presented as the interests of everyone (Hall *et al.* 1978). This conceals both the divergence of interests within countries and the alignment of class interests across national borders.

PRODUCTIVITY AND BUSINESS INVESTMENT

Another piece in the puzzle of low wages is low productivity. This was barely mentioned in the sampled media coverage: in the entire sample, it was cited as a cause of any of the economic problems only twice. However, in finance pages and specialist publications it receives regular attention. In a comments piece from 2015, the *Guardian*'s Heather Stewart referred to Britain's 'woefully weak productivity record'. She continued,

> Rising productivity – the amount of output each worker produces – is the key to generating sustainable economic growth and higher living standards.
>
> But while the UK economy has been creating jobs at the rate of more than 100,000 a quarter, allowing Osborne to claim that 'Britain

is working', the fact is these workers are producing far less – and so being paid much less generously – than economists would predict (Stewart 2015).

Mainstream economics holds that labour productivity determines pay. Labour productivity is usually defined as the output produced per worker or worker hour. Increased productivity means less labour for more output. In theory, higher productivity means a higher rate of profit, which means companies can pay their workers more. Britain has a particular problem with low productivity, but in recent years falling productivity growth has been observed in several major economies (see Roberts 2017).

Missing from Heather Stewart's piece is *why* UK productivity is low. Seumas Milne, in another article in the *Guardian* from 2014, gives one of the most comprehensive explanations for low pay in Britain. He begins by setting out the extent of precarious employment and linking it to low productivity:

> Four out of five jobs created under Osborne have been in sectors where average wages are less than a quarter of average earnings. Just under 80 per cent are in London and most are involuntary part-time, zero hours or enforced self-employed: the flexible labour market in action.
>
> That's one reason real earnings have fallen continuously for four years, the longest decline in living standards since the 1870s. Behind that lies the slump in British productivity. While the productivity of other advanced economies has bounced back since the crash, Britain's has stagnated as employers have switched to low-wage, low-skilled labour, rather than invest to raise output and efficiency (Milne 2014).

Milne thus ultimately traces low wages back to a lack of investment by private firms:

> That failure to invest is what lies behind the 'productivity puzzle', the fall in real wages and the feebleness of Osborne's much acclaimed recovery. Low investment has long been the Achilles heel of the British economy, running far behind other comparable economies. But the collapse in private-sector investment has been by far the greatest factor in the crisis of the past six years and is still 15 per cent down in real terms.

Meanwhile, UK corporations are sitting on a £750bn cash mountain, while paying out a record £65bn in shareholder dividends last year. Small- and medium-sized businesses still face a credit squeeze seven years after the start of the crisis, and public investment is down 35 per cent on pre-crash levels (Milne 2014).

Milne therefore takes us back to the issues of business investment and share buybacks, discussed in Chapter 3. He explains that a lack of private investment in training and equipment has led to low productivity, which has in turn led to low wages. At the same time, the lack of worker protection has allowed companies to rely on 'low-waged, low-skilled labour' rather than invest to increase efficiency. Thus low wages appear to be both cause and effect of low business investment.

In the entire sample of media items, low business investment is cited only three times as a cause of any of the economic problems.

THE GLOBAL DIVISION OF LABOUR

In Chapter 3 we saw that one other factor behind the lack of business investment was the outsourcing of production to much lower-waged countries – i.e. globalisation. Interestingly, globalisation was not mentioned as a reason for low wages in the sample. It seems it only entered the spotlight in 2016, with Brexit and particularly the election of Donald Trump in the US. Those momentous events have led to public discussions about the extent to which outsourcing has led to lower wages in rich countries. While publics appear to have voted for protectionism, believing that they have lost out to workers in China and elsewhere, some economists have argued that rich-country job losses are more attributable to technology advancements and automation – discussed in the next section – than globalisation.

Public debates about globalisation and low pay tend to revolve around the effects on workers in rich countries, rather than the effects of globalisation globally. Political economist John Smith examines wages and inequality globally. He sets out many problems associated with gathering and comparing this kind of data. However, he argues that there is extensive evidence to support the theory that outsourcing has exerted a downward pull on rich-country pay, reflected in the decline in the wage share discussed above (Smith 2016: 153–4). But he also finds that the wage share (the share of national income going to workers as wages) in emerging and developing countries has fallen even more than in rich countries. The ILO found that Asia's wage share decreased by around 20 per cent between 1994 and 2010. In China, the wage share had declined by 10 percentage points since 2000. In Africa the wage share declined by 15 per cent between 1990 and 2010. The most gradual decline was in Latin America, where the wage share had fallen by 10 per cent since 1993 (Smith 2016: 148).

As seen above, not only is labour's share of income declining, this share is itself being distributed more unequally. Wage inequality has widened, as the wages of high-skilled workers have increased while those of low-skilled workers have grown more slowly, stagnated or declined. This is the case in the UK, the US and across much of the developed world. But again, the trend is even more pronounced in emerging and developing countries. According to the ILO, 'on average, wage inequality is higher in countries with a lower GDP per capita' (Smith 2016: 156). Smith deconstructs the common theory that pay and living standards between richer and poorer countries will 'converge' as the poorer countries 'catch up'. If the wage share in developing countries is falling, and that share is itself distributed more unequally, catching up is unlikely, especially since the economic growth experienced by those countries appears to be slowing down.

Smith also shows that the low wages in emerging and developing countries are *not* due to low labour productivity in those places, describing a 'high degree of autonomy of wages from productivity' (Smith 2016: 167). This is contrary to mainstream economic theory. Rather, for Smith, low wages in those regions are a result of a combination of a large supply of surplus labour, as globalisation has brought more people into the formal labour market, and the suppression of international labour mobility through immigration controls (while capital is not subject to such controls) (Smith 2016: 171).

In addition, in emerging and developing countries the wage share takes a big hit during economic crises – which have been frequent in the neoliberal era. These crises have been opportunities for governments, firms and international bodies such as the IMF to apply what Naomi Klein (2008) calls the shock doctrine: 'southern governments were brought to heel, trade unions broken, and labor protection swept away, breaking resistance to downwardly mobile wages' (Smith 2016: 162). The ILO found, for 83 developed and developing nations between 1995 and 2006, that during times of GDP growth, real wages rose by only 0.65 per cent for every 1 per cent rise in per capita GDP. But during periods of negative growth, real wages declined by more than 1.5 per cent for each 1 per cent decline in GDP. One World Bank economist described 'the transfer of assets away from Labour during the crisis period' as 'staggering ... the world average is 33.7 per cent of GDP per financial crisis' (quoted in Smith 2016: 162–3).

Defenders of modern globalisation argue that, while inequality within nations is increasing, and global inequality in the sense of the gap between the richest and poorest in the world is widening, relative inequality *between* countries is narrowing. However, these claims are also disputable, especially given the high and increasing levels of wage inequality within countries. One study tried to get round this by analysing international wage differentials *within occupations* in the periods 1983–9 and 1992–9. The researchers concluded that 'Inequality of wages across countries in the same occupation increased over this period despite globalisation, which should have reduced inequality' (quoted in Smith 2016: 158). Others argue that apparent reductions in inequality between countries all but disappear when China is taken out of the equation. The same goes for the claim that globalisation has taken millions out of absolute poverty.

Inequality is therefore not just a class issue, it is a global class issue. Understanding inequality means understanding the global dynamics of capitalism, and the power relations that exist between and across countries. Although headline figures about global inequality occasionally make it into the news, the vast majority of the sample focused exclusively on the UK. Of the media items with a primary focus on poverty, living standards and inequality, only 3.8 per cent mentioned emerging and developing countries. Moreover, 81.5 per cent of the items failed to give any global context to the UK problems.

THE ROBOTS ARE COMING

Productivity growth can mean higher wages, but it can also mean fewer jobs. There have been warnings lately that we are in the midst of a 'fourth industrial revolution' based around robotics and artificial intelligence (AI). The Bank of England's chief economist Andrew Haldane (2015) has claimed that over time, 15 million jobs in the UK could be automated. Research by Citi and Oxford University estimated that 57 per cent of jobs across the OECD are at risk of automation. Machines now substitute not only manual human tasks but cognitive ones too, with mid-skill jobs increasingly at risk. In this sense, productivity growth can increase rather than decrease inequality, with unemployment or under-employment for many while wages for skilled work explode. Moreover, automation could also lead to an even more dramatic fall in labour's share of national income, as the profits created by robots are taken by their owners. Bank of England Governor Mark Carney has said that Britain is facing 'the first lost decade since the 1860s' when 'Karl Marx was scribbling in the British Library' (Giles 2016). For Carney, a com-bination of globalisation and automation is leading people in the rich countries to abandon ideas of free trade and open societies.

There appears to be a paradox at work here. On the one hand, economists are worried about low productivity leading to low pay and rising inequality. On the other hand, they worry about soaring produc-tivity resulting in the same things. Nick Srnicek and Alex Williams, in *Inventing the Future,* try to resolve this contradiction. They explain that roboticisation is gathering steam, for example with 150,000 profes-sional service robots sold in the past fifteen years (Srnicek and Williams 2015: 110). However, it has yet to reach its full potential. Out of the US companies that could benefit from incorporating industrial robots, less than 10 per cent have done so (112). The reason given for this is that low wages are repressing investment in productivity-enhancing technol-ogies: 'why purchase new machines when cheaper workers will do the same for less?' Again, low wages appear to be both a cause and a conse-quence of low productivity growth.

Automation was not given at all as an explanation for inequality, depressed living standards or poverty in the sample for this study. However, it does now seem to be gaining traction in the media. Yet, no major political party has so far dared to take on this medium-term problem – a problem at the heart of capitalism itself. Karl Marx (1990) predicted that capitalism's productivity gains would eventually make its system of wage labour obsolete. Paul Mason offers an updated version of this idea in *Postcapitalism* (2015). Again, the lack of sustained media attention to these issues is linked to the narrow range of opinions on offer. News content tends to be structured by the actions and statements of those occupying the corridors of political power, and they have little to say on this issue.

DEATH AND TAXES

Interestingly, while explanations are given more frequently for the problems associated with falling living standards, poverty and inequality than for the other economic problems explored here, solutions are offered relatively less frequently. In 24.5 per cent of the items focusing primarily on these issues, no possible solutions are mentioned. For the sample as a whole, the figure is 9.4 per cent. Puzzlingly, although austerity is the most cited cause of the problems, the option of partially reversing or ending austerity was only mentioned five times, mainly in the *Mirror*. Reversing austerity completely was never mentioned. Solutions addressing the financial sector were mentioned only twice. As will be seen, though, solutions that do address some of the other problematic aspects of neo-liberalism – especially the deregulation of the labour market – have by contrast made it into the news.

The most frequently mentioned solution was tax cuts for the general population (as opposed to tax cuts for the wealthy, discussed in Chapter 3). This made up 19.1 per cent of all the possible solutions to the problems of living standards, poverty and inequality mentioned, and was endorsed in the *Sun*, the *Mirror* and especially the *Telegraph*. As shown in Table 2.3, tax cuts for the general population were also a popular solution to all the aspects of the crisis combined in all the outlets. For the sample as a whole, it was the sixth most frequently mentioned possible response, and was endorsed 25 times more frequently than it was rejected. These measures included the rise in the tax-free personal allowance brought in by the coalition government, and a freeze in fuel duty and cuts in alcohol duty also brought in by the coalition. Labour under Ed Miliband also advocated tax cuts, such as a cut in business rates for small firms and a lower starting rate for income tax.

Conversely, tax *rises* on the wealthy comprised 10.9 per cent of all the possible responses – the third largest category. This option was endorsed in the *Mirror* and the *Guardian*, but not even mentioned in the *Telegraph*, the *Sun* or BBC news. As seen in Chapter 2, for the sample as a whole and as a response to the UK deficit, this option was strongly rejected in the *Telegraph* and the *Sun*. In the *Guardian*, Polly Toynbee quotes the Secretary General of the OECD, Angel Gurria, who she points out 'is not some socialist ideologue, but the head of a historically conservative organisation that traditionally preaches free markets and state austerity':

Gurria calls for 'top marginal taxes to be raised and the role of taxes on all forms of property and wealth to be reassessed'. The money is needed for 'high quality public services, such as education, health and family care' (Toynbee 2012a).

Other items in the *Guardian* also (fleetingly) mentioned Oxfam's proposal of a wealth tax and a financial transaction tax, claiming the latter could raise £20 billion in Britain alone (Elliott 2014).

These kinds of progressive tax proposals are attracting more serious attention, even from free-market institutions like the OECD. The 2017 Oxfam report on global inequality cites the IMF as advocating top income-tax rates of between 50 per cent and 70 per cent. A figure of 60 per cent has been recommended for the UK. Thomas Piketty (2014) proposes a *global* wealth tax (though he admits it does not look very politically viable). Developing this concept, Oxfam (2017b) calculates that a 1.5 per cent tax on wealth in excess of $1 billion would raise $70 billion a year (33). Andrew Sayer advocates strong capital gains and progressive property taxes, pointing out that the largest fortunes tend to grow at 6–7 per cent every year. Sayer also proposes a tax on inheritances over £20,000 or £50,000. On Piketty's global wealth tax idea, Sayer writes, 'talk of global taxes may make you think "in your dreams" but the nightmares of global warming and the growing power of the plutocracy are already reality … radical responses are necessary' (Sayer 2015: 357). These kinds of options, however, are not yet attracting sustained or widespread media attention.

TAX HAVENS

The (illegal) evasion or (legal) avoidance of tax through offshore tax havens periodically becomes a hot-button issue, though tackling tax avoidance or evasion only accounts for 5.5 per cent of possible solutions mentioned in the sampled items on living standards, poverty or inequality. Again, this option was endorsed in the *Mirror* and the *Guardian* but not mentioned in the other outlets. For the full sample covering all the aspects of the crisis, this option comprised only 1.6 per cent of the possible solutions mentioned. Both the government and the Labour opposition have promised to clamp down on tax havens, and Jeremy Corbyn has tried to put this high on Labour's agenda. Again, the *Guardian* quoted the Oxfam reports, underlining the importance of tackling tax avoidance: 'The charity calls for a fairer burden for the rich, pointing out that the [British] government admits £35bn a year is lost to tax avoidance' (Ramesh 2012).

Nicolas Shaxson, in his book *Treasure Islands*, shows what a central role tax havens have played in the neoliberal era. In the 2008 financial crash, for example, most of the risky securitisations described in Chapter 1 took place offshore (Shaxson 2011: 186). Shaxson explains that tax havens aren't just about small tropical islands doing dodgy deals on the margins of the economic system. The City of London in the UK is at the centre of the most important part of the offshore system (Shaxson 2011: 15). The US is now, by some measure, 'the world's single most important tax haven in its own right' (18).

Shaxson defines tax havens, also known as secrecy jurisdictions, as places that seek to 'attract business by offering politically stable facilities to help people or entities get around the rules, laws and regulations of jurisdictions elsewhere' (Shaxson 2011: 184). He explains that 'More than half of world trade passes, at least on paper, though tax havens. Over half of all banking assets and a third of foreign direct investment by multinational corporations, are routed offshore' (8). Media corporations are among those using tax havens and avoiding tax. The *Economist* found in 1999 that Rupert Murdoch's News Corp paid tax in the UK at the rate of just 6 per cent (13). The island of Brecqhou houses 'the luxury offshore castle hideaway of the Barclay brothers, owners of Britain's *Telegraph* newspaper' (16).

According to Shaxson, tax havens have been central to the transfer of resources upwards: 'Offshore is a project of wealthy and powerful elites to help them take the benefits from society without paying for them' (Shaxson 2011: 10). Offshore is not only about avoiding or evading tax, it also helps force down tax rates for corporations and the rich onshore, through tax competition and the 'race to the bottom'. Tax havens are also a key vehicle for modern imperialism. Britain controls a 'spider's web' of offshore centres based in its former colonies, such as the Cayman Islands, Bermuda and the British Virgin Islands. Britain retains 'a large degree of control over and involvement with the vast amount of wealth in and out of these places, under the table' (18).

Moreover, developing countries lose vast sums through the use of tax havens by individuals and, above all, transnational corporations. The Global Financial Integrity (GFI) programme estimated that developing countries lost $1.2 trillion in illicit financial flows in 2008 alone – losses that have grown at 18 per cent per year. This is compared to $100 billion in total foreign aid. Thus, in the words of the GFI's Raymond Baker, 'for every dollar we have been generously handing out across the top of the table, we in the West have been taking back some $10 billion of illicit money under the table' (Shaxson 2011: 27). 'Transfer pricing', a practice frequently deployed by transnational corporations, uses subsidiaries to shift profits into low-tax jurisdictions and costs into high-tax countries, where they can be offset against tax. Developing countries lose an estimated $160 billion a year just to corporate transfer pricing (12).

Shaxson writes that the governments of the rich OECD nations have been quite successful in persuading their publics that they have conducted a major crackdown on secrecy jurisdictions. However, 'OECD member states, notably Britain, the United States and several big European havens, are guardians of the offshore system' (Shaxson 2011: 22). In January 2013, then-Chancellor George Osborne cut the tax paid by UK multinationals on profit attributed to offshore subsidiaries that make loans to other units to 5.75 per cent, thereby making it more worthwhile for corporations to shift income to tax havens. In March 2013, the same George Osborne publicly denounced tax avoidance as 'morally repugnant' (Sayer 2015: 264). Shaxson concludes, 'when the fox says it has done an excellent job of beefing up the security of the henhouse, we should be very cautious indeed' (Shaxson 2011: 22).

Addressing the tax burden in a variety of ways is important. During the neoliberal era, the tax burden has shifted away from the rich and onto the shoulders of everybody else. Tax havens have ballooned. Onshore, taxes paid by the wealthy – such as top levels of income tax, corporation tax and capital gains tax – have tended to fall, while indirect taxes such as VAT have risen. Indirect taxes are regressive in their effects – the lower your income the higher a proportion of your income you pay. Not only that, privatisation has led to increases in what James Meek (2014) calls 'private taxes'. When essential services such as water, energy and transport are privatised, citizens have no choice but to pay the amount charged. In the UK, water bills have risen by nearly twice as much as inflation since privatisation, and energy costs and train fares have soared, the latter by 17 per cent in real terms.

Despite the high-profile tax cuts for the general population that governments have brought in since the 2008 crisis, overall, post-crisis tax measures have been regressive. Polly Toynbee claims that the increase in the tax-free allowance actually benefits the better off rather than those at the bottom:

> As Resolution Foundation research shows, 5 million of the low-paid get not a penny more. Only 10 per cent of the high cost of this policy goes to lifting anyone out of income tax. Only 15 per cent of the money goes to anyone earning less than the £26,000 median, the rest all goes up the scale to above-average earners (Toynbee 2014).

Regressive taxes such as VAT, meanwhile, have increased. Moreover, 'Universal Credit [the new benefits system] sees every penny of a tax cut taken away in lower credits' (Toynbee 2014).

Taxing middle and low earners less and taxing the rich more, partly through cracking down on tax havens, would be an important step towards reducing inequality. However, yet again, the kinds of measures that get the most attention are those announced by the government, and these, as we have seen, have been predominantly regressive. If the opposition does not offer much of an alternative, or is weak or delegitimised in the media, strongly progressive tax measures are unlikely to gain much traction. A good example of this is the Panama Papers, millions of leaked documents containing information on hundreds of thousands of offshore entities. *Guardian* journalists were part of the research and document review team and the *Guardian* devoted considerable resources to covering the leaks. The Panama Papers were at the top of the media agenda for a while. However, in a clear case of media amnesia, they were quickly forgotten as the news agenda – led by Westminster and ultimately controlled by media corporations that in many cases use tax havens – moved on. Further revelations about the scale of tax avoidance were contained in the Paradise Papers, which hit the headlines in November 2017. Time will tell how long they remain in the public eye, and whether they will lead to any meaningful change.

'BAD LABOUR IDEAS'

As important as tax reforms are in tackling inequality, focusing on redistribution through tax ignores the exploitation that takes place when goods and services are being produced and consumed. After tax cuts, the most frequently cited solution was re-regulating business through wage and price controls – especially through a living wage and the capping of energy prices. Re-regulating business made up 15.5 per cent of possible responses mentioned in those media items focusing primarily on inequality, poverty or living standards. For the entire sample covering all aspects of the crisis, this option comprised only 1.3 per cent of the possible responses mentioned (these figures do not include the discussions of financial regulation explored in Chapter 1). It was frequently endorsed in the *Guardian* and the *Mirror*, received mixed reviews in the *Telegraph*, was barely mentioned in the *Sun* and was reported neutrally by the BBC news.

The Labour Party under leader Ed Miliband decided to make living standards part of its election agenda for 2015, pledging a rise in the minimum wage to £8 an hour, energy price freezes till 2017, and an end to zero-hours contracts. Oxfam had called for the institution of a living wage in 2014, which received some media attention, and in the same year the *Mirror* launched a campaign for both a living wage and price controls (Wynne-Jones 2014). Interestingly, the *Mirror*'s content mix endorsed these regulatory measures frequently, even though the *Mirror* was on the whole also supportive of business-friendly measures such as deregulation and especially tax breaks for business, as explored in Chapter 3.

Perhaps surprisingly, since its shock election win in 2015, the Conservative Party has adopted some of these ideas on wage regulation. In its July 2015 budget, as well as £12 billion in welfare cuts, the new all-Conservative government caused a stir by announcing a living wage. It was interpreted by sections of the press as a political coup aimed to capture the centre ground, with a piece in the *Sun* describing it as 'a major land grab' from Labour (Dunn and Schofield 2015). The new 'National Living Wage' would be £7.20 an hour for those aged 25 and over, rising to over £9 an hour by 2020. The chancellor at the time, George Osborne, announced that the budget would 'keep moving us from a low wage, high tax, high welfare economy, to the higher wage, lower tax, lower welfare country we intend to create' (Dominiczak 2015a).

It was received with caution by both the left and right. The Confederation of British Industry (CBI) called it 'a big gamble' and questioned whether firms could absorb the increases without having to lay people off (Dunn and Schofield 2015). Free-marketeer Fraser Nelson (2015), in the *Telegraph*, chastised the government for adopting 'bad Labour' ideas, noting that the living wage might sound good, but 'the problem with adopting Left-wing ideas is that they tend not to work'. Interestingly, in another opinion piece in the *Telegraph*, Jeremy Warner tentatively supported the move, even though he described himself as 'someone who broadly believes in as little government as possible'. In the piece, Warner gives one of the most in-depth explanations for low pay, including globalisation, the lack of business investment, and even the decline of the trade union movement ('Not that we want to go back to that world'). He writes that, under circumstances in which markets are not delivering expected wage growth at the lower end of the scale, 'forcing wages up by diktat is certainly worth a try' (Warner 2015).

The political opposition, on the other hand, with the help of the Institute for Fiscal Studies (IFS) post-budget analysis, soon figured out that the living wage didn't compensate for the cuts in tax credits the government announced at the same time. Reductions in the welfare bill were expected to save the Treasury £12 billion by the end of the decade, while the gross pay increase from the higher minimum wage was £4 billion. The *Guardian* reported that the IFS analysis also showed that the working poor would be hardest hit by the budget, and IMF figures indicated that the poorest two deciles had suffered the most from all the budget changes since 2010 (Elliott 2015b). Meanwhile, business would gain £6.6 billion in the form of another corporation tax cut, changes to investment allowances and incentives to increase the number of apprenticeships (Goodley 2015). The government was forced to make a series of u-turns on its budget measures, including on tax credits, but has not ended its austerity drive.

The Brexit vote in June 2016 was followed by a change of prime minister and chancellor. New prime minister Theresa May continued the government discourse around low pay and living standards, promising to work in the interests of the 'JAMs' – those 'just about managing'. However, at the time of writing, the rhetoric has yet to be translated into meaningful policy. At the same time, Chancellor Phillip Hammond has warned his Brexit EU negotiating partners that Britain could 'change its economic model' if denied access to the single market, meaning even lower corporation taxes and even less regulation (BBC 2017).

At the other end of the pay spectrum, Labour leader Jeremy Corbyn has said that he supports a cap on high incomes, though the party does not at the time of writing have a policy on this issue (Elgot 2017). During his time as Business Secretary in the coalition government, Vince Cable of the Liberal Democrats also proposed implementing indirect measures to curb executive pay (BBC 2012).

The solutions to the problems of inequality, poverty and depressed living standards attracting the most media attention were once again those announced by the government or, to a lesser extent, the opposition party. These revolved around tinkering with the tax burden on one hand, and regulating business mainly through a slightly higher minimum wage on the other. That the idea of increasing regulation on pay has been at least flirted with by all the main parties, and that it is accepted by a number of free-market commentators, shows how severe the problems have become in recent years and how much public dissatisfaction there is about the current state of affairs. Time will tell how far these policies and proposals will go. However, at the time of writing, the direction of travel seems to be in continuing the transfer of resources from labour to capital.

GOING FURTHER

In previous chapters, we saw that media amnesia about the causes of the crisis helped to legitimise the escalation of the very policies that caused the crisis in the first place. When it comes to the media coverage analysed in this chapter, however, this is not the case. Neoliberal solutions such as social spending cuts, tax breaks for the rich, privatisation and deregulation did not receive the most attention. However, we can say that the amnesiac media framing of the problems of depressed living standards, inequality and poverty has enabled the monopolisation of a very limited set of responses – mostly those offered by politicians. This section will attempt to fill in some of the gaps, and explore some possible solutions that have not received a thorough hearing in the mainstream media.

Apart from a wealth tax, briefly mentioned in the media, other measures proposed by Oxfam (2017b) for tackling inequality struggled even harder to make it into the news. These included intergovernmental agreements on minimum wages and working conditions, such as an ASEAN (Association of South-east Asian Nations) minimum wage, or a requirement that multinational companies invest more in their supply chains, thereby ensuring decent work across national borders (31), and pay limits for those at the top. In addition, Oxfam proposed different business models, moving away from shareholder capitalism to a more mixed economy worldwide, supported by government tax breaks and other incentives for cooperative, employee-owned businesses. As with the idea of deglobalisation, discussed in Chapter 3, Oxfam puts international collaboration and the needs of those living in developing countries at the heart of its analysis.

Both Oxfam and Andrew Sayer see reforming democracy as key to reducing inequality. We have explored in previous chapters the idea that the form politics assumes in the neoliberal era is postdemocracy, where democratic institutions remain in place in many countries but have been hollowed out and hijacked by corporate interests. Sayer claims that instead of living in a democracy – the rule of the people – we are currently living in a plutocracy – the rule of the rich. He acknowledges how difficult a task it is to rebuild democracy and remove the political capture of states by the rich. Yet he continues that, 'the plutocracy of the early 20th century was pushed back by democratic political pressure' and we can do the same today (Sayer 2015: 364).

Sayer supports severely limiting political donations; introducing elements of proportional representation in countries without it; restricting the 'revolving door' between politics and big business, whereby politicians can expect to earn huge sums after leaving office (à la Tony Blair); and controlling corporate lobbying. Sayer also notes that the ownership of the media by the rich is part of the problem. We will explore options for media reform in Chapter 6.

Although Oxfam emphasises the need to shift away from fossil fuels to sustainable energy, and advocates moving away from GDP growth as the only indicator of progress, it does not address the problem that infinite growth is incompatible with continued human existence on planet earth – nor does it advocate 'degrowth'. Sayer, like some ecological economists, floats ideas of reducing consumption in developed countries, nationalising major energy companies, creating more locally-based economies, and reducing the working week. Moving away from growth in this vision goes hand in hand with more equal ways of producing and distributing wealth.

Universal basic income

Another idea mentioned by Sayer is universal basic income (UBI), which is gaining some limited traction in public debate. This is the idea that every citizen or resident would be given a set amount of money every month, without means-testing, whether they are working or not. It would replace benefits such as unemployment and housing benefit. It is a concept with a long pedigree, and is being trialled in certain places

(Sayer 2015: 118). It is a slippery idea and has proponents both on the left and from fans of free markets. It could easily be made compatible with the neoliberal form of capitalism, if a small universal basic income came to replace not only benefits that were previously higher but had to be used to pay for an increasingly privatised range of public services as well.

Srnicek and Williams, in *Inventing the Future* (2015), put forward a very different vision. They insist on a universal basic income that is sufficient to provide a dignified life, is truly universal, and is a supplement to the welfare state rather than a replacement. Thus, everyone would have enough to live on, without stigma, without having to work. If people wanted to earn extra, they would take on paid work on top of their basic income. Though this might sound financially impractical, according to Srnicek and Williams, research indicates that it would be possible to finance through 'some combination of reducing duplicate programmes, raising taxes on the rich, inheritance taxes, consumption taxes, carbon taxes, cutting spending on the military, cutting industry and agriculture subsidies, and cracking down on tax evasion' (123).

For Srnicek and Williams, the campaign for a UBI should include an insistence on reducing the working week. Furthermore, they argue that we should campaign not to prevent robots from taking our jobs, but to accelerate automation and implement a universal basic income so that automation becomes a blessing not a curse. They write that 'the success of these efforts will be clear when media discussions about automation shift from fear-mongering over lost jobs to celebrations of the freedom from drudgery' (Srnicek and Williams 2015: 176). This would mean moving away from the work ethic and the deeply embedded notion that somehow it is morally right that we endure unnecessary toil and suffering just in order to survive. As we saw in Chapter 3, most jobs are 'bullshit jobs' – only 13 per cent of people say they find their jobs engaging (Srnicek and Williams 2015: 176). Moreover, as we have seen, we need to reduce both production and consumption in order to preserve the conditions for human life on earth. Therefore, 'the classic social democratic demand for full employment should be replaced with the future-orientated demand for full *un*employment' (123, emphasis added).

These ideas go further than those that tend to structure debate in the mainstream media. They don't necessarily solve all the problems. Many of these proposals can be seen as envisioning an updated version of the social democracy that dominated the postwar developed world until the 1970s. That period ended in crisis, which is how the neoliberal restructuring of capitalism came about in the first place.

David Graeber writes that the economic crises of the 1970s were in many ways 'crises of inclusion'. He explains that the postwar 'Keynesian settlement' was offered only to a relatively small slice of the world's population. Over time, more and more people wanted in on the deal. This went for civil rights and feminist movements in the rich countries and national liberation movements in former colonies. The economy buckled under the pressure: 'it would appear that capitalism, as a system, simply cannot extend such a deal to everyone.' Graeber continues, 'Quite possibly, it wouldn't even remain viable if all its workers were free wage laborers. Certainly it will never be able to provide the sort of life lived by, say, a 1960s auto worker in Michigan or Turin with his own house, garage, and children in college – and this was true even before those children started demanding less stultifying lives' (Graeber 2014: 375). What is more, even the postwar 'golden age' of capitalism, though less unequal than today, was still unequal. And it could still be considered imperialist, as the former colonial powers continued to struggle to ensure that they retained their place in the global pecking order and that their businesses continued to capture global markets (Arrighi 2010).

The kind of economic system advocated by Srnicek and Williams, based around accelerated automation, shorter working weeks and universal basic income, can be seen as a post-social-democratic vision, combining the traditional welfare state with a new autonomy from waged work. The authors do not fully address the issue of the global division of labour. Nor do they fully consider the problem of growth – would this system not still be reliant on economic growth to fund UBI, even if it does entail cutting consumption and jobs? Indeed, Srnicek and Williams understand the long-term limitations of their social vision, and see it as a transitional phase from capitalism to postcapitalism. After all, as long as there is a class system, there will always be inequality. As long as there is capitalism, there will need to be economic growth. As long as there are nation-states, we can ask if imperialism in one form or other will ever end. All of these issues and ideas, from the more modest to the more ambitious, urgently require sustained public deliberation from across the social spectrum. Yet again, the mainstream media fails to ask the right questions.

ON YOUR BIKE

One particularly creative solution to child poverty was implemented by former work and pensions secretary Iain Duncan Smith (known as IDS). It was simply to change the definition of poverty. This was first announced in 2012 and brought in in 2015. The Child Poverty Act had been passed in 2010 under the previous Labour government, and defined a child as living in relative poverty if it lived in a household with an income below 60 per cent of the UK average. This was to be replaced by a definition that shifted the focus from income to 'lifestyle' issues of work-lessness, drug and alcohol consumption, and educational achievement. This change in the definition of poverty was accompanied by the intro-duction of Universal Credit to replace six means-tested benefits, which was expected to save more than £2 billion a year in cuts to the work allowance (Chakelian 2017). The Child Poverty Act is to be repealed or replaced, and its target of eradicating child poverty by 2020 abandoned.

The *Telegraph* introduced the story with the headline: 'Get a job, IDS tells parents on dole'. It emphasises that poor people need to take responsibility for themselves and get into work: 'FAMILIES will be told today that they should work at least 35 hours a week, rather than rely on state handouts, if they want to avoid their children living in poverty.' It quotes, unchallenged, IDS's statement that 'For those who are able to work, work has to be seen as the best route out of poverty. For work is not just about more money – it is transformative. It's about taking responsibility for yourself and your family' (Winnett 2012). The report also contains the idea that 'throwing money at the problem' does not work, complaining about the 'huge amount of taxpayers' money' spent on tackling child poverty.

In the *Guardian*, Polly Toynbee (2012b) gave a thorough critique of this proposal, explaining that it is important to define poverty in terms of money (something that one might have thought self-evident), and showing how the new definition scapegoats the poor and places the burden of responsibility onto the individual rather than conceiving of poverty as a societal problem. Toynbee reminds the reader that the majority of the poor are in work ('repeat that three times, for you will hear no ministers say it. Only 4 per cent are addicts'). In March 2016 IDS resigned as Work and Pensions Secretary because he felt that the government had abandoned its commitment to help the poor and had turned Universal Credit into a simple cost-cutting exercise.

Toynbee accused the government of waging a 'campaign of vilification' against the poor. Other recent soundbites from former Conservative ministers support this claim. Former Chancellor George Osborne, for example, conjured the image of 'the shiftworker, leaving home in the dark hours of the early morning, who looks up at the closed blinds of their next-door neighbour sleeping off a life on benefits' (Osborne quoted in Grice 2013). Former Prime Minister David Cameron rehearsed soundbites created by spin-doctor Lynton Crosby, such as 'workers and shirkers' and 'strivers and skivers' (Garland 2015: 6).

The scapegoating of the poor is a widespread cultural phenomenon, about which there is a substantial amount of scholarship. Studies consistently find that those in poverty are stereotyped and placed into the categories of the deserving and undeserving poor (Golding and Middleton 1982; Redden 2011; Harkins and Lugo-Ocando 2016). The 'undeserving' poor are subject to abusive media campaigns, employing themes of moral corruption, pathology and welfare abuse. Individualising narratives that blame poverty on personal failings are common, as is an emphasis on the cost of welfare to the taxpayer rather than the financial difficulties of those experiencing poverty. Scapegoating of the poor is accompanied by attacks on the welfare state for being inefficient and a corrupting influence, and calls for it to be rolled back, reinforcing the sense that the undeserving poor should be disciplined and punished.

In their UK study from 1982, Peter Golding and Sue Middleton identified a period of intense media 'scroungerphobia' during an economic crisis in 1976–7. By the time Margaret Thatcher was elected in 1979, opposition to the welfare state had become widespread in the press, accompanied by the idea that the work ethic needed to be reinvigorated and law and order restored. These ideas were not invented in the 1970s but had a long lineage: 'underneath the acrid "scroungerphobia" of the late 1970s was the musty odour of the workhouse' (Golding and Middleton 1982: 75). It was this powerful cultural reserve that could be tapped during a time of crisis and used to reform society under Thatcher. It connected with an anti-state sentiment stretching back hundreds of years. In a more recent study, Harkins and Lugo-Ocando (2016) found that since 2008 the British tabloids have drawn on a centuries-old Malthusian ideology that frames poverty in terms of scarcity of resources and sees it as the disgrace of the poor individual.

Golding and Middleton suggest that 'public opinion' (that 'most nebulous and evasive of political concepts' (229)) shifted alongside the increased anti-welfare sentiment in the media. In the early 1960s, polls showed a 'broadly expansive' attitude towards welfare. By 1975, twice as many thought unemployment benefit was too high as thought it too low (228–9). More recently, Mike Berry (2018) found that, in focus groups, large numbers blamed immigrants and welfare recipients, as well as public sector 'waste', for the deficit. These are arguments commonly found in the right-leaning press. Although a direct causal link between media coverage and public attitudes can't be proven, it seems likely that at least an indirect link exists. Berry's focus group participants often cited stories they had read in the papers as the basis for their beliefs. Berry and Golding and Middleton also point out, however, that media scapegoating was not always accepted uncritically by members of the public.

Owen Jones (2015: 87) describes a campaign by the *Sun* in 2010 that asked readers to 'Help us Stop £1.5 Billion Benefits Scroungers'. He also identified cases of scapegoating in the *Daily Mail* and the *Sunday Times*. Though they are less likely to wage campaigns against the poor, the *Guardian* and the *Mirror* also implicitly reproduce the deserving and undeserving poor dichotomy. While it is important to highlight that the majority of those claiming benefits are in work, an exclusive focus on this group could be interpreted as designating those who are not in work as 'unworthy'. The *Mirror* contains pieces strongly supporting the public sector and human-interest pieces following those using food banks, but these also rely on images of the 'deserving poor' who have a strong work ethic and behave 'respectably' (Skeggs 2004).

On the other hand, Joanna Redden (2011) found an alternative framing of poverty in her 2011 study comparing mainstream and alternative media coverage of poverty in Britain and Canada. Alternative news sites contained a 'social justice frame', which situated poverty in historical and political context, presented poverty as an issue of rights, and explicitly or implicitly advocated social solutions.

Redden suggests that, while children are the most common representatives of the 'deserving poor', one group most often designated as 'undeserving' are working-class immigrants. She highlights particularly virulent messages in the *Daily Mail*, which is well known for its anti-immigrant sentiment. As Sukhwant Dhaliwal and Kirsten Forkert indicate in their (2016) study on public distinctions between 'deserving' and 'undeserving' migrants, media anti-immigrant campaigns dovetail with government anti-immigrant rhetoric. David Cameron described asylum-seekers entering the UK from Calais as a 'swarm', and in her former position as Home Secretary, Theresa May had overseen a campaign involving a publicly-funded 'go home' van that travelled around five areas in London carrying a billboard with the slogan 'In the UK illegally? Go Home or Face Arrest', next to a picture of handcuffs. Language around illegality has been an important means of coding immigrants as 'undeserving'.

Explaining media scapegoating

As to why the media treat poverty as they do, as well as the important issue of sources, news values have also been found to be an important factor. Golding and Middleton (1982: 240) found that journalists tended to associate their profession with ideals of self-help, individualism, anti-bureaucracy and the work ethic, values that inevitably filter the coverage of poverty.

Golding and Middleton placed these journalistic norms into the political and economic context of journalism in Britain at the time. The 1960s and 1970s had seen a concentration of media ownership, so that by 1981 three groups controlled 73.5 per cent of the national daily circulation and 89.6 per cent of the national Sunday circulation. Accompanying this trend had been an 'obliteration of a left and social democratic tradition in the press' (Golding and Middleton 1982: 217). This happened in three ways: through the death of individual titles, the deradicalisation of the surviving working-class press, and through barriers to entry by new titles. These three processes were caused by market dynamics. Several left-wing titles closed in the 1960s, not because they had insufficient readers but because they had the kind of readers that failed to attract enough advertising revenue – those in lower income groups (218). Increased concentration of ownership produced a 'textbook crush in the centre of the market', diminishing the range of newspaper opinion (219). At the same time, production costs were high, barring new titles from entering the market. It is impossible to tell if alternative framings of poverty and welfare would have been more widespread under different economic conditions. However, we do know that due to market forces, 'the contemporary press is predetermined to lack a political commitment to the poorest and weakest in society' (222).

Golding and Middleton's study predated online news and social media. Have things changed since then? It is certainly true that there has been a huge proliferation of information online. However, as we will see in Chapter 6, though barriers to entry have lowered in the internet age, barriers to prominence remain high (Chakravartty and Schiller 2010). In other words, if you have a decent internet connection you can say whatever you want. But that doesn't mean that anyone will hear it – at least no one outside your social media bubble. Redden (2011) found that her alternative news sites offering a 'social justice' framing of poverty, described above, did not turn up on the first ten pages of a Google search using the term 'poverty' (837). On Twitter, some 0.05 per cent of all users attract almost 50 per cent of all attention on the network – probably those with existing resources and influence (in Freedman 2014: 96).

And as we know, the problem of concentrated media ownership has not gone away. This could help explain why the problems of inequality, living standards and poverty get relatively little attention in the news media, and mainly from the 'independent' *Guardian*. It could also shed light on why certain solutions get the kinds of sustained, in-depth coverage that are likely to have more impact on public opinion while others get no attention at all or only short-lived or minimal attention.

JEZ WE CAN

Labour lost the 2015 general election, and was virtually wiped out in Scotland by the Scottish National Party (SNP). This triggered the resignation of the Labour leader Ed Miliband and the contest for a new leader. To the amazement of the political establishment, media pundits, and probably to himself, longtime left-wing MP Jeremy Corbyn won by a landslide. A year after he had become leader, he was forced into a second leadership contest, after his own MPs called a vote of no confidence. He won the second election by an even bigger landslide. Then, in 2017, the Conservative government called a snap election, in the belief that they would obliterate the opposition. The Labour Party under Corbyn lost the election but won enough seats to undermine the Tory majority – an upset that led to stunned disbelief among journalists and politicians. Corbyn's popularity is at least partly based on his clear anti-austerity stance (as opposed to Miliband's 'austerity lite') and his more strongly egalitarian orientation.

There have been a number of studies on media representations of Jeremy Corbyn, which found that he has been ridiculed and delegitimised especially by the right-wing press but also by left-wing papers and broadcasters (Cammaerts *et al.* 2016; Media Reform Coalition

2016). The study for this book found similar trends. The *Sun* was particularly virulent in its personal attacks, repeatedly painting Corbyn, his Shadow Chancellor John McDonnell and their allies as the 'loony left'. One particularly extreme piece was headlined 'Too late to put down rabid underdog Jez'. Another referred to John McDonnell as a 'fellow socialist firebrand' and an 'IRA sympathiser' (Dunn and Hawkes 2015). In *Manufacturing Consent*, Herman and Chomsky (1988: 29) identify anti-communist ideology as the fifth filter through which news content becomes conformist and defends the status quo. Their book was written during the cold war and one might have expected this aspect of it to have become outdated. However, it appears that anti-communism as a control mechanism is alive and kicking.

Another of Herman and Chomsky's filters is 'flak'. As well as the extreme flak heaped on Corbyn by the right-wing press, he faced more subtle delegitimation from across the media spectrum. A common narrative found before the 2017 elections was that Corbyn was 'unelectable'. Journalists and pundits appear to have based these unelectabilty claims on opinion polls, taking these to be representative of the elusive thing that is 'public opinion'. They were trying to reflect this public opinion in their coverage. They seem to have been oblivious to the potential impact media coverage can have on public opinion. One former section editor at the *Guardian* told me that as well as the idea that Corbyn was 'unelectable', another implicit narrative circulating at that paper was that Corbyn and his ideas did not constitute 'grown-up politics'. These narratives help to contain political debates within certain parameters – the 'centre ground'. However, there are constant struggles being fought both within the *Guardian* and in the broader public sphere around what is considered 'grown up', 'electable', 'realistic' and the 'centre ground'. Corbyn has proven that he is potentially electable, despite the media flak. Time will tell how far the political ground will shift and what role the media will play.

CONCLUSION

Thomas Piketty (2014: 571) writes that the consequences of the current dynamics of wealth distribution are 'potentially terrifying', if levels of private wealth compared to national income and trends in income inequality converge. In order to have an informed public debate about issues of inequality, living standards and poverty, we need our news media to offer a range of explanations for the problems, including those that are historically in-depth and take a global perspective, and to create space to debate a wide range of possible solutions. As with the other aspects of the economic crisis, instead we have been offered coverage that rarely takes into account many of the causal factors since the 2008 crash, never mind the longer-term dynamics of capitalism that got us there. The kinds of solutions getting the most sustained attention are too often those offered by the government, which tend to be unambitious and in many cases turn out not to be solutions at all. Indeed, the problems of inequality, poverty and depressed living standards receive relatively little media attention, certainly not from the conservative and free-market sections of the press, though this may be changing as governments and international organisations are becoming increasingly concerned at the effects of inequality on the economy and the role it is playing in the rise of nationalism.

The factors explaining why the coverage has been so limited and superficial are the usual suspects that have reappeared throughout this book and are consistently found in media research. These include media ownership and political stance, advertising pressures, the impacts the increasingly ferocious search for profits are having on journalists' time and ability to produce quality news, the drive towards 'infotainment', sourcing practices, journalistic values and routines, and flak. As we have seen, there are feedback loops between media, politics and audiences. News is led by those in political power, who are in turn influenced by powerful media proprietors. Journalists try to reflect 'public opinion' but in the process help to shape that opinion. Politicians try to manipulate 'public opinion' through the media, but need in turn to please voters, or at least not alienate them too much. These processes help to create a centre ground which Tariq Ali (2015) claims has become an 'extreme centre', dominated by market fundamentalism and what Stuart Hall termed 'authoritarian populism' back in 1983. The current combination of free-market and authoritarian politics is plain to see. In order collectively to find a way out of the current interlocked economic and political crises, we need media that serve the interests of the many. Some possible options for creating this will be explored in the next chapter.

6

Curing Media Amnesia

Previous chapters have shown how the mainstream news coverage of the economic turmoil post 2008 has suffered from acute media amnesia. It has forgotten not only the deep roots of the crisis in the dynamics of neoliberal capitalism, but has erased the immediate past of the crisis – its development over the past few years or even months. It has thereby left citizens unable to understand the situation in which they find themselves or to negotiate a viable way out. Instead, this amnesia has served the interests of those who wish to escalate the kinds of policies that helped cause the crisis in the first place, and that transfer resources upwards. It has helped to legitimise virtually unconditional bank bailouts, quantitative easing, austerity, tax cuts for the rich and further privatisation and deregulation. It has led to lowered living standards, increased inequality, rising nationalism and to political decisions that will probably worsen the situation even further. It has short-circuited the possibility of discussing fundamental questions about how our societies should be organised.

We have seen that there are three main elements of media amnesia: a lack of historical context; a narrow range of elite perspectives; and a lack of global context. With some notable exceptions, coverage tends to be shallow, often not offering any explanation at all for the problems. When explanations are given, they are vague or superficial. Sometimes – as with the public profligacy frame – they are inaccurate. This links to the second element. Those controlling the narrative tend to be politicians, other officials or spokespeople for financial services or the business community. When there is controversy, it is usually because the political establishment is split (Brexit being a notable example). The two sides of the argument will be those given by the two sides of the establishment division. These two sides do not represent the range of views existing in society and neither side usually represents the interests of the majority. This issue is thus to do with the *plurality* of views gaining prominence. Thirdly, the news coverage tends to inhibit understanding of the global dimensions of the crisis. Related experiences of those elsewhere that might help us understand our own predicament are ignored. The links between what is happening to our communities and what is happening to communities thousands of miles away are obscured. Current calls in the UK for overseas aid budgets to be cut to pay for services at home display in extremis this lack of awareness of the global nature of capitalism and its crises.

I have tried to explain the factors behind this amnesiac coverage. Particular emphasis has been on news values and journalistic norms and routines on the one hand and the political and economic pressures on journalism on the other. This chapter will explore some of the different options for tackling the problems of contemporary journalism. In doing so, it will range over some of the major debates about not just journalism but media more broadly. We begin with optimistic claims that despite the pressures faced by news organisations, the internet is leading to a renaissance in journalism, and that a new journalism ecosystem is flowering. In this view, all we need to do is seek the outlets that best suit our individual needs out of the myriad on offer. Relatedly, others claim that mainstream media is beyond hope, that we should abandon it altogether and use alternative media instead, of which there are plenty to be found both on- and offline. We then move on to some of the debates around social media, which do not produce news, but through which people are increasingly accessing it. Do social media offer a greater plurality of news and the freedom to communicate with each other on equal terms? Or are they exacerbating the anti-democratic tendencies of media? Finally, we'll look at different options for public intervention in media, from mild forms of regulation to degrees of public ownership and control.

All of these fields in themselves are vast, and it will be impossible to do more than touch on a few of the discussions most relevant to the issues at stake in this book. Although many of the media trends analysed throughout these chapters are international, media systems are different in different places, and the problems with media and therefore good solutions to them will vary. The possibilities discussed here come from the context of Western Europe and especially the UK, as well as the US. I hope that what follows will at least provide some ideas for ways forward.

MAINSTREAM NEWS ADAPTS

Mainstream media companies are having to adjust to the new economic reality for journalism and adapt their business models. Some are optimistic that the most innovative enterprises will survive and indeed flourish.

However, all of the strategies currently being pursued by the major commercial media come with their own drawbacks and do not necessarily address the problems with content explored throughout this book. Many large corporations have responded to declining audiences and revenues with portfolio development strategies. According to Picard (2014: 368), most media companies now produce multiple media products in an attempt to reduce risk and profit from economies of scale and scope. So far, though, this does not seem to have had much of a positive impact on content. Another option is some form of consumer payment model, where consumers pay either a subscription or a micro-payment per article. This has been working for some providers, such as the *Financial Times*, which offer particular kinds of consumer value. However, others have had less success in putting up paywalls and it is uncertain how far consumers are willing to pay directly for news. An advertising-based solution uses branded content, where companies pay to insert advertorials in news copy – articles that are in fact marketing material (see the Branded Content Research Network website). This has been a deepening trend, but, given what we know about the effects of advertising and PR on journalism, we can hardly expect this to lead to improved content.

Another trend has been billionaires from other industries taking over media outfits. To give just a couple of high-profile examples, in 2012, financial investor Warren Buffett bought a controlling stake in the Media General newspaper group. In 2013, Jeff Bezos, the founder of Amazon, bought the *Washington Post* for $250 million. In these cases, the motivation for buying newspapers is something other than profit. As Des Freedman (2014: 47) notes, these interventions signal 'a desire to see a return on their investment measured less in profits than in influence'. Todd Gitlin points out that these wealthy new owners will bring to their titles their existing dispositions, which, in the case of Jeff Bezos, include an opposition to tax increases on the wealthy and a commitment to tax avoidance (quoted in Freedman 2014: 55). Relying on billionaires to fund journalism does not seem likely to address the problem of the extent to which the existing media serve the interests of the rich and powerful. We will have to look elsewhere for solutions.

A NEW JOURNALISM ECOLOGY?

There are some who believe that the internet has produced or will lead to a renaissance in journalism (Curran 2010b), as bloggers, citizen journalists and journalism start-ups take over cyberspace. In this view, the monopolistic industrial model of journalism is giving way to a pluralistic networked model based on profit and non-profit, individual and organised journalistic practices (Benkler in Curran 2010b: 467). The internet results in processes of decentralisation and disintermediation (Freedman 2014). Because the costs of creating and sharing something online are so low in comparison with traditional media, news provision can become less centralised. And because the internet is conducive to horizontal, peer-to-peer and interactive communication, middle men and gatekeepers controlling information will be a thing of the past. Guido Fawkes argues that 'the days of media conglomerates determining the news in a top-down Fordist fashion are over ... Big media are going to be disintermediated because the technology has drastically reduced the cost of dissemination' (in Curran 2010b: 467).

These new, web-based forms of journalism can be either for-profit or non-profit. Funding models include advertising, subscription, philanthropic foundations, crowd-funding, volunteering and publishers investing their own resources. The US-based *Huffington Post* and Politico are well-known examples of successful new forms of for-profit journalism (though the *Huffington Post* is no longer independent, having been acquired by internet giant AOL in 2011). These kinds of sites have also been known to exert influence on the coverage of mainstream media (Curran 2010b: 470). Crowd-sourcing is another option. According to the Pew Research Center (Vogt and Mitchell 2016), between 28 April 2009 and 15 September 2015, 658 journalism-related projects proposed on the crowd-funding site Kickstarter received full – or more than full – funding, to the tune of nearly $6.3 million.

Charles Lewis (2011: 356), founder of the Center for Public Integrity, writes of a 'new investigative journalism ecosystem' rising up in response to the crisis in journalism in the US, Canada and parts of Europe, Africa, Latin America and Asia. In this new ecosystem, some of the most ambitious investigative journalism is emanating from the non-profit sector rather than commercial outlets. These are online publishing centres founded and staffed by professional journalists whose jobs have been lost or are threatened, or 'disconcerted veterans who are excited to be doing major important reporting projects once again' (356). The new class of non-profit investigative journalism includes ProPublica and the Investigative Reporting Workshop, both founded in 2008. In 2009, 20 US non-profit news publishers came together for three days and issued the Pocantio Declaration, announcing that 'We have hereby established, for the first time ever, an investigative news network' (358). Half of the groups represented had only been in existence since 2007.

This ecosystem has a strong global dimension. For example, the International Consortium of Investigative Journalism consists of 100 reporters from 50 countries on 6 continents who produce cross-border content. Non-profit organisations have also joined together to form the Global Investigative Journalism Network. Much of the funding comes from philanthropic foundations. Between 2005 and 2009, at least 180 US foundations spent nearly $128 million on news and information projects, half of that for investigative reporting by non-profit centres – not including support for public broadcasting (357). In the UK, the Centre for Investigative Journalism based at Goldsmiths, University of London, is a non-profit also funded by foundations.

Slow news

A related phenomenon is the rise of 'slow news'. The slow-news movement directly confronts some of the problems of media amnesia. According to Megan Le Masurier (2015), it was inspired by the slow-food movement, which emphasises local produce, careful cooking and taking pleasure in sharing an unhurried meal. From there, the 'slow' movement has emerged in different spheres of life. The term 'slow journalism' was first used by Susan Greenberg to praise long-form journalism, which has a pedigree stretching back centuries (in Le Masurier 2015: 141–2). It has since been applied to different forms of journalism that are critical of the effects of speed on the practice of journalism, and experiment with publishing that addresses those effects. Its features include allowing time for deeper reflection and research on its subject, often at some length. The periodicity of its delivery is slowed down as well, allowing more time for production and consumption. This kind of journalism can use narrative story-telling techniques, rather than just 'the mechanistic expository style of hard news stories' (143). It treats its subjects and producers ethically and avoids sensationalism and herd reporting. It is not scoop-driven. On top of that, for Le Masurier, the slow approach values transparency. It should not only be factually accurate but sources should be verifiable, for example by linking or citing sources or methods in the text. The work is relevant to a particular community, and it takes a collaborative, non-competitive approach. This kind of journalism is produced in alternative spaces, usually on a small scale, in order to realise its values.

Among the examples Le Masurier gives are the New York based Narratively, which offers in-depth, human-driven stories 'that might otherwise fall through the cracks'. Each week, Narratively explores a different theme about a particular place and publishes one story per day, in whatever medium suits the story – animated documentary, long-form article, photo essay (144). Finnish online start-up Long Play (LP) produces one story per month with unpaid work from eight journalists, two designers, and one photographer, who form 'a democratic collective'. It is an example of the growing 'e-single' phenomenon in long-form journalism where articles are sold as digital singles. The French quarterly magazine *XXI* contains 'flashbacks' of shorter news stories from the preceding three months, to counter the tendency of the news to move on from even recent, high-profile events in the search for newer stories (146). Dutch for-profit website De Correspondent is funded by subscribers. It publishes stories every day, but the focus is background, analysis, investigative reporting and long-form writing. The site's publisher expects correspondents to be 'factual, accurate and fair', but they are not asked to hide their own opinions. Rather, they are expected to make their position explicit.

These media reject news values leading to a focus on the very latest events and the information overload it can cause. They encourage us to reflect on questions like 'how much news do I need?', 'when do I need it?' and 'what really matters in the news?' (le Masurier 2015: 148). They recognise the problems that can arise when news has to operate at warp speed, including inaccurate and poorly-informed journalism that is more likely to reproduce the views of elites, and the forgetting, rewriting or misremembering of even the most recent events. Many of these slow-news outfits identify internet technologies as exacerbating the problems of speed, and some emphasise offline, printed products. Others try to carve out a slow space within the online media torrent. From the perspective of media amnesia, the slow-news movement can be considered an important part of the new journalism ecosystem.

Alternative media

Perhaps a special part of this ecology is comprised of what is variously called 'alternative', 'oppositional' or 'radical' media. Chris Atton defines alternative media as 'a range of media projects, interventions and networks that work against, or seek to develop different forms of, the dominant, expected (and broadly accepted) ways of "doing" media' (in Dowmunt and Coyer 2007: 3). Tony Dowmunt and Kate Coyer explain that alternative media play a double role: they provide content that differs from the dominant media, and they offer examples of alternate modes of production that are 'more democratic and participatory and organised horizontally rather than hierarchically' (3). Both these functions can be considered as counter-hegemonic, in that they challenge the 'common sense' of mainstream media in both content and form. The fact that they are consciously counter-hegemonic is what distinguishes them from other small-scale news outfits that form part of the 'new journalism ecosystem'. However, alternative media have a complex relationship with mainstream media. They offer both an alternative to and a critique of dominant media. At the same time, though, they often adhere to the ethos, values and practices of professional journalism – to 'provide independent, reliable, accurate, wide-ranging and relevant information that a democracy requires' (Bowman and Willis in Lievrouw 2011: 145).

Alternative media tend to be non-commercial. Indeed, the fact that they are not primarily driven by commercial imperatives is one of their most important distinguishing features. Indymedia is perhaps the quintessential recent example of an alternative media organisation. It was set up during the Seattle World Trade Organisation protests in 1999. It is a radical, autonomous, decentralised and highly participatory news project with over 170 independent media centres worldwide, more than half of them outside the US (Lievrouw 2011: 136).

Alternative media can help counter the tendencies of media amnesia. They are often run by those marginalised or misrepresented in mainstream media, and they can offer perspectives not usually found there. In this way, they can illuminate events from different angles and focus on events and processes that are not covered in the mainstream media. As discussed in Chapter 5, for example, Joanna Redden found a 'social justice' frame in the coverage of poverty in alternative media that was not to be found in mainstream media. Lievrouw (2015: 125) points to instances in which amateurs have broken important stories on alternative media, such as the political purges of US attorneys by the Bush administration, reported by Talking Points, or undertaken critical fact-checking such as the independent monitoring of casualties in the

Iraq War by the Iraq Body Count and Iraq Coalition Casualty Count sites.

Alternative media can also counter the geographic myopia of mainstream media. Many alternative news sites are intentionally international. Given the internet's ability to connect people in distant parts of the world in real time, some of the barriers to creating global participatory journalism have come down (Curran and Witschge 2010). These media can also pay more attention to historical context. In some cases they are more issues-based rather than event-driven, so that they can explore processes and interconnections in a way neglected by mainstream media. They are not so constrained by the commercial imperative to break stories or get the very latest news, or by conventions which cram stories into small spaces or time-slots and separate content into different sections, obscuring interconnections.

There are also alternative social media sites. Fuchs (2015: 366) lists Diaspora*, N-1, Occuppii, InterOccupy, OccupyTalk, Occupy News Network, Occupy Streams, Riseup, Lorea, identi.ca, StatusNet, Quitter, Vinilox, Load Average, Thimbl and Crabgrass. In a survey of activists, respondents said that they saw these as good alternatives to Facebook, Twitter and YouTube because they do not profit from users' activities and have better privacy protection. We will explore issues around social media and their implications for journalism and democracy more broadly in the next section.

Given the rich diversity of the new journalism ecology, it is tempting to say that the remedy for the evils of media amnesia is to forget about mainstream media altogether. This is certainly the view of some on the left. After all, if mainstream media functions (intentionally or not) to create a 'common sense' that serves the interests of the rich and powerful at the expense of everyone else – a theory somewhat borne out by the research for this book – surely the answer is to reject mainstream media in favour of the available alternatives? There are, however, problems with this approach.

First, the new journalism ecology is not without its inequalities. For-profit media can be problematic. The *Huffington Post*, for example, has been accused of exploitative practices, profiting from the labour of a host of unpaid contributors. Even non-profit, alternative media, although they offer a range of different perspectives, do not always represent the views of marginalised groups. Their power dynamics can't help but reflect those of the wider society (Curran and Witschge 2010). Indeed, research has found a high degree of cannibalisation in online news. Many news sites lack the resources or capability to gather 'raw' news in the way that professional organisations can. They often copy stories from other sites, frequently mainstream sites, giving those stories their own spin. Even when not cannibalised, big media tend to set the news agenda for smaller sites. Meanwhile, professional journalists themselves are increasingly cannibalising each other's stories. As well as offering diversity, then, in some ways the internet leads to increased journalistic homogeneity (Phillips 2012; Redden and Witschge 2010).

A different problem is related to concerns over 'fake news'. With all the thousands of sites out there, how do we know which ones to trust (Lievrouw 2015: 130)? The only way to is to cross-check sources against other sources, which takes time and doesn't necessarily get us anywhere. Many people use mainstream media despite being sceptical of it because they do not have time to sort through the myriad of alternative news options for one they find credible. Additionally, we might find a site that we like for news on certain topics but that site may not contain news on other topics we find important. The fragmentation of non-mainstream news online and the lack of time to navigate all the choices on offer are problematic.

One of the most serious issues with non-mainstream media is their scale. This is in turn related to resources. For-profit start-ups have to compete with their much bigger rivals. Those that are not-for-profit have no choice but to operate within a profit-orientated context. Their sources of funding can be precarious and limited. If they do manage to secure funding from, say, a foundation, there are worries about cooptation by wealthy benefactors, which would defeat their purpose. This means that most alternative media organisations tend to be small scale and their audiences tend to be minuscule in relation to mainstream media. Especially with alternative media, this can mean groups of like-minded people talking amongst themselves without connecting to other sections of society. This goes equally for alternative social media. Using and supporting trustworthy non-mainstream or alternative media (either on- or offline) is important, and is a key component of a multi-pronged attempt to create a better journalism field. However, on its own it is not enough. As McChesney and Nichols argue about the hegemonic coverage of US mainstream media:

It is the result of relentless lobbying from big business interests that have won explicit government policies and subsidies permitting [corporate media] to scrap public interest obligations and increase commercialization and conglomeration. It is untenable to accept such massive subsidies for the wealthy, and to content ourselves with the 'freedom' to forge alternatives that only occupy the margins (in Hardy 2014: 211).

As well as using alternative media, we need to change the ways the media are regulated and organised. We will return to these questions. But first, let's turn to some of the debates around the new facilitators and gateways to news, which nowadays exert a powerful influence on the news agenda without actually making news.

SOCIAL MEDIA

Many of the news ventures discussed above operate online, and support the claim that the internet offers the potential for decentralisation and disintermediation. However, the internet has also given rise to competing trends. As well as decentralisation and proliferation there has been extreme concentration. And while the internet contains the potential for disintermediation, new gatekeepers have emerged to exert a strong influence over news. We are all aware of the media giants that have colonised the internet. This concentration is no accident, but is rather a characteristic of capitalist development. Large companies with economies of scale and scope are able to buy up or price-out smaller companies, leading to increased centralisation. Des Freedman (2014: 101) explains that by 2013, Google had spent $20 billion acquiring 127 companies. According to McChesney, the internet has created the largest monopolies in economic history (in Fenton 2016a: 151).

These companies are, of course, highly financialised, and they contribute to the risks posed by financialisation. The dot.com crash of 2000 shed light on the risks of speculating on tech companies. Those risks have not disappeared. Des Freedman (2014: 112–13) recounts the story of when Facebook floated on the stock exchange in 2012. Its share price plummeted to half its original price after 6 months before climbing back up to its original level. Not only that, soon after its initial public offering (IPO), it emerged that the company, with the help of its bank, Morgan Stanley, had effectively hidden reduced growth forecasts; the bank had set the share price too high and had been forced to intervene to protect the share price. The deal has since faced a number of official investigations, with Morgan Stanley fined $5 million by the financial authorities. Fuchs (2018) relates how, while Facebook and Google are very profitable as a result of their domination of the online ad market, Twitter and the Chinese social media company Weibo are struggling financially. Both companies listed on the stock market in 2013, even though they were making losses – $645.32 million for Twitter and $38.12 million for Weibo. Their share prices are not matched by their actual profits, and they are therefore especially risky. We know that financial crashes can have serious impacts on real people's lives.

The new intermediaries

Google, Facebook, Twitter and YouTube are among the new inter-mediaries through which millions of us access news. Media scholar Justin Schlosberg (2016) refers to them as 'gateways'. Manuel Castells (2009), though critical of global media corporations, argues that social networking sites offer the means of 'mass self communication'. They enable users to produce meaning interactively. Anyone can tweet, post or upload a video. The dark side of this freedom, which has been making headlines lately, is 'fake news' circulating on social media.

Despite these claims, and despite the multiplicity that no doubt exists on social media, gateways actually tend to lead users back to mainstream news brands. For example, Schlosberg (2016: 120–3) reveals that Google's news algorithm systematically favours large-scale and incumbent providers. Its ranking of stories is not only matched to the keywords of a search: it gives prior weighting to news providers based on a range of what it considers indicators of news quality. These include the size of audience, the size of newsroom, and the volume of output. When it comes to volume, it favours providers that offer a breadth of coverage over specialist media, *and* those that produce a lot of coverage on topics that are also receiving a lot of attention on the web as a whole. Thus, the algorithm favours established providers that pursue a dominant news agenda. Google would no doubt argue that mainstream outlets – it specifically mentioned CNN and the BBC in its patent filing – are those that users trust and want to access. However, we can see another feedback loop at work here. Because these outlets are dominant, Google prioritises them, which in turn reinforces their dominance. As

Schlosberg points out, given its stated preference for sources like CNN and the BBC, it may also be reinforcing a news agenda with a 'western' bias (122).

For its Trending Topics news operation, along with its algorithm, Facebook uses a team of editors who help to decide which stories to prioritise. It 'relies heavily on just 10 news sources to determine whether a trending news story has editorial authority ... BBC News, CNN, Fox News, the *Guardian*, NBC News, the *New York Times*, *USA Today*, the *Wall Street Journal*, *Washington Post*, and Yahoo News or Yahoo' (Thielman 2016). Twitter's Trending Topics algorithm prioritises topics that produce spikes in user attention over consistent and sustained activity. One major catalyst for such spikes is of course attention from mainstream news brands (Schlosberg 2016: 75–6). In 2015, Facebook launched its 'instant articles', based on a revenue-sharing model that allows the site to host articles directly. Google, Twitter and Apple quickly followed suit. Instant articles will be likely to favour the larger, mainstream news brands which have the resources to plough into regular and high volumes of content and the brand clout to attract users (Schlosberg 2016: 78).

These examples show how mainstream news brands and social media giants are mutually reliant. Social media platforms depend on mainstream outlets. At the same time they have extraordinary power to direct traffic and therefore set news agendas, power that is often hidden. Given their gatekeeping power over news and given the editorial decisions embedded in their personalisation algorithms, there is ongoing debate as to whether these social media companies should be deemed publishing companies rather than, as they insist, tech companies. Labelling them as publishing companies would make them subject to legislation around libel and defamation as well as certain anti-monopoly laws.

It should also be remembered that technologies that do not provide gateways to news content but *facilitate* access – internet service providers, browsers, mobile operators and app platforms – are also dominated by huge corporations. They have no direct bearing on news consumption, but they do have varying degrees of power over traffic management (Schlosberg 2016: 134–5). Even the cable and routers forming the internet backbone are owned by private corporations. While the internet started out as a publicly-funded project, it has been privatised at the deepest levels (see Curran, Fenton and Freedman 2016). All of these issues need to be taken into consideration when assessing the role of media in society.

Personalisation

The purpose of the algorithms these intermediaries use is to personalise content. The purpose of personalisation in turn is to maximise advertising revenue. The platforms want to provide users with content that will pique their interest enough to make them click and then sustain their interest enough to keep them on the page. Some claim these personalisation filters have exacerbated the problems around infotainment and the 'dumbing down' of news, discussed in previous chapters. Facebook's newsfeed algorithm in particular has come under attack for favouring stories that are 'highly emotive, trivial and partisan' (Schlosberg 2016: 76). Given Facebook's power over the direction of news traffic, a worry is that its bias towards this kind of content could have a knock-on effect on editorial decision-making and news-gathering priorities *at large*.

Perhaps more concerning, the rise of personalised content has been linked to 'filter bubbles' and social fragmentation. Some claim that it means we are enclosed in our own bubbles or echo chambers where the only views we are exposed to are those similar to our own. Eli Pariser (2012) points to the example of different users performing identical searches on Google but getting radically different results. Personalisation is not in the users' hands and is controlled by algorithms. Often we are not even aware of the process. As Schlosberg (2016: 67) writes, 'This may not be such a problem when we are searching for information about yoga classes or football results. But if we are searching for information about climate change, for instance, or stem cells, the results are likely to be shaped by an ideological bias that comports with our previous searches, clicks, purchases, communications and connections.' The shock election of Donald Trump in 2016 caused a panic about such social fragmentation and polarisation. Thus, although it is possible to find a large variety of news options on social media, not only are mainstream brands given prominence but users may be fed the kinds of sources – whether mainstream or not – that confirm their existing views. We can find information that suits our purposes, but it is more difficult to dialogue with those different from ourselves about that information.

Consumerism and individualism

A great deal has been made of the role of social media in political mobilisations, with the Arab Spring giving rise to talk of 'Twitter revolutions'.

It is true that social media have enabled activists to communicate effectively and mobilise people quickly. However, it is often forgotten that these mobilisations could not happen without people actually mobilising – that is, it is not the technology that is causing the revolutions but rather that people who are politically engaged are using social media to communicate. Counter to the view that social media enhance democracy and produce social change, scholars like Jodi Dean (2009) describe a situation of 'communicative capitalism' whereby millions of people are blurting out their views but nobody is listening to or engaging with them.

Some claim that communication on social media is highly self-referential and motivated by personal fulfilment. Indeed, as Natalie Fenton (2016a: 158) points out, it may be conducive to the neoliberal idea espoused by Margaret Thatcher that there is no such thing as society, only individuals – in this case a mass of networked but only superficially connected individuals. And the ways in which people are communicating are increasingly consumption-oriented and self-commodifying. For example, the Facebook profile structure is not neutral but encourages users to construct themselves in certain ways. Marwick writes:

> Generally, the user is portrayed not as a citizen, but as a consumer … applications encourage people to define themselves through the entertainment products they consume … Not only are users treated as consumers, they are encouraged to consume others in a concept of networking that privileges social capital over friendship or community building. 'Networking', in business terms, is a goal-oriented process in which one's social circle is constantly expanded in order to connect with as many people as possible, in order to gain business advantages (quoted in Fenton 2016a: 150).

Fenton also describes the rise of bots and astroturf marketing. Bots are automated software operating fake accounts that are hard to spot. Some estimates put them at one in 20 accounts. They can inflate followers, influence the stock market and sway political discourse as well as 'massively enhance marketing campaigns' (Fenton 2016a: 149). Astroturfing uses software to disguise the sponsor of a message to make it look as if it comes from a member of the general public and so give the impression of grassroots support for a product. These automated programmes promote not just particular products but the consumer ethic itself. The concerns expressed in this book over media amnesia are ultimately about the ability of people to understand and make meaningful decisions about society. It could be that the wider digital environment in which journalism is increasingly consumed is in some ways detracting further from that ability.

Data

As with PR, the marketing techniques described above have leached into political communications. Bots can be used to try to sway public opinion. Concerns over 'dark ads' have been raised in connection with the US 2016 election and the Brexit referendum and the 2017 general election in the UK. Political parties are able to micro-target key constituencies, using information gleaned from Facebook usage. Thousands of different iterations of an ad can be used, and people would not necessarily know that they are seeing a version that others aren't seeing. Moreover, the ads disappear after they are viewed, so it's impossible to know whether they are fraudulent – whether parties are 'talking out of both sides of their mouth'. Facebook has employed former political aides to help with targeting. In the UK, the information commissioner has launched an investigation into this kind of social media targeting, which is currently far less regulated than other forms of political advertising.

The furore over the data analytics company Cambridge Analytica shows how sinister this kind of activity can become. Cambridge Analytica uses a method it calls psychographics. It targets users according to their personality type, which the company analyses based on Facebook usage. Thus it can allow parties to adjust ads for people who are 'conscientious', 'neurotic' or 'agreeable' (Booth 2017). Cambridge Analytica has been linked to the Ted Cruz, Donald Trump and Leave.EU campaigns. However, it now claims that it didn't use psychographics on the Trump campaign and never worked for Leave.EU. Currently it looks as if the original claims made by the company were exaggerated and that the method itself is not particularly successful. However, it gives a glimpse into a not-so-distant dystopia.

A related problem is around 'fake news', delivered by social media during key moments of public life such as elections. Fake news websites deliberately publish incorrect information, usually for propaganda purposes. The World Economic Forum recently identified the rapid spread of misinformation online as one of the top ten threats to society.

Fake news can be spread on social media using dissemination algorithms or through bots that promote content in a pre-programmed way. A study of the way social media was used during the 2017 UK election found that 'junk' news accounted for 11.4 per cent of relevant information shared; 53.6 per cent of relevant information shared came from professional news organisations. In the US 2016 election, fake news was more prominent, in one case accounting for one third of relevant information shared (Kaminska et al 2017). Thus, on the one hand, social media compounds the problems associated with mainstream media. On the other, it exacerbates a host of other problems, around echo chambers, polarisation, political manipulation and fake news. The solution to fake news is not to fall back on 'real', mainstream news, which as we have seen gives only a partial and often superficial account of reality. More viable solutions are discussed shortly.

Antisocial media

Scholars and commentators (Fuchs 2015; Freedman 2014; Mason 2016) have pointed out that under these circumstances, social media are not really that social. They are used to fulfil social needs, but they are ultimately for the benefit of private interests. Christian Fuchs (2018) points out that the likes of Google, Facebook, Twitter and the Chinese companies Weibo and Baidu are first and foremost huge advertising agencies. In 2014, Facebook made 92 per cent of its revenues from advertising. For Google it was 89 per cent. Baidu derived 98.9 per cent of revenue from online marketing services. These companies are constantly monitoring users' behaviour and collecting data about their lives from which they can profit. The contradiction between social media and private interest can lead to some quite antisocial behaviour on the part of these corporations.

In 2013, Edward Snowden revealed that state security agencies, especially the NSA in the US and the UK's GCHQ, were operating vast surveillance programmes to eavesdrop on phone conversations, emails and social media. They have done this with the connivance of telecoms giants like AT&T and Verizon as well as tech companies like Google, Facebook, Microsoft and Cisco Systems. UK telecoms companies such as BT and Vodafone have also been implicated (Freedman 2014: 103).

As well as privacy issues and concerns over security with all this data being stored and shared, there is also concern about the potential for discrimination attached to big data. Algorithms that sort through our data are by no means objective but are 'as susceptible to bias as the human decisions embedded within them' (Freedman 2014: 109). The difference is that the biases within algorithms are harder to spot. Just as there have been news stories about racist dating apps, there are fears that discrimination could be unwittingly carried out on an industrial scale through the use of big data. For example, at least in the US, Facebook profiles are increasingly being used as a basis for credit-rating scores. Facebook's vast repository of data has strong indicators of users' socioeconomic status— where they attend school, where they work, who their friends are and so on. Financial services ads – including those services with extortionate interest rates aimed at low-income groups – are targeted accordingly (Taylor and Sadowski 2015). This raises two issues. It illuminates how social media companies 'literally spread financialization' through data collection and advertising (Skeggs and Yuill 2016). And it shows how the algorithms used by social media can potentially lead to hidden discrimination on a major scale.

As Fuchs points out, while social media corporations continually violate their users' privacy, they are very protective of their own – especially their finances. Thinking back to the discussion about tax avoidance and evasion in Chapter 5, social media companies are notorious tax avoiders. In 2011, Amazon paid corporation tax in the UK at the rate of 0.05 per cent, Facebook 0.1 per cent and Google 1.5 per cent (Fuchs 2015: 348–9).

However, only 42 per cent of the world's population even uses the internet (Fenton 2016b: 15), showing that the 'digital divide' is still deep. Rich countries experience far more internet usage overall than poorer ones: 95 per cent of the population uses the internet in Norway and Sweden, 90 per cent in the UK and 88 per cent in North America. In contrast, in China the figure is 47 per cent, in Egypt 53 per cent, Pakistan 15 per cent and Iraq 9 per cent (13). Within nations there are also inequalities when it comes to online. In the UK, almost all of the wealthiest people use the internet, while for those earning less than £12,500 it is only 58 per cent. In the US, 93 per cent of those earning $100,000 or more are internet users versus 48 per cent of those earning less than $25,000.

Meanwhile, lower down the value chain, digital media involves:

Digital labour slaves extracting conflict minerals in Africa, hardware assemblers working often under toxic and extremely hard conditions [for example the Foxcomm workers in China], highly paid and highly stressed software engineers in the West, precarious call-centre workers, freelance digital media professionals, and e-waste workers facing dangerous conditions (Fuchs 2015: 348).

The issues explored throughout this book to do with the global division of labour and the ecological impacts of capitalist production and consumption apply to media as much as any other sector of the economy. To give one example, by 2007, between 20 and 50 *million tons* of e-waste were being generated annually, mostly in the global north, and increasingly India and China, and dumped in the global south (Maxwell and Miller 2012: 3).

Again, these issues are not directly connected to journalism, but to the wider media environment in which it is increasingly consumed. While the internet offers enormous potential for more equal, diverse and pluralistic ways of communicating, learning about the world and participating in society, that potential is constrained by the context in which it exists. As long as we have economies that run on the basis of private profit, the internet and social media can't be fully social, and certainly cannot in their current form solve the problems of journalism. The next section looks at possible solutions based on increased public control over media.

REGULATION

Media policy varies by geographical location and is often contradictory. However, in many parts of the world, during the neoliberal era, trends have been – surprise, surprise – broadly neoliberal, in the sense of being more at the disposal of corporations than the public. In their history of British media, Curran and Seaton explain that in the UK deregulatory policies were adopted by successive Conservative administrations during the 1980s and 1990s and under New Labour after 1997 (Seaton and Curran 2010: 370). For example, the 1990 Broadcasting Act inaugurated the sale of ITV franchises. It also established a 'light touch' regulator (Independent Television Commission) and weakened public obligations on commercial broadcasters. The subsequent 1996 Broadcasting Act relaxed restrictions on ITV and commercial radio concentration

(371). The 2003 Communications Act allowed a further increase of commercial radio and television concentration. It allowed British terrestrial television channels to be bought by proprietors outside the EU. And it set up a new regulator, Ofcom (the Office of Communications), with a brief to 'roll back regulation promptly when regulation becomes unnecessary' (372).

Some EU media policy has also been deregulatory. Seaton and Curran (372) write that the EU's 2007 Audiovisual Media Services Directive established a 'country of origin' principle. This meant that satellite TV companies can only be regulated in the country where their programmes are 'uplinked', not in the countries where they are received. Some feared that this would lead to a race to the bottom whereby countries competed for investment by lowering regulation. Ultimately this did not occur on a significant level. Only two countries extensively deregulated their satellite television companies – Luxembourg and Britain. Another proposal that was successfully resisted came from the European Commission's Competition Directorate in 1998. It proposed that public service broadcasters should be prevented from making programmes of a kind made by commercial broadcasters. There have been various attempts from parties within the EU to prevent public broadcasters from developing online services. So far these have not met with success (373). There have also been attempts to impose free-market media policies through the World Trade Organisation (WTO). Through this route, neoliberals succeeded in securing the international deregulation of telecommunications, completed in Europe in 1998. Less successful have been attempts multilaterally to outlaw subsidies for media production (including the television licence fee) and eliminate programme quotas (373).

Although broadcasting regulation has become increasingly deregulatory, in the UK governments have been much more willing to intervene when it comes to broadcasting than with the press. Not only does the UK have a huge public broadcaster, funded largely through a licence fee, but commercial broadcaster ITV and Channel 4 are – at least for now – required to meet public service obligations. The press, meanwhile, is largely self-regulated. There is a powerful lobby coming from the media barons that harnesses seemingly 'common sense' arguments about freedom of the press and democracy. In reality, this 'freedom' seems to be the freedom for media corporations to protect their commercial interests. In 2010–11, the phone-hacking scandal led to the Leveson Inquiry, which exposed criminal behaviour on the part of media companies and evidence of intimate relationships between media moguls and top politicians (Freedman 2014: 78). The Leveson Report of 2012 recommended an improved system of self-regulation, which included setting up a recognition body with oversight of the independent regulator, a low-cost arbitration service, and the possibility of third-party complaints. This body would have no authority whatsoever to demand changes to press content. However, even this mild suggestion was met with a fierce lobby led by the *Daily Mail*'s editor, Paul Dacre, proclaiming that the proposals constituted the 'end of 300 years of press freedom' (Freedman 2014: 71). The government compromised and instead worked similar proposals through a Royal Charter – a 'medieval instrument' – agreed in 2013 (Freedman 2014: 134). The press refuse to abide by this and have instead set up their own self-regulator, the Independent Press Standards Organisation, in 'a determined effort to maintain [the] status quo' (134). The government has delayed part two of the Leveson Inquiry, and there are doubts about whether it will ever go ahead.

Media activists and even some journalists have called for a strengthening of regulation around the right to privacy, the right to reply, the publication of corrections and the process of lodging complaints against media companies. These proposals aim to protect members of the public from having their privacy violated or from being misrepresented in the media. Allowing third-party complaints, for example, might allow an organisation to complain on behalf of a group of asylum-seekers about racist coverage. Another demand concerns the transparency of media policy – particularly contacts between senior government officials and media owners or executives. Leveson urgently called for the quarterly disclosure of relationships of this kind and meetings and discussions of media policy issues, including interactions by phone, text or email. Schlosberg (2016: 150) writes that since 2010, UK governments have been proactive in publishing details of their meetings with stakeholders. But these are published separately by different government departments at different times, on different web pages, with varying titles and in different file formats, resulting in a 'fog of transparency'. Instead, Schlosberg recommends that details of these kinds of meetings should be published on a central register, made available in spreadsheet format and updated at regular intervals.

These relatively mild proposals to do with media law are 'behavioural' rather than structural. Another, stronger, behavioural proposal is legally to underwrite the independence of editors from pressure exerted by owners. An approach adopted in the Austrian press is for the editorial independence of journalists to be protected in legally-binding contracts (Curran 2002: 245). Schlosberg (2016: 146), meanwhile, cites calls for editorial boards consisting of a rotating panel of staff journalists with veto power over the appointment or dismissal of editors, and the redistribution of shareholder voting rights among staff journalists. One journalist I spoke to suggested that news organisations should also adopt quotas for staff coming from state rather than private schools, to address the issue of journalists' unconscious class bias.

Given the power of gateways like Google, Facebook, Twitter and YouTube to direct attention to news providers online, it is necessary to consider top-down legislation on that level too. As a first step, Schlosberg advocates some kind of algorithm governance. Given its infancy and complexity, he acknowledges the need for further deliberation on this issue – preferably at the supranational level. At this stage, algorithm *transparency* could be the focus of governance, especially because of 'the hidden qualities of algorithm filters that can make news agendas appear natural and spontaneous rather than the work of complex code' (Schlosberg 2016: 146). Major news algorithms could also be periodically audited by independent bodies to ensure they vest the power of selection with users as well as meeting baseline plurality objectives.

Further removed from these online gateways are what Schlosberg calls 'facilitators' such as internet service providers (ISPs). They do not produce news content, nor do they direct attention to certain content, as the gateways do. Rather, they have power over admission, exclusion and prioritisation. They have been at the centre of fierce 'net neutrality' debates, focused in the US and Europe on ISPs charging content-providers for access, which would privilege providers who are able to pay for preferential treatment. For Schlosberg (2016: 144), net neutrality rules should at the very least prohibit tiered pricing. And they should allow regulators to intervene in response to complaints by providers of unfair treatment.

These represent desirable first steps. However, given the depth and extent of the problems with contemporary journalism, deeper changes will also need to be made if we are seriously to address the problems with news content that result in media amnesia. Public intervention is needed not just to regulate existing media systems from the top down but to reorganise them from the bottom up.

PUBLIC MEDIA

As we have seen again and again, one of the major problems with journalism is the lack of pluralism. Only a narrow range of perspectives is offered and these tend to be the perspectives of politicians and other elites. Increasing pluralism should therefore be one of the most important aims of media policy. The Leveson Report recommended that the UK government develop an appropriate measurement framework for plurality and consider a 'menu of potential remedies'. The most obvious of these remedies is to tackle the concentration of media ownership, which, as we have seen, is one of the most important filters through which content comes to serve the interests of the rich and powerful. During his appearance at the Leveson Inquiry, then-Labour leader Ed Miliband called for a cap on newspapers owning between 20 and 30 per cent of the news market. Former Conservative Prime Minister John Major argued for a cap of about 15–20 per cent. Leveson passed the buck to the government, which has refused to clamp down on the market power of the largest media groups (Freedman 2014: 81).

The outcome of the BSkyB case will be revealing in this respect. In 2011–12, Rupert Murdoch's News Corp tried to take full control of BSkyB, a move that would have substantially increased Murdoch's already immense media power. Because of the phone-hacking scandal, the attempt was dropped. However, another attempt was launched in 2016. The takeover was approved by the EU regulator in April 2017 and at the time of writing (January 2018) is being assessed by the UK regulator, which is considering whether it will give Murdoch too much control of news media in the UK, and whether he is a 'fit and proper' owner of Sky. If the proposed deal with Disney goes through, the stakes in Sky would pass to Disney, one of the world's biggest media conglomerates.

Breaking up media oligopolies, if necessary through enforced divestment, is essential, and is one of the key demands of campaign groups like the UK's Media Reform Coalition. In addition to that, there are other kinds of structural reform that can serve the public interest, as opposed to the usual kinds of structural reforms we have been dealing with here. Press subsidies, for example, exist in Sweden and Norway. In Sweden, a compensatory grant is given to newspapers with a minority market share. The size of the grant is determined by circulation and the volume of newsprint (with no reference to editorial content), and administered by a public body with all-party representation to prevent political partiality (Curran 2010b: 377). This increases diversity by supporting smaller-circulation papers that lack the economies of scale of their larger competitors. Breaking up media oligopolies and public subsidies for small newspapers are two basic steps that could help widen the range of views to which publics are routinely exposed.

Reforming the BBC

In countries like the UK, with a strong public service broadcasting tradition, protecting and reforming the public broadcasters is another essential piece of the puzzle. The BBC is under sustained attack. Its funding is again under threat and there are those who wish to curb its presence online. Austerity Chancellor George Osborne accused the BBC of having 'imperial ambitions' and of 'crowding out' national newspaper companies with its website (Syal 2015). Cutting back the BBC would of course benefit the media barons who are its competitors. Protecting the funding of public service media and their online presence is imperative. But the BBC should also be reformed. As we have seen, BBC news is far from immune to the problems associated with media amnesia.

A recent report on the future of public service television in the UK recommends that the BBC licence fee should be replaced by a more progressive funding mechanism such as a tiered platform-neutral household fee, a supplement to council tax or funding via general taxation. To help protect the BBC's independence, the government should hand over decision-making on BBC funding to an independent advisory body that would work on fixed settlement periods. The Royal Charter should be abolished and the BBC should be reconstituted as a statutory body. Appointments to the BBC's new unitary board should be entirely independent from government and the process should be overseen by a new independent appointments body. The regulator would be given the resources and the structures to regulate the BBC independently of both government and its commercial rivals. The other public service channels – ITV, Channel 4 and Channel 5 – should increase public service provision and in the case of Channel 4 (which is a public trust) be protected from privatisation (Goldsmiths 2016).

Public service principles include a commitment to reporting the news impartially and giving due prominence to news and current affairs; high programme standards that cater to the diversity of the public; and binding together and 'integrating an increasingly privatised society' (Curran 2010b: 380–1). An important additional reform would be to redefine the purpose of public broadcasting to include both representative pluralism and internationalism. Curran (2010b: 384) argues that 'broadcasting organizations should be charged with a duty to give adequate expression to the different viewpoints and concerns of the public. Broadcasters' existing obligation to inform could also contain an explicit reference to the need to give due prominence to events and developments outside Britain.'

Going further

Some propose that public funding and oversight over media should go much further. In the US context, McChesney and Nichols (2011) advocate an intervention costing some $35 billion. It would include wide-ranging direct and indirect subsidies for news media, paying for part of journalists' salaries in non-corporate newspapers, a graduated postal subsidy, and financial support for high school journalism and trainees. In addition, every American adult would get an annual $200 voucher to donate to a news medium (or media) of their choice, on the condition that it passes a modest threshold of audience demand, is a non-profit or low-profit venture, and makes its content freely available online.

In those countries that already have a strong tradition of public service media (unlike in the US), there are calls from several quarters to establish funds to pay for expanded public service journalism, especially online. Veteran media scholar James Curran (2010c), for example, has suggested a Fund for Independent Journalism, which would provide grants for low-cost, web-based journalistic initiatives. The funding body would include all-party and civil society representation, ensuring a diversity of viewpoints and backgrounds. He argues that PSB (public service broadcasting) websites could offer the opportunity to experiment with different kinds of format, including user-generated content and interactions, wide-ranging access to archives, and the creation of a search engine with different prioritisation criteria than the 'ratings-driven Google' (Curran 2010b: 388). He emphasises that public funding could also harness the opportunities offered by the internet for global journalism, opportunities that are not being properly used now due to the pressures of the free market.

Where would this level of funding come from? Media taxes. Suggested funding sources include a tax on broadcast spectrum, a surcharge on internet service providers, or an advertising tax. In their book *Misunderstanding the Internet*, Curran, Fenton and Freedman (2016: 208–9) claim that a 1 per cent tax on the operating profits of computer software and hardware, internet services and retailing, entertainment and telecoms companies in the Fortune 500 list alone would raise some $1.7 billion annually worldwide. This could be distributed by participatory commissioning through non-profit agencies. It could be used to support public journalism start-ups as well as endeavours that address the problems of online conglomeration more widely, such as 'the development of non-proprietorial content, community broadband initiatives ... and public access software labs'. Given their agenda-setting power, their enormous profits and their tax-avoiding antics, a levy on the advertising revenues of the giant digital intermediaries like Google and Facebook to pay for independent journalism is a recurring suggestion (see Schlosberg 2016: 149). There are two crucial features of these kinds of proposals. They call for public funding through the state, but insist on public journalism ventures being *independent* from the state as well as the market. And they recommend that funding be created through *progressive* taxation.

Christian Fuchs (2015) argues for both public and civil society provision of social media too – the new gateways to news. He writes that YouTube-type user-generated content sites that need large storage capacity but do not hold a lot of personal data, could increasingly be organised by public service institutions like the BBC. Social networking sites like Facebook that are personal-data intensive could be run by civil society organisations, to reduce the risk of data being shared with secret services. He argues that we 'need a YouTube run by the BBC and a Facebook organised by Wikipedia or a global network of public universities' (363). Fuchs puts forward similar funding proposals. A fund could be created through a tax on the revenues of online media giants and a progressive extension of the licence fee. The money could be used partly to fund public service media's online presence directly and partly to provide an annual voucher to every citizen to be given to their chosen non-profit social media. The voucher would therefore not replace BBC funding but would be additional to it. In this way, non-commercial versions of Twitter, Facebook and YouTube could be run either by public institutions or civil society, thereby 'strengthen[ing] the democratic character of communications' (368).

A mixed media economy

In his 2002 book, *Media and Power*, James Curran suggests a working model of a democratic media system, drawing on existing practices in different European countries. At the core is public service media, reaching large audiences. The core sector would be fed by four peripheral media sectors: the civic sector, the social market sector, the professional sector and the private sector. The civic sector would support the activist organisations of civil society, including political parties, social movements, interest-groups and sub-cultural networks. It could be enabled by public subsidies as well as practical support. The social market sector would consist of minority media, operating within the market and supported by the state. Its purpose would be to promote media pluralism and diversity of ownership. This builds on the idea of press subsidies found in Nordic countries, mentioned above. The professional sector would be controlled by media professionals. It would be publicly funded but not regulated, and would enjoy greater independence than the other sectors. For Curran (245), 'This should assist their fearless oversight of the state and other centres of power .... journalists in the professional sector should be guided by truth-seeking.' The private sector would be similar to the existing private sector. It would 'make the media system as a whole more responsive to popular pleasures'. The public service core would give prominence to public affairs and would be the space where all the different groups in society came together to discuss the management of society. It would be organised in such a way as to be inclusive and reflect the diversity of the country, and would cover the news with due impartiality.

This vision, as well as several of the ideas outlined above, could be described as radical social-democratic proposals for media reform. They certainly seem preferable to the media systems we have now. Above all, they emphasise plurality. And they fundamentally grasp the fact that the concentration of media ownership and control threatens plurality, and that the only way to enable plurality is to diversify structures of ownership and control. They also acknowledge that market as well as state pressures curb the freedom and ethical behaviour of journalists and can lead to narrow, homogeneous, elite-driven – not to mention inaccurate – kinds of journalism. Through bottom-up reform, the boundaries between mainstream and minority or alternative media would begin to blur, as social power became less concentrated.

These recommendations could also address the other two elements of media amnesia: the lack of either global context or historical context. Some of them stress the need to enable journalism to look outward and engage in dialogue with those in other parts of the world. They also emphasise giving journalists the time and freedom to engage in thorough investigation so as to be able to explain their societies more adequately. Pluralism would also mean offering a wider range of explanations and interpretations.

How stable these mixed media economies would be is hard to tell. Presumably, they would exist in the context of social-democratic (as opposed to neoliberal) societies. As we have seen, in the past, these have not evaded capitalism's crises. And they have not so far managed to avoid imperialistic international relations that mean some areas of the world benefit at the expense of others (recall the relationship between tax and exploitation in developing countries discussed in Chapter 2, for example). However, many of these proposed reforms would certainly represent great improvements and should be supported. They might serve as stepping stones to greater transformations. For instance, they might in due course lead to reconsideration of the ownership of other assets, such as media infrastructure.

Worker control

Some proposals are more ambitious still. Back in the 1960s, the late Marxist cultural scholar Raymond Williams (1966) argued that media workers should have collective control over the means of mass communication:

> Where the means of communication can be personally owned, it is the duty of society to guarantee this ownership and to ensure that distribution facilities are adequate, on terms compatible with the original freedom. Where the means of communication cannot be personally owned, because of their expense and size, it is the duty of society to hold these means in trust for the actual contributors, who for all practical purposes will control their use (122).

In this scenario, both the BBC and commercial broadcasting would be replaced by public trusts. These trusts would lease facilities on a long-term basis to companies that would control programme-making.

The companies would be independent and run democratically, with all members having an equal say over policy. Newspapers would also be taken into public ownership, and leased to their editors and journalists, who would determine editorial policy. Media workers would thus be protected 'alike from the bureaucrat and the speculator'. This vision is based on the principle that people 'should grow in capacity and power to direct their own lives – by creating democratic institutions, by bringing new sources of energy to human work, and by extending the expression and exchange of experience on which understanding depends' (Williams 1966: 125–6).

Public commissioning

More recently, Dan Hind (2012) has put forward a proposal for a public commissioning system in the contexts of the UK and US, which puts the link between media professionals and the public at its centre. In this vision, a public commissioning system would sit alongside existing public service and commercial broadcasters and publishers. An amount of money from tax revenues or licence fees would be placed into trusts. Journalists and researchers would pitch ideas for areas they want to research and produce content about. Their proposals would be made available online and in public spaces. The public would then vote on the proposals it wanted to support. Every citizen would have an equal say in how to allocate resources. Votes could be split to support a number of projects according to an expressed set of priorities (158). Each round of voting would be preceded by official and unofficial public meetings, where those bidding for funding would set out their ideas and objectives and raise awareness of issues of concern to them. Public meetings could also be held after a report is completed to discuss the content and consider how it should be disseminated.

The public would have control not only over the kinds of investigation carried out but also over how findings are published. It could decide to make the results of inquiries available to commercial and state-owned media. In the UK version, the different nations and regions would have a statutory body that published results as well as dispersing funds. Companies providing regional news on the independent TV networks could be required to publish the results of publicly commissioned research. Where large-scale public or commercial operators wanted to make extensive use of the material, they could be charged and the proceeds fed back into the commissioning system. Small-scale media outfits could use the material for low cost or for free. According to Hind, a sum of £80 million could pay for 3,000 publicly commissioned full-time journalists and researchers, including 250 investigative journalists. Public commissioning could help ensure that citizens received the kinds of information about society that they found useful, including about global and historical processes. It could enable journalists to develop deep knowledge in their fields and strong professional networks, and would give them the time to carry out thorough research. And it would support pluralism, giving everybody a say in what counts as 'news'.

A similar system could be set up in the US. Hind points out, as do McChesney and Nicols (2011) and others, that this would not be going against American values, because US media have always enjoyed different kinds of state support (168–9). Funds could be levied from commercial broadcasters in exchange for their right to make use of broadcast frequencies, which are public assets. The broadcasters would also be required to publish the findings of the research. In return, 'they could be relieved of their onerous public service functions and could focus instead on producing entertainment' (168–9). Over time, more funds might be made available to public commissioning. For example, part of the $4.7 billion spent by the Pentagon on public relations could be 'diverted into a system of public oversight of defense contracts and independent assessments of the country's military needs' (169).

This proposal can also be seen as strongly social democratic. It does not seek to supplant the capitalist societies that we have but to work within them to support more democratically informed public opinion. However, within it are contained the seeds of a much more ambitious transformation. With his public commissioning idea, Hind wishes to take on the media barons. And in his vision, the public commissioning of journalism would sit alongside a much more extensive system for the public production of knowledge, especially science research. This would confront, for example, the might of the military-industrial complex and pharmaceutical companies, which currently dominate much of the direction of scientific research. While these systems would initially supplement rather than replace the private sector, Hind opens up the possibility that, as publics become more involved with the production of knowledge, they will increasingly gain in experience and acquire the skills for self-governance. Over time, public self-governance over all areas of life could increase, until a new type of society – free from the tyranny of both bureaucrat and speculator – could emerge.

Think back to Chapter 5 and Srnicek and Williams' proposals for a social-democratic universal basic income. In this conception, a radically reformed capitalism is not seen as an end in itself but as a starting point that can shift into something else. These kinds of visions for a reformed media ecology can be seen in a similar light. Both Raymond Williams' and Hind's suggestions seem to assume strong state intervention initially. But they emphatically emphasise people themselves – workers for Williams and the public for Hind. Both insist on independence from the state as well as markets. Indeed, if one were anarchistically inclined, one could conceive of these kinds of systems operating in societies that do not have states but do have informal, democratically-run institutions that are able to coordinate social affairs on a large scale.

Of course, there are all kinds of objections that can be raised to all of these proposals, and there are likely to be many devils in the detail. Some might point out the dire obstacles in even beginning to make these moves, given the place we are starting from. But the point is that other media systems are possible, just as other societies are possible. As should have become abundantly clear, the media and the wider society are entirely connected. Media industries are currently some of the drivers of capitalism. In turn, they influence how we perceive the world and the way we interact with each other. To change the media we need to change society and to change society we need to change the media. We will need to engage in long-term multi-pronged action if we are to solve the problems with the media and the wider social, economic and political problems described here. The kinds of change envisioned in this book might not seem 'realistic' or 'grown up'. But to escape an increasingly dangerous status quo we might need to leave the comfort of safe ideas and imagine other possible worlds.

Glossary

Current account   One of the main components of a country's balance of payments – a record of the country's transactions with the rest of the world over a given time period. The current account consists of the country's balance of trade plus net income and direct payments. It measures international transfers of capital as well as exports and imports.

Debt-to-GDP ratio   The ratio of a country's public debt to its gross domestic product (GDP). By comparing a country's debt to its economic output, the debt-to-GDP ratio indicates the ability of the country to repay its debt. For that reason, the debt-to-GDP ratio is sometimes considered a more useful measure of a country's debt than the nominal figure (the amount of the debt) alone.

Deficit, budget   Usually refers to a government's budget deficit, which indicates that the government's revenues are lower than its expenditures over the course of a year. The government debt is the accumulation of the yearly budget deficits.

Deficit, trade   Refers to the balance of trade between countries. If a country is running a trade deficit, the value of its imports exceeds that of its exports. Conversely, a trade surplus is when a country exports a greater value than it imports. A trade deficit can act as a drag on GDP.

ECB   European Central Bank.

Fiscal   Relating to taxes and government expenditure. Fiscal policy is the government's use of tax and spend to influence the economy.

GDP   Gross Domestic Product. The monetary value of all the final goods and services produced within a country's borders in a given time period. GDP is commonly used to measure the economic health of a country.

ILO   International Labour Organization.

IMF   International Monetary Fund.

Labour productivity   The output produced per unit of labour input. Measures the economic efficiency of labour.

Monetary policy Policy related to the money supply, usually determined by central banks. Monetary policy is implemented through modifying the interest rate, buying or selling government bonds, and changing the amount of money banks are required to keep in the vault (bank reserves). Monetary policy is used to control inflation and encourage economic growth.

OECD The Organisation for Economic Cooperation and Development. An economic organisation of 35 high-income countries that are democratic and support free-market economies.

Share buybacks Also known as share repurchases. When a company purchases its own shares, decreasing the number of its shares on the open market and thereby increasing their value.

Sovereign debt Also known as national debt, government debt, country debt or public debt. The amount that a country owes. Sovereign debt is an accumulation of a government's annual deficits. Sovereign debt is usually financed through issuing sovereign bonds.

Surplus value The difference between the value a worker produces and their wages. In Marxist political economy, all economic value is created by workers. The surplus value they create is captured by the capitalist and is the source of profit.

TNC Transnational Corporation. A commercial enterprise that is registered and operates in more than one country at a time.

Wage share Also known as labour share. The part of national income allocated to wages as opposed to capital.

References

All URLs last accessed 21 September 2017.

Ali, T. (2015) *The Extreme Centre*. London: Verso.

Allan, S. (2004) *News Culture*. Maidenhead: Open University Press.

Ampuja, M. (2012) Globalization Theory, Media-Centrism and Neoliberalism: A critique of recent intellectual trends. *Critical Sociology* 38 (2).

Arrighi, G. (2010) *The Long Twentieth Century*. London: Verso

Ashley, J. (2008) Are the Guardianistas Rats? *Guardian*, 29 April.

BBC (2008a) *News at Ten*, 18 September.

BBC (2008b) *News at Ten*, 8 October.

BBC (2008c) *News at Ten*, 13 October.

BBC (2009) *News at Ten*, 23 January.

BBC (2010a) *News at Ten*, 22 March.

BBC (2010b) *News at Ten*, 2 May.

BBC (2011) *News at Ten*, 26 March.

BBC (2015) *News at Ten*, 6 July.

BBC (2012) Government Executive Pay Curbs Plans Announced. *BBC Online*, 23 January. bbc.co.uk/news/uk-politics-16688925

BBC (2016) What is Quantitative Easing. *BBC Online*, 6 August. bbc.co.uk/news/business-15198789

BBC (2017) Brexit: UK 'could change economic model' if single market access denied. *BBC Online*, 15 January. bbc.co.uk/news/uk-politics-38628428

BBC Radio 4 (2011) Radical Economics: Escaping credit serfdom. bbc.co.uk/programmes/booy6qtb

Beattie, J. (2013) Gran Larceny. *Mirror*, 22 March.

Belfried, C., Cribb, J., Hood, A. and Joyce, R. (2016) Living Standards, Poverty and Inequality in the UK: 2016. *Institute for Fiscal Studies*, July.

Bello, W. (2013) *Capitalism's Last Stand?* London: Zed Books.

Berglez, P. (2008) What is Global Journalism? *Journalism Studies* 9 (6): 845–58.

Berry, M. (2012) The *Today* Programme and the Banking Crisis. *Journalism* 14(2).

Berry, M. (2016a) No Alternative to Austerity: How BBC broadcast news reported the deficit debate. *Media, Culture, Society* 38 (6): 844–63.

Berry, M. (2016b) The UK Press and the Deficit Debate. *Sociology* 50 (3): 542–59.

Berry, M. (2018) Austerity, the Media and the UK Public. In: L. Basu, S. Schifferes and S. Knowles (eds) *The Media and Austerity*. Oxon: Routledge. In press.

Bickes, H., Otten, T. and Weymann, L.C. (2014) The Financial Crisis in the German and English Press. *Discourse and Society* 25 (4): 424–45.

Biressi, A. and Nunn, H. (2013) *Class and Contemporary British Culture.* Hampshire: Palgrave Macmillan.

Blyth, M. (2013) *Austerity.* Oxford: Oxford University Press.

Booth, R. (2016) More Than 7m Britons Now in Precarious Employment. *Guardian*, 15 November. theguardian.com/uk-news/2016/nov/15/more-than-7m-britons-in-precarious-employment

Booth, R. (2017) Free Software to Reveal How Facebook Election Posts Are Targeted. *Guardian*, 3 May. theguardian.com/technology/2017/may/03/free-software-reveal-facebook-election-posts-targeted-chrome-extension

Bourdieu, P. and Wacquant, L. (2001) New Liberal Speak: Notes on the new planetary vulgate. *Radical Philosophy* 105: 1–5.

Branded Content Research Network [website]. brandedcontentresearchnetwork. org/

Brignall, M. (2007) Northern Rock Crisis: Darling throws out rules in bid to end turmoil. *Guardian*, 17 September.

Browning, G. (2008) Castoffs of the Universe. *Guardian*, 11 October.

Burleigh, M. (2011) The Bond at Breaking Point. *Telegraph*, 16 September.

Butler, E. (2011) A Huge Incentive to Work. *Guardian*, 24 March.

Byttebier, K. (2017) *Towards a New International Monetary Order.* Cham: Springer.

Cammaerts, B., DeCillia, B., Magalhães, J.C. and Jimenez-Martínez, C. (2016) Journalistic Representations of Jeremy Corbyn in the British Press. *LSE* report. lse.ac.uk/media@lse/research/Mainstream-Media-Representations-of-Jeremy-Corbyn.aspx

Carlin, B., Porter, A. and Wallop, H. (2007) Politics as Tories Blame Labour's 'Decade of Debt'. *Telegraph*, 17 September.

Castells, M. (2009) *Communication Power.* Oxford: Oxford University Press.

Chakelian, A. (2017) What Welfare Changes did Philip Hammond Make in his Budget 2017? *New Statesman*, 8 March. newstatesman.com/politics/welfare/2017/03/what-welfare-changes-did-philip-hammond-make-his-budget-2017

Chakrabortty, A. (2015) The £93bn Handshake. *Guardian*, 7 July.

Chakravartty, P. and Schiller, D. (2010) Neoliberal Newspeak and Digital Capitalism in Crisis. *IJOC* 4: 670–92.

Chan, J.M. and Lee, C.C. (1984) The Journalistic Paradigm on Civil Protests: A Case Study of Hong Kong. In: Arno Andrew, Dissanayake Wima (eds) *The News Media in National and International Conflict*, 183–202. Boulder: Westview.

Chang, H.J. (2011) *23 Things They Don't Tell You About Capitalism.* London: Penguin.

Conway, E. (2008) Financial Markets Face Their Biggest Test Since the 1930s. *Telegraph*, 15 March.

Conway, E. (2010) Does the Coalition Have the Courage to Carry Out These Cuts? *Telegraph*, 24 June.

Corlett, A. and Clarke, S. (2017) Back to the '80s. *Resolution Foundation*, 1 February. resolutionfoundation.org/media/blog/back-to-the-80s-projections-for-living-standards-and-inequality-in-the-uk/

Corporate Watch (2014) *False Dilemmas*. London: Freedom Press.

Cox, A. (2018) Reform in Retreat: The media, the banks and the attack on Dodd-Frank. In: L. Basu, S. Schifferes and S. Knowles (eds) *The Media and Austerity*. Oxon: Routledge. In press.

Cox, J. (2016) $12.3 Trillion of QE Has Added Up to ...This?. *CNBC*, 12 February. cnbc.com/2016/02/12/123-trillion-of-qe-has-added-up-tothis.html

Crouch, C. (2000) *Postdemocracy*. Cambridge: Polity.

Crouch, C. (2011) *The Strange Non-Death of Neoliberalism*. Cambridge: Polity.

Cruddas, J. (2008) A Ready Made People's Bank. *Guardian*, 13 October.

Curran, J. (2002) *Media and Power*. London: Routledge.

Curran, J. (2010a) Press History. In: J. Curran and J. Seaton, *Power without Responsibility*. Oxon: Routledge.

Curran, J. (2010b) Media Reform: Democratic choices. In: J. Curran and J. Seaton, *Power without Responsibility*. Oxon: Routledge.

Curran, J. (2010c) The Future of Journalism. *Journalism Studies* 11(4): 464–76.

Curran, J., Fenton, N. and Freedman, D. (2016) *Misunderstanding the Internet*. Oxon: Routledge.

Curran, J. and Witschge, T. (2010) Liberal Dreams and the Internet. In: N. Fenton (ed.) *New Media, Old News*. London: Sage.

Curtis, P. (2011) Reality Check: How much did the banking crisis cost taxpayers? *Guardian*, 12 September. theguardian.com/politics/reality-check-with-polly-curtis/2011/sep/12/reality-check-banking-bailout

Cushion, S,, Kilby, A., Thomas, T., Morani, M. and Sambrook, R. (2016) Newspapers, Impartiality and Television News. *Journalism Studieses* D. DOI: 10.1080/1461670X.2016.1171163.

Dahlgreen, W. (2014) Voters Choose Greater Equality over Greater Wealth. *YouGov*, 30 April. yougov.co.uk/news/2014/04/30/equality-more-important-wealth/

Dardot, P. and Laval, C. (2017) *The New Way of the World*. London: Verso.

Davies, N. (2009) *Flat Earth News*. London: Vintage.

Davis, A. (2002) *Public Relations Democracy*. Manchester: Manchester University Press.

Davis, A. (2011) Promotion, Propaganda and High Finance. In: Gerald Sussman (ed.) *The Propaganda Society: Promotional Culture and Politics in Global Context*. London: Bloomsbury: 251–66.

Davis, A. (2013) *Promotional Cultures*. Cambridge: London.

Dean, J. (2009) *Democracy and Other Neoliberal Fantasies*. Durham: Duke University Press.

De Cock, C. (2018) Ideologies of Time: How elite corporate actors engage the future. *Organization*. Forthcoming.

De Cock, C., Cutcher, L. and Grant, D. (2012) Finance Capitalism's Perpetually Extinguished Pasts. *Culture and Organization* 18 (2): 87–90.

De Quetteville, H. (2010) A Nation at War with Itself. *Telegraph*, 7 May.

Deuze, M. (2007) *Media Work*. Cambridge: Polity.

Dhaliwal, S. and Forkert, K. (2016) Deserving and Undeserving Migrants. *Soundings* 16: 49–61.

Dominiczak, P. (2015a) From Welfare to Work. *Telegraph*, 9 July.

Dominiczak, P. (2015b) Unions Threaten Chaos after Corbyn Win. *Telegraph*, 14 September.

Dowmunt, T. and Coyer, K. (2007) Introduction. In: K. Coyer, T. Dowmunt and A. Fountain (eds) *The Alternative Media Handbook*. Oxon: Routledge.

Dunn, T.N. and Hawkes, S. (2015) Corbyshambles. *Sun*, 15 September.

Dunn, T.N. and Schofield, K. (2015) The Osborne Supremacy. *Sun*, 9 July.

Eleftheriadis, P. (2015) Where Did Greece Go So Wrong? *Telegraph*, 11 July.

Elgot, J. (2017) Jeremy Corbyn Calls for Maximum Wage Law. *Guardian*, 10 January. theguardian.com/politics/2017/jan/10/jeremy-corbyn-calls-for-maximum-wage-law

Elliott, L. (2008a) Commentary. *Guardian*, 20 September.

Elliott, L. (2008b) This Week the Crash Went Nuclear, and Britain Will Feel the Worst of the Fallout. *Guardian*, 16 September.

Elliott, L. (2012) Eurozone's Mood Music is Still Downbeat. *Guardian*, 11 June.

Elliott, L. (2014) Divided Britain: Five families own more than poorest 20%. *Guardian*, 17 March.

Elliott, L. (2015a) George Osborne Talks a Good Game, But His Strategy Has Been a Flop. *Guardian*,18 March.

Elliott, L. (2015b) IFS Picks the Budget to Pieces ... Again. *Guardian*, 10 July.

Elliott, L. and Stewart, H.(2008a) Financial Services: Less profit, more regulation to come, says watchdog. *Guardian*, 13 October.

Elliott, L. and Stewart, H. (2008b) Economic Outlook: Housing slump will help push UK into recession next year, warns IMF. *Guardian*, 9 October.

Emmerson, C., Johnson, P. and Joyce, R. (2017) Spending Cuts to Accelerate as Tax Burden Rises to Highest Level in Over 30 Years. *Institute for Fiscal Studies*, 7 February. ifs.org.uk/publications/8891

Entman, R. (1993) Framing: Toward clarification of a fractured paradigm. *Journal of Communication* 43 (4): 51–8.

European Commission (2012) Facts and Figures on State Aid in the EU Member States. *European Commission*, autumn update. http://ec.europa.eu/competition/state_aid/studies_reports/2012_autumn_working_paper_en.pdf

Evans-Pritchard, A. (2008) Countries 'Face Going Bust'. *Telegraph*, 11 October.

Fay, S. (2011) Big City, Bright Lights. *British Journalism Review* 22: 48–53.

Feldner, H. and Vighi, F. (2015) *Critical Theory and the Crisis of Contemporary Capitalism*. London: Bloomsbury.

Fenton, N. (2010) Drowning or Waving. In: N. Fenton (ed.) *New Media, Old News*. London: Sage.

Fenton, N. (2016a) The Internet of Radical Politics and Social Change. In: J. Curran, N. Fenton and D. Freedman (eds) *Misunderstanding the Internet*. Oxon: Routledge.

Fenton, N. (2016b) *Digital, Political, Radical*. Cambridge: Polity Press.

Financial Times (2016a) S&P: QE 'Exacerbates' Inequality. *Financial Times*, 10 February. ft.com/content/b4e604c8-b61a-362e-b741-a78f7009a569

Financial Times (2016b) Mr Trump's Victory, Coming After the Brexit Referendum Vote in Britain, Looks Like Another Grievous Blow to the Liberal International Order. *Financial Times* [editorial], 9 November. ft.com/content/a4669844-a643-11e6-8b69-02899e8bd9d1

Franklin, B. (1997) *Newszak and News Media*. London: Arnold.

Fraser, M. (2009) Five Reasons for Crash Blindness. *British Journalism Review* 20 (4): 78–83.

Freedland, J. (2008) Our Leaders Are Impotent To Tame the Beast. *Guardian*, 8 October.

Freedman, D. (2010) The Political Economy of the 'New' News Environment. In: N. Fenton (ed.) *New Media, Old News*. London: Sage.

Freedman, D. (2014) *The Contradictions of Media Power*. London: Bloomsbury.

Froud, J., Johal, S., Leaver, A., Moran, M. and Williams, K. (2011) Groundhog Day. *CRESC Working Paper Series*, Working Paper No.108, November.

Fuchs, C. (2010) *Foundations of Critical Media and Information Studies*. New York: Routledge.

Fuchs, C. (2015) *Reading Marx in the Information Age*. New York: Routledge.

Fuchs, C. (2018) Social Media and the Capitalist Crisis. In: L. Basu, S. Schifferes and S. Knowles (eds) *The Media and Austerity*. Oxon: Routledge. In press.

Fuchs, C. and Sandoval, M. (2012) Introduction: Critique, social media and the information society in the age of capitalist crisis. In: C. Fuchs and M. Sandoval (eds) *Critique, Social Media and the Information Society*. Oxon: Routledge.

Garland, C. (2015) Framing the Poor. *Triple C* 13 (1).

Gentleman, A. (2015) Austerity Cuts Will Bite Even Harder in 2015 – Another £12bn will go. *Guardian*, 1 January. theguardian.com/society/2015/jan/01/austerity-cuts-2015-12-billion-britain-protest

Ghosh, J. (2011) Spooked Into Austerity, We Dig Our Own Economic Grave. *Guardian*, 14 September.

Giles, C. (2016) UK Suffering 'First Lost Decade Since 1860s' Says Carney. *Financial Times*, 5 December. ft.com/content/c0c36268-bbod-11e6-8b45-b8b81dd5do80

Gimson, A. (2008) The One Thing Sure To Cheer No 10. *Telegraph*, 9 October.

Giroux, H.A. (2014) *The Violence of Organized Forgetting*. San Francisco: City Lights.

Gitlin, T. (1980) *The Whole World Is Watching: Mass Media in the Making and Unmaking of the New Left*. Berkeley: University of California Press.

Gitlin, T. (2001) *Media Unlimited*. New York: Metropolitan Books.

Golding, P. and Middleton, S. (1982) *Images of Welfare*. Oxford: Basil Blackwell.

Goldsmiths (2016) A Future for Public Service Television. *Goldsmiths* [report], June. futureoftv.org.uk/

Goodley, S. (2015) Chancellor Hands Businesses £6.6bn in Tax Cuts and Giveaways. *Guardian*, 9 July.

Goodman, G. (2009) Thankless Times Can Only Be Tackled by a Labour Which Finds its Soul. *Mirror*, 24 April.

Graeber, D. (2013) On the Phenomenon of Bullshit Jobs. *Strike Magazine*, 17 August.

Graeber, D. (2014) *Debt: The First 5,000 Years*. Brooklyn: Melville House.

Gramsci, A. (1971) *Selections From the Prison Notebooks*. New York: International.

Greenslade, R. (2016) Telegraph Media Group Made £51m Operating Profit in 2015. *Guardian*, 17 February.

Grice, Andrew (2013) Voters 'Brainwashed By Tory Welfare Myths', Shows New Poll. *Independent*, 4 January. independent.co.uk/news/uk/politics/voters-brainwashed-by-tory-welfare-myths-shows-new-poll-8437872.html

Grusin, R. (2010) *Premediation: Affect and Mediality after 9/11*. Hampshire: Palgrave Macmillan.

Guardian (2008) Financial Crisis: Economics through the looking-glass. *Guardian*, 11 October.

Guardian (2010) Newspaper Support In UK General Elections. *Guardian* [datablog]. theguardian.com/news/datablog/2010/may/04/general-election-newspaper-support

Hague, W. (2015) Why I Was Right To Oppose Euro From the Start. *Telegraph*, 7 July.

Haldane, A. (2011) Control Rights (and Wrongs). Wincott Annual Memorial Lecture, 24 October. bis.org/review/r111026a.pdf

Haldane, A. (2015) Labour's Share. *Bank of England*, 12 November. bankofengland.co.uk/publications/Pages/speeches/2015/864.aspx

Hale, T. (2017) How the ECB's Purchases Have Changed European Bond Markets. *Financial Times*, 8 February. ft.com/content/c5568324-ec8f-11e6-930f-061b01e23655

Hall, S. (1983) The Great Moving Right Show. In: S. Hall and M. Jacques (eds) *The Politics of Thatcherism*. London: Lawrence and Wishart.

Hall, S., Critcher, C., Jefferson, T., Clarke, J. and Roberts, B. (1978) *Policing the Crisis*. Hampshire: Palgrave Macmillan.

Hallin, D. (1986) *The 'Uncensored War': The Media and Vietnam*. New York: OUP.

Hallin, D. (1994) *We Keep America on Top of the World*. New York: Routledge.

Hardy, J. (2014) *Critical Political Economy of the Media*. Oxon: Routledge.

Harkins, H. and Lugo-Ocando, J. (2016) How Malthusian Ideology Crept into the Newsroom: British tabloids and the coverage of the 'underclass'. *Critical Discourse Studies* 13 (1): 78–93.

Harvey, D. (1989) *The Condition of Postmodernity*. Oxford: Basil Blackwell.

Harvey, D. (2011) *The Enigma of Capital*. London: Profile Books.

Hastings, M. (2008) Many of These Bankers are Horrible People, but We Will Still Need Them. *Guardian*, 15 September.

Hawkes, S. (2011) Do the Business. *Sun*, 24 March.

Heffer, S. (2007) If We Take Away All the Risk, Then Capitalism is Finished. *Telegraph*, 19 September.

Heffer, S. (2011) Reputations Are Built on Actions, not the Half-Truths of Spin Doctors. *Telegraph*, 23 March.

Herman, E.S. and Chomsky, N. (1988) *Manufacturing Consent*. New York: Pantheon.

Hesmondhalgh, D. (2015) *The Cultural Industries*. London: Sage.

Hind, D. (2012) *The Return of the Public*. London: Verso.

Hobsbawm, E. (2008) The £500bn Question: A welcome step forward, or a reckless handout? *Guardian*, 9 October.

Hood, A. and Phillips, D. (2015) Substantial Cuts Made, But Biggest Changes To the Benefit System Yet To Come. *Institute for Fiscal Studies*, 28 January. ifs. org.uk/publications/7541

Hood, A. and Waters, T. (2017) Living Standards, Poverty and Inequality In the UK: 2016–17 to 2021–22. *Institute for Fiscal Studies*, 2 March. ifs.org.uk/publications/8957

Hope, W. (2011) Crisis of Temporalities: Global capitalism after the 2007–08 financial collapse. *Time and Society* 20 (1): 94–118.

Horvit, B. (2004) Global News Agencies and the Pre-War Debate. In: R.D. Berenger (ed.) *Global Media go to War*. Spokane: Marquette Books.

Hoskins, A. and Tulloch, J. (2016) *Risk and Hyperconnectivity: Media and Memories of Neoliberalism*. Oxford: OUP.

Hudson, M. (2017) *J is for Junk Economics*. ISLET.

Hunt, T. (2008) Groundhog Capitalism. *Guardian*, 20 September.

Hutton, W. (2008) Brown and Darling Have Bitten the Bullet – And Set the World an Example. *Guardian*, 9 October.

Ipsos Mori (2009) *Public Spending Index*, June. ipsos.com/sites/default/files/migrations/en-uk/files/Assets/Docs/poll-public-spending-charts-june-2009.pdf

Ipsos Mori (2015) *Veracity Index*. January.

Islam, F. (2016) Why Labour Lost Election: By Margaret Beckett. *Sky News* [website]. news.sky.com/story/why-labour-lost-election-by-margaret-beckett-10144153

Jackson, T. (2011) *Prosperity without Growth*. Oxon: Routledge.

Jenkins, S. (2011) Europe is Returning to National Identity – And Brussels Oligarchs Can't Stop it. *Guardian*, 16 September.

Jenkins, S. (2012) This May be the Last Hurrah for the Tory-Lib Dem Accord. *Guardian*, 21 March.

Johnson, B. (2008) In Times as Dire as These, the Only Thing to do is Dig for Victory. *Telegraph*, 14 October.

Johnston, P. (2010) Danger: Turbulence ahead. *Telegraph*, 26 June.

Jones, O. (2015) *The Establishment*. London: Penguin Books.

Jubilee Debt Campaign (2015) At Least 90% of the Greek Bailout has Paid off Reckless Lenders. *Jubilee Debt Campaign*, 18 January. jubileedebt.org.uk/press-release/least-90-greek-bailout-paid-reckless-lenders

Kaminska, M., Gallacher, J.D., Kollanyi, B., Yasseri, T. and Howard, P.N. (2017) Social Media and News Sources during the 2017 UK General Election. COMPROP Data Memo, 5 June.

Kavanagh, T. (2008a) Darling's Hands are Tied by You Know Who. *Sun*, March 10.

Kavanagh, T. (2008b) We're All Paying for Gord's Inflated Ego. *Sun*, 13 October.

Kavanagh, T. (2009) Only You Can Save Us All Now, Darling. *Sun*, April 20.

Kavanagh, T. (2012) We Must Step Back from Euro Plughole. *Sun*, 11 June.

Kay, J.B. and Salter, L. (2014) Framing The Cuts: An analysis of the BBC's discursive framing of the ConDem cuts agenda. *Journalism* 15 (6): 754–72.

Klein, N. (2008) *The Shock Doctrine*. London: Penguin.

Klein, N. (2014) *This Changes Everything*. New York: Simon and Schuster.

Klein, N. and Butselaar, E. (2008) Expert Views: After a week of turmoil, has the world changed? *Guardian*, 20 September.

Klingberg, K. (2008) *The Overflowing Brain*. Oxford: OUP.

Knowles, S., Phillips, G. and Lidberg, J. (2017) Reporting the Global Financial Crisis: A longitudinal tri-nation study of mainstream financial journalism. *Journalism Studies* 18 (3): 322–40.

Krugman, P. (2016) The Mitt-Hawley Fallacy. *New York Times* [blog], 4 March. krugman.blogs.nytimes.com/2016/03/04/the-mitt-hawley-fallacy/

Kurz, R. (2009) *Schwarzbuch Kapitalismus. Ein Abgesang auf die Marktwirtschaft.* Frankfurt am Main: Eichborn. Translation by J Robinson.

Kynaston, D. (2010) Austerity Was a Hard Sell In the 40s. *Guardian*, June 22.

Kyriakidou, M. and Garcia-Blanco, I. (2018) Safeguarding the Status Quo: The press and the emergence of a new left in Greece and Spain. In: L. Basu, S. Schifferes and S. Knowles (eds) *The Media and Austerity*. Oxon: Routledge. In press.

Labour Press (2017) The Tories £70bn Tax Giveaways to the Super-Rich and Big Business. *Labour Press*, 12 March. press.labour.org.uk/post/158315410419/the-tories-70bn-tax-giveaways-to-the-super-rich

Lambert, R. (2010) Fall-Out from Greece Heads Our Way. *Guardian*, 8 May.

Lamont, L. (2010) George's Unpalatable Medicine. *Telegraph*, 21 June.

Lapavitsas, C. (2010) Germany: A euro laggard. *Guardian*, 22 March.

Lapavitsas, C. (2011) Greece Must Default and Quit the Euro. *Guardian*, 20 September.

Lapavitsas, C. (2013) *Profiting without Producing*. London: Verso.

Lapavitsas, C. (2014) State and Finance in Financialised Capitalism. Think piece for the Centre for Labour and Social Studies, June.

Laws, D. (2011) We Must Tackle the Economy and Mend Our Broken Society. *Sun*, September 16.

Lea, R. (2007) The Tories' Solid Economic Legacy Has Been Squandered. *Telegraph*, 17 September.

Leckie, B. (2008) Bradford and Bingley, HBOS ... RBS ... Lehman Bros ...You Took One Helluva Beating! *Sun*, 9 October.

Leeson, N. (2009) Escape of the Bankrupt. *Guardian*, 19 September.

Le Masurier M (2015) What is Slow Journalism? *Journalism Practice* 9(2): 138–152.

Leonard, T. (2008) If the Left has its Way the Bad Times will be Even Worse. *Telegraph*, 13 October.

Levitin, M. and Samuel, H. (2008) Drastic Action Was Needed to Save Banks, Says Merkel. *Telegraph*, 14 October.

Lewis, C. (2011) Civil Society and Public Journalism. In: M. Edwards (ed.) *The Oxford Handbook of Civil Society*. Oxford: OUP.

Lewis, J., Inthorn, S. and Wahl-Jorgenson, K. (2005) *Citizens or Consumers?* Maidenhead: Open University Press.

Lewis, J. and Thomas, R. (2015) More of the Same. In: G. Murdock and J. Gripsrud (eds) *Money Talks*. Bristol: Intellect.

Lewis, J., Williams, A. and Franklin, B. (2008) A Compromised Fourth Estate? *Journalism Studies* 9 (1): 1–20.

Lievrouw, L.A. (2015) *Alternative and Activist New Media*. Cambridge: Polity.

Littunen, M. (2017) An Analysis of News and Advertising in the UK General Election. *Open Democracy*, 7 June. opendemocracy.net/uk/analysis-of-news-and-advertising-in-uk-general-election

Lumina, C. (2015) Greek Debt Audit – Definition of Terms. *Committee for the Abolishment of Illegitimate Debt*, 18 January. cadtm.org/Greek-debt-audit-Definition-of

Luyendijk, J. (2016) *Swimming with Sharks*. London: Guardian Faber Publishing.

Maguire, K. (2008a) Gordon's Chance to Become a Super Hero. *Mirror*, 8 October.

Maguire, K. (2008b) Gamble Will Cost Labour Dear if Public Picks up Tab. *Mirror*, 9 October.

Maguire, K. (2014) Osborne Keeps Us Locked to Austerity. *Mirror*, 17 March.

Maguire, K. (2015) Osborne's War on Low Wage Workers. *Mirror*, 6 July.

Marquand, D. (2008) Situation Vacant. *Guardian*, 11 October.

Martin, I. (2008) Brown Should Enjoy Himself While He Can. *Telegraph*, 10 October.

Martinson, J. (2016) Guardian Media Group to Cut 250 Jobs in Bid to Break Even Within Three Years. *Guardian*, 17 March. theguardian.com/media/2016/mar/17/guardian-media-group-to-cut-250-jobs

Marx, K. (1990 [1867]) *Capital, Volume I*. London: Penguin.

Mason, P. (2011) How Will the Two Speed Europe get into Gear? *BBC Online*, 9 December. www.bbc.co.uk/news/business-16112447

Mason, P. (2016) *Postcapitalism*. London: Penguin.

Maxwell, R. and Miller, T. (2012) *Greening the Media*. Oxford: OUP

Mazzucato, M. (2013) Patchy Boosts Aren't Enough. *Guardian*, 20 March.

McChesney, R. (1999) *Rich Media, Poor Democracy*. Urbana: University of Illinois Press.

McChesney, R. and Nichols, J. (2011) *The Death and Life of American Journalism*. New York: Nation Books.

McDonagh, M. (2010) Unlike the Greeks, the Irish Are Facing up to their Plight. *Telegraph*, 3 May.

McDonnell, J. (2008) The £500bn Question: A welcome step forward, or a reckless handout? *Guardian*, 9 October.

McElroy, D. and Anast, P. (2010) Three Die as Greek Militants Set Bank Ablaze. *Telegraph*, 6 May.

McLeod, D.M. and Hertog, J.K. (1999) Social Control, Social Change and the Mass Media's Role in the Regulation of Protest Groups. In: D. Demers and

V. Kasisomayajula (eds) *Mass Media, Social Control and Social Change: A Macrosocial Perspective.* Ames: Iowa State University Press: 305–30.

McNair, B. (1999) *News and Journalism in the UK.* London: Routledge.

McNally, D. (2011) *Global Slump.* Oakland: PM Press.

Media Reform Coalition (2015) Who Owns the UK Media? *Media Reform Coalition Report.* mediareform.org.uk/who-owns-the-uk-media

Media Reform Coalition (2016) Should He Stay or Should He Go? *Media Reform Coalition Report.* mediareform.org.uk/featured/stay-go-television-online-news-coverage-labour-party-crisis

Meek, J. (2014) *Private Island.* London: Verso.

Mercille, J. (2014) The Role of the Media in Fiscal Consolidation Programmes: The case of Ireland. *Cambridge Journal of Economics* 38: 281–300.

Milligan, B. (2017) UK Household Debt Now a Record £13,000, Says TUC. *BBC Online*, 8 January. bbc.com/news/business-38534238

Mills, T. (2016) *The BBC: The Myth of a Public Service.* London: Verso.

Milne, S. (2008) The Political Class Can't Face up to the Scale of this Crisis. *Guardian*, 18 September.

Milne, S. (2010) Osborne's Claims of Fairness Are Now Exposed as a Fraud. *Guardian*, 24 June.

Milne, S. (2012) Osborne is Stuck in a Failed Economic Model, Circa 1979. *Guardian*, 21 March.

Milne, S. (2014) Osborne's Record is a Dismal Failure Even in His Own Terms. *Guardian*, 20 March.

Mirowski, P. (2013) *Never Let a Serious Crisis go to Waste.* London: Verso.

Mirror (2011) 13.5m Live in a Britain Where Parents Face a Choice . . . Feed Their Children or Keep Them Warm at Night. *Mirror*, 19 September.

Mitchell, A., Gottfried, J., Barthel, M. and Shearer, E. (2016) The Modern News Consumer. *Pew Research Center*, 7 July. journalism.org/2016/07/07/the-modern-news-consumer/

Monbiot, G. (2008) This Stock Collapse is Petty When Compared to the Nature Crunch. *Guardian*, 14 October.

Monbiot, G. (2017) The Election's Biggest Losers? Not the Tories but the Media, Who Missed the Story. *Guardian*, 13 June. theguardian.com/commentisfree/2017/jun/13/election-tories-media-broadcasters-press-jeremy-corbyn

Moor, M. (2008) Asia Traders Overwhelmed by 'Panic and Fear'. *Telegraph*, 11 October.

Moore, C. (2008) At Least the Crash Will Not Make Britain the Sick Man of Europe. *Telegraph*, 11 October.

Moore, C. (2012) As the Eurozone Breaks Apart, Britain Must Go its Separate Way. *Telegraph*, 9 June.

Mylonas, Y. (2012) Media and the Economic Crisis of the EU: The 'culturalization' of a systemic crisis and *Bild-Zeitung*'s framing of Greece. *Triple C* 10 (2): 646–71.

Needham, D. (2015) 'Goodbye, Great Britain'?: The press, the Treasury, and the 1976 IMF crisis. In: S. Schifferes and R. Roberts (eds) *The Media and Financial Crises: Comparative and Historical Perspectives.* Oxon: Routledge.

Nelson, F. (2013) Britain's Fortunes Rest on the Bank's Great Money-printing Machine. *Telegraph*, 22 March.

Nelson, F. (2015) The Living Wage Sounds Like a Good Idea – But Tax Cuts Are Better. *Telegraph*, 10 July.

Norfield, T. (2011) What the 'China Price' Really Means. *Economics of Imperialism* [blog], 4 June. economicsofimperialism.blogspot.nl/2011/06/what-china-price-really-means.html

Norfield, T. (2016) *The City*. London: Verso.

Novarra Media (2017) Interview with Paul Mason. YouTube, 7 June. youtube.com/watch?v=1z5_mRdcB14

Oborne, P. (2011) Some European Countries are in the Habit of Going Bankrupt. *Telegraph*, 25 March.

Oborne, P. (2015) Why I Have Resigned from the Telegraph. *Open Democracy*, 17 February. opendemocracy.net/ourkingdom/peter-oborne/why-i-have-resigned-from-telegraph

OECD.Stat. stats.oecd.org/index.aspx?DataSetCode=ANHRS

Ofcom (2015) *News Consumption in the UK*. ofcom.org.uk/research-and-data/tv-radio-and-on-demand/tv-research/news-consumption-2015

O'Reilly, L. (2016) The 30 Biggest Media Companies in the World. *Business Insider*, 31 May. businessinsider.com/the-30-biggest-media-owners-in-the-world-2016-5

Ortiz, I., Chai, J. and Cummins, M. (2011) Austerity Measures Threaten Children and Poor Households. *UNICEF* [report], September. unicef.org/socialpolicy/files/Austerity_Measures_Threaten_Children.pdf

Oxfam (2014a) A Tale of Two Britains [press release], 17 March. policy-practice.oxfam.org.uk/publications/a-tale-of-two-britains-inequality-in-the-uk-314152

Oxfam (2014b) Even it Up. [report]. oxfam.org/en/campaigns/even-it-up

Oxfam (2017a) Just 8 Men Own Same Wealth as Half the World [press release], 16 January. oxfam.org/en/pressroom/pressreleases/2017-01-16/just-8-men-own-same-wealth-half-world

Oxfam (2017b) An Economy for the 99%. *Oxfam*, January [briefing report]. www.oxfam.org/en/research/economy-99

Papahelas, A. (2010) The Task Appears Sisyphean. But Don't Write Greece Off. *Guardian*, 7 May.

Pariser, E. (2012) *The Filter Bubble*. London: Penguin.

Parsons, T. (2008) So Many Suffer for the Grimy Greed of a Few. *Mirror*, 11 October.

Peston, R. (2012) *How Do We Fix this Mess?* London: Hodder and Stoughton.

Phillips, A. (2010) Old Sources: New Bottles. In: N. Fenton (ed.) *New Media, Old News*. London: Sage.

Phillips, A. (2012) Faster and Shallower: Homogenisation, cannibalisation and the death of reporting. In: P. Lee-Wright, A. Phillips and T. Witschge, *Changing Journalism*. Oxon: Routledge.

Phillips, M. (2016) The World's Debt is Alarmingly High. *Bloomberg*, 22 February.

Philo, G. ed. (1995) *Glasgow Media Group Reader, Volume 2*. London: Routledge.

Picard, R.G. (2014) The Future of the News Industry. In: J. Curran (ed.) *Media and Society*. London: Bloomsbury.

Piketty, T. (2014) *Capital in the Twenty-first Century*. Cambridge: Belknap Harvard.

Pirie, I. (2012) Representations of Economic Crisis in Contemporary Britain. *British Politics* 7: 341–64.

Ponsford, D. (2017) Print ABCs. *Press Gazette*, 23 January.

Porter, A. (2009) Cameron Calls for Action on Banks. *Telegraph*, January 27.

Prince, R. (2009) Families Will Pay Price for Labour's Decade of Debt, Says Cameron. *Telegraph*, April 23.

Quiggin, J. (2010) *Zombie Economics*. Princeton: Princeton University Press.

Ramesh, R. (2012) UK in a Perfect Storm of Inequality – Oxfam. *Guardian*, 14 June.

Raynor, G. (2008a) Vulture Capitalists Shot Down. *Telegraph*, 19 September.

Raynor, G. (2008b) How a £500 Billion Bank Bail-out Became an Historic State Buyout. *Telegraph*, 13 October.

Reade, B. (2008) Make all These Greedy Bankers Feel the Pain. *Mirror*, 9 October.

Reade, B. (2012) Euro Joking! *Mirror*, 14 June.

Redden, J. (2011) Poverty in the News. *Information, Communication and Society* 14 (6): 820–49.

Redden, J. and Witschge, T. (2010) A New News Order? Online news content examined. In: N Fenton (ed.) *New Media, Old News*. London: Sage.

Reece, D. (2008) Paying Price for Creating Illusion of Wealth from a Pile of Debt is Coming to a Bloody End. *Telegraph*, October 11.

Roberts, B. (2010) Hammer the Rich… to Help the Poor. *Mirror*, 25 March.

Roberts, B. and Manning, C. (2008) The Rate Escape. *Mirror*, 9 October.

Roberts, M. (2015) Keynes, Marx and the Effect of QE. *The Next Recession* [blog], 11 November. thenextrecession.wordpress.com/2015/11/11/keynes-marx-and-the-effect-of-qe/

Roberts, M. (2016a) Will China Pull Down the World? *The Next Recession* [blog], 14 January. thenextrecession.wordpress.com/2016/01/14/will-china-pull-down-the-world/

Roberts, M. (2016b) From China to Mars. *The Next Recession* [blog], 5 September. thenextrecession.wordpress.com/2016/09/05/from-china-to-mars/

Roberts, M. (2016c) The End of Globalisation and the Future of Capitalism. *The Next Recession* [blog], 11 September. thenextrecession.wordpress.com/2016/09/11/the-end-of-globalisation-and-the-future-of-capitalism/

Roberts, M. (2016d) The Global Debt Hangover. *The Next Recession* [blog], 9 October. thenextrecession.wordpress.com/2016/10/09/the-global-debt-hangover/

Roberts, M. (2016e) Britain at the Crossroads. *The Next Recession* [blog], 5 November. thenextrecession.wordpress.com/2016/11/05/britain-at-the-crossroads-the-class-conference/

Roberts, M. (2017) ASSA 2017 – Part One: Productivity and inequality. *The Next Recession* [blog], 9 January. thenextrecession.wordpress.com/2017/01/09/assa-2017-part-one-productvity-and-inequality/

Roberts, R. (2015) The Pound and the Press, 1919–1972. In: S. Schifferes and R. Roberts (eds) *The Media and Financial Crises: Comparative and Historical Perspectives*. Oxon: Routledge.

Roberts, R. (2018) The 'Geddes Axe': The Press and Britain's First Austerity Drive. In: L. Basu, S. Schifferes and S. Knowles (eds) *The Media and Austerity*. Oxon: Routledge.

Robertson, J.W. (2011) The Propaganda Model in 2011. *SCAC* 1 (1): 24–33.

Rosa, H. (2015) *Social Acceleration*. New York: Columbia University Press.

Rosenberg, H. and Feldman, C.F. (2008) *No Time to Think*. New York: Continuum.

Routledge, P. (2008) City Fall-out Just Criminal. *Mirror*, 19 September.

Sayer, A. (2015) *Why We Can't Afford the Rich*. Bristol: Policy Press.

Schifferes, S. and Knowles, S. (2015) The British Media and the 'First Crisis of Globalization'. In: S. Schifferes and R. Roberts (eds) *The Media and Financial Crises*. Oxon: Routledge.

Schechter, D. (2009) Credit Crisis: how did we miss it?. *British Journalism Review* 20: 19–26.

Schlosberg, J. (2016) *Media Ownership and Agenda Control*. Oxon: Routledge.

Schlosberg, J. (2017) Do the Voices of Mainstream Media Still Dominate Public Conversation? Maybe. *Media Reform Coalition* [blog], 22 June. mediareform.org.uk/blog/voices-mainstream-media-still-dominate-public-conversation-maybe

Screpanti, E. (2014) *Global Imperialism and the Great Crisis*. New York: Monthly Review Press.

Seager, A. (2008a) British Economy: City's pain could be industry's gain. *Guardian*, 16 September.

Seager, A. (2008b) Banking Crisis: Tax rises and public expenditure reductions grow ever more likely. *Guardian*, 9 October.

Seager, A. (2009) The Verdict: 50p tax rate may end up costing government money, warns IFS. *Guardian*, 24 April.

Seager, A. and Wintour, P. (2009) Deepest Cuts Since 70s to Fill '£45bn Hole'. *Guardian*, 24 April.

Seaton, J. and Curran, J. (2010) Contradictions in Media Policy. In: J. Curran and J. Seaton, *Power without Responsibility*. Oxon: Routledge.

Seth, S. (2015) World's Top Ten News Companies. *Investopedia*, 18 February.

Shaxson, N. (2011) *Treasure Islands*. London: Vintage Books.

Shaxson, N. (2012) Quack Medicine Built on Economic Fallacies. *Guardian*, 22 March.

Simanowitz, S. (2011) Iceland Has Jailed 29 Bankers. Why Can't the UK and US Do the Same? *HuffPost*. huffingtonpost.com/stefan-simanowitz/iceland-has-jailed-29-bankers_b_8908536.html

Skeggs, B. (2004) *Class, Self, Culture*. Oxon: Routledge.

Skeggs, B. and Yuill, S. (2016) Capital Experimentation with Person/a Formation: How Facebook's monetization refigures the relationship between property, personhood and protest. *Information, Communication and Society* 9 (3): 380–96.

Slattery, J. (2010) UK Journalists' Jobs Down by a Quarter to a Third. [Blog]. jonslattery.blogspot.nl/2010/09/uk-journalists-jobs-down-by-quarter-to.html

Smith, H. (2010) Athens Burns – and Crisis Strikes at Heart of the EU. *Guardian*, 6 May.

Smith, H. (2012) Will Syriza Leader's Radical Message of Hope Lead Eurozone into Chaos? *Guardian*, 12 June.

Smith, J. (2016) *Imperialism in the Twenty-first Century*. New York: Monthly Review Press.

Sorrell, M. and Butselaar, E. (2008) After a Week of Turmoil, has the World Changed? *Guardian*, 20 Sept 2008.

Srnicek, N. and Williams, A. (2015) *Inventing the Future*. London: Verso.

Stalker, P. (2015) *The Money Crisis*. Oxford: New Internationalist.

Starkman, D. (2014) *The Dog that Didn't Bark: The Financial Crisis and the Disappearance of Investigative Journalism*. New York: Columbia University Press.

Stein, B. (2006) In Class Warfare, Guess Which Side is Winning. *New York Times*, 26 November.

Stewart, H. (2015) Britain's Fragile Recovery is Based on an Act of Political Conjuring. *Guardian*, 19 March.

Stiglitz, J. (2010a) Reform the Euro or Bin it. *Guardian*, 6 May.

Stiglitz, J. (2010b) *Freefall*. New York: Norton.

Stiglitz, J. (2016) Globalization and its New Discontents. *Project Syndicate* [blog], 5 August. project-syndicate.org/commentary/globalization-new-discontents-by-joseph-e--stiglitz-2016-08

Streeck, W. (2016) *How Will Capitalism End?* London: Verso.

Streeck, W. (2017) *Buying Time*. London: Verso.

Strupczewski, J. (2013) Does Size Matter? *Reuters*, 21 March. reuters.com/article/us-eurozone-cyprus-banking-size-idUSBRE92K0YK20130321

Sum, N.L. and Jessop, B. (2013) *Towards a Cultural Political Economy: Putting culture in its place in political economy*. Cheltenham: Edward Elgar.

Sun (2015) Too Late to Put Down Rabid Underdog Jez. *Sun*, 14 September.

Syal, R. (2015) Osborne Accuses BBC of 'Imperial Ambitions' and Calls for Savings. *Guardian*, 5 July. theguardian.com/uk-news/2015/jul/05/osborne-accuses-bbc-of-imperial-ambitions-and-calls-for-savings

Tambini, D. (2010) What Are Financial Journalists For? *Journalism Studies* 11 (2): 158–74.

Taylor, A. and Sadowski, J. (2015) How Companies Turn Your Facebook Activity into a Credit Score. *The Nation,* 27 May. thenation.com/article/how-companies-turn-your-facebook-activity-credit-score/

Telegraph (2009) Put Faith in the Market – and Get Confidence Back. *Telegraph,* 22 January.

Temple, M. (2008) *The British Press.* Maidenhead: Open University Press.

Thielman, S. (2016) Facebook News Selection is in Hands of Editors not Algorithms, Documents Show. *Guardian,* 12 May. theguardian.com/technology/2016/may/12/facebook-trending-news-leaked-documents-editor-guidelines

Thompson, G. (2009) What's in the Frame? How the financial crisis is being packaged for public consumption. *Economy and Society* 38 (3): 520–4.

Thurman, N.J., Cornia, A. and Kunert, J. (2016) *Journalists in the UK.* Reuters Institute for the Study of Journalism. http://reutersinstitute.politics.ox.ac.uk/sites/default/files/research/files/Journalists%2520in%2520the%2520UK.pdf

Toussaint, E. (2016) History of the CADTM Anti-debt Policies. *CADTM,* 14 June. cadtm.org/History-of-the-CADTM-Anti-Debt

Toynbee, P. (2008) Brown May be Today's Saviour, but Only by Cleansing the City of Greed and Restoring Trust Will he Find Redemption. *Guardian,* 14 October.

Toynbee, P. (2010) Public Backing for Cuts Will Dissolve When Reality Strikes. *Guardian,* 26 June.

Toynbee, P. (2012a) Now it's Full-steam Ahead for Osborne's Inequality Drive. *Guardian,* 20 March.

Toynbee, P. (2012b) This Vilification Campaign against the Poor Is So Clever. *Guardian,* 12 June.

Toynbee, P. (2014) Look Out for Even More of Osborne's Sham Pledges. *Guardian,* 18 March.

Tracy, J.F. (2011) Covering 'Financial Terrorism'. *Journalism Practice* 6 (4): 513–29.

Traynor, I. (2013) Britons' Savings Exempt from Bailout Levy. *Guardian,* 18 March.

Treanor, J. (2008) A New Age of Austerity. *Guardian,* 9 October.

Treanor, J. (2011) It's Pretty Good News, Say Business Leaders as Osborne Springs Surprise Corporation Tax Cut. *Guardian,* 24 March.

Treanor, J. (2013) UK Experts Fly in as Cyprus MPs Pass Banking Reforms. *Guardian,* 23 March.

Treanor, J., Seager, A. and Wintour, P. (2009) Day the Markets Breathed Again. *Guardian,* 14 October.

Tremlett, G. (2012) Europe's Crisis: Greed, cronyism and payoffs – the scandal of Spain's failed banks. *Guardian,* 9 June.

Tremlett, G. and Traynor, I. (2012) Spain to Agree Bank Bailout. *Guardian,* 9 June.

Trinity Mirror website. trinitymirror.com.

Trussell Trust (2017) UK Foodbank Use Continues to Rise. *Trussell Trust,* 25 April. trusselltrust.org/2017/04/25/uk-foodbank-use-continues-rise/

Truth Committee on Public Debt (2015) Preliminary Report. www. hellenicparliament.gr/UserFiles/f3c70a23-7696-49db-9148-f24dce6a27c8/ Report_web.pdf

Tulloch, J. (2009) From Amnesia to Apocalypse: Reflections on journalism and the credit crunch. In: J. Mair and R.L. Keeble (eds) *Playing Footsie with the FTSE? The Great Crash of 2008*. Suffolk: Abramis. Special book issue of *Ethical Space.*

Van Reenen, J. (2013) Hopeless Case. *Mirror,* 21 March.

Varoufakis, Y. (2015) *The Global Minotaur.* London: Zed Books.

Vaughan and Macalister, T. (2015) The Nine Green Policies Killed off by the Tory Government. *Guardian,* 24 July.

Vogt, N. and Mitchell, A. (2016) Crowdfunded Journalism: A small but growing addition to publicly driven journalism, 20 January. journalism.org/2016/01/20/ crowdfunded-journalism/

Wahl-Jorgensen, K., Berry, M., Garcia-Blanco, I., Bennett, L. and Cable, J. (2016a) Rethinking Balance and Impartiality in Journalism? *Journalism* 10.1177/1464884916648094.

Wahl-Jorgensen, K., Williams, A., Sambrook, R., Harris, J., Garcia-Blanco, I., Dencik, L., Cushion, S., Carter, C., and Allan, S. (2016b) The Future of Journalism. *Journalism Studies* 17 (7): 801–7.

Warner, J. (2012) The Chancellor's Long Walk to Recovery. *Telegraph,* 22 March.

Warner, J. (2015) Our New Living Wage Might Just Pay its Way. *Telegraph,* 11 September.

Watt, N. (2008) Financial Storm Turns Party Ideologies Upside Down. *Guardian,* 9 October.

Watt, N. (2009) Spending: The party's over – cuts will wipe out decade of growth. *Guardian,* 24 April.

Watt, N. and Treanor, J. (2008) Financial Crisis: Seven days of turmoil. *Guardian,* 11 October.

Weeks, J. (2014) *Economics of the 1%.* London: Anthem.

White, M. (2010) Emergency Budget: Glossary of Osbornese. *Guardian,* June 22.

Whittaker, M. Corlett, A. and Finch, D. (2016) Household Incomes Have Finally Surpassed Previous Peak. *Resolution Foundation,* 15 February. resolutionfoundation.org/media/press-releases/8686/

Whyte, P. and Tilford, S. (2008) This is No Time to Listen to the Siren Call of the Euro. *Guardian,* 14 October.

Wile, R. (2014) Guess How Many Pages of Thomas Piketty's 700-Page Book on Inequality Most People Actually Read. *Business Insider,* 7 July. businessinsider. com/least-read-book-of-the-year-2014-7

Williams, A. (2013) The Crisis in Newspapers, and What to Do About It. *SciScreen* [blog], 30 August. cardiffsciscreen.co.uk/article/crisis-newspapers-and-what-do-about-it-new-york-times-western-mail

Williams, R. (1966) *Communications.* London: Chatto and Windus.

Williams, Z. (2011) This 'Neutral' Budget's First Principle is to Attack Equality. *Guardian,* 24 March.

Winnett, R. (2008) Bank Under Siege. *Telegraph*, 17 September.

Winnett, R. (2009) Ministers Rule Out State-owned Banks. *Telegraph*, January.

Winnett, R. (2011) Britain 'Open for Business' as Cut Saves Firms £4.2bn. *Telegraph*, 24 March.

Winnett, R. (2012) Get a Job, IDS Tells Parents on Dole. *Telegraph*, 14 June.

Winnett, R., Porter, A. and Kirkup, J. (2011) Standard of Living to Fall for Two Years. *Telegraph*, 25 March.

Wintour, P. (2008a) Banking Crisis: Downing St forced to acts as events started to look out of control. *Guardian*, 8 October.

Wintour, P. (2008b) Brown: 'Sometimes it takes a crisis': PM calls for biggest financial overhaul since 1944. *Guardian*, 14 October.

Wolf, M. (2014) *The Shifts and Shocks*. London: Allen Lane.

Wolff, R. (2012) *Democracy at Work*. Chicago: Haymarket Books.

Wolff, R.D. and Resnick, S.A. (2012) *Contending Economic Theories: Neoclassical, Keynesian, and Marxian*. Cambridge: MIT Press.

Wren-Lewis, S. (2015) The Austerity Con. *London Review of Books*. 19 February: 9–11. www.lrb.co.uk/v37/n04/simon-wren-lewis/the-austerity-con

Wynne-Jones, R. (2014) Wanted: Budget to end the misery of our hungry poor. *Mirror*, 19 March.

Index